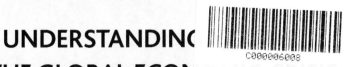

UNDERSTANDING
IN THE GLOBAL ECONOMIC CRISIS

Alan France

First published in Great Britain in 2016 by

Policy Press
University of Bristol
1-9 Old Park Hill
Bristol
BS2 8BB
UK
+44 (0)117 954 5940
pp-info@bristol.ac.uk
www.policypress.co.uk

North America office:
Policy Press
c/o The University of Chicago Press
1427 East 60th Street
Chicago, IL 60637, USA
t: +1 773 702 7700
f: +1 773-702-9756
sales@press.uchicago.edu
www.press.uchicago.edu

© Policy Press 2016

British Library Cataloguing in Publication Data
A catalogue record for this book is available from the British Library

Library of Congress Cataloging-in-Publication Data
A catalog record for this book has been requested

ISBN 978 1 44731 576 6 paperback
ISBN 978 1 44731 575 9 hardcover

The right of Alan France to be identified as author of this work has been asserted by him in
accordance with the Copyright, Designs and Patents Act 1988.

Cover design by Liam Roberts
Front cover image: istock
Printed and bound in Great Britain by CPI Group (UK) Ltd,
Croydon, CR0 4YY
Policy Press uses environmentally responsible print partners

For Ruth, Laurie, Maria and Alex
– the next generation

Contents

List of tables and figures

Tables

Figures

About the author

Alan France is Professor of Sociology in the School of Social Sciences – Te Pokapū Pūtaiao Pāpori – at the University of Auckland in New Zealand. Born in the UK, he was a co-founder of the Centre for the Study of Childhood and Youth at the University of Sheffield (2002) and between 2006 and 2010 he was Director of Centre for Social Policy at Loughborough University. His research interests are on the sociology of youth and the youth question. He has published on a wide range of areas such as youth and citizenship, youth crime, youth and risk taking, and youth policy. His previous publications include *Understanding Youth in Late Modernity* (2007, Open University Press) and *A Political Ecology of Youth and Crime* (with Dorothy Bottrell and Derrick Armstrong) (2012, Palgrave Macmillan).

Acknowledgements

I was helped in this project by a number of people and it is important they are acknowledged. I would like to thank Derrick Armstrong, Rob MacDonald, Phil Mizen, Dorothy Bottrell, Howard Williamson, Line Nyhagen, Edward Haddon and Ewa Krzaklewska, who made the time to read sections of the book and provide important feedback. Having these 'critical friends' was invaluable and, while the final analysis is mine, I am aware that they have made a contribution to my thinking and writing. I would also like to thank Tracey Sharpe and Bertalan Magyar, who helped me gather and collate important information on the eight case study areas. They provided insightful comments and very useful information on localised developments. They had an almost impossible task of trying to respond to my relentless search for answers. Thanks also to Isobel Bainton and her team at Policy Press. Her patience and guidance at difficult stages was always valuable and I appreciate the support they have offered throughout the process. I would also like to thank the University of Auckland, which provided me with resources and the time to complete this task. Special thanks also to Judy McDonald and Angela Maynard, who helped with the proof reading. Finally, I want to thank Jan, my partner and best friend of 41 years, who has always encouraged and supported me.

Introduction

Background

Over the last thirty years it has become increasingly clear that significant changes have taken place worldwide, that are reconfiguring and changing the experience of growing up for those leaving compulsory education at sixteen. Of course, these experiences are not uniform but it is safe to say that the world for the young today now looks significantly different to that experienced by their parents and grandparents. Major changes across the previous three decades, especially in young people's experiences and opportunities to education, training and employment, have seen the process of growing up in many countries extended and redefined. With the coming of the 2007[1] financial crisis it also seemed that the young were adversely affected especially as a result of high unemployment. This event undoubtedly created an economic and social rupture in a number of 'epicentre' nations, but it also had a global ripple effect, creating significant political and economic impact in countries that were not central to the crisis (Konzelmann, 2014). The question then arose of what impact this crisis, and the great recession that followed, had on what it might mean to be young today. Yet to make sense of this we need to locate the discussion in a historical context, exploring some of the major economic and political changes which have been taking place that provided the setting and environment of how nation states responded to the 2007 crisis.

To achieve this the book will undertake a detailed examination of developments in eight nation states to illuminate young people's experiences of growing up today. These countries are the United Kingdom, Australia, New Zealand, Canada, Spain, Japan, Poland and Norway. It is important to recognise that this is not a global analysis; in such a diverse world that task would be impossible. The analysis is of a range of countries defined as belonging to 'developed' or 'advanced economies' (OECD, 2014a). While such terms are a reflection of Western-Northern hegemony, rooted in a colonising history that sees 'modernisation' or 'advancement' as 'natural' or 'evolutionary', the

---

[1] The financial crisis officially started in February 2007 but its development extended into 2008 and 2009. In the discussions that follow the crisis will be defined by this start date. For a timeline see: https://www.stlouisfed.org/financial-crisis/full-timeline

1

term does define a group of countries that have significant economic power and influence over the rest of the world (Hoogvelt, 2001). This classification includes countries such as the US, the United Kingdom (UK), Germany, France, Australia and many others (OECD, 2014a).

Youth is a social construct that is defined by age categorisations. It can include those aged between 11 and 30, depending on a wide range of factors (Wallace and Kovatcheva, 1998). In this analysis I am concentrating on how social change has affected young people aged 16 to 24. The focus is particularly on young people's progress through this age period and concentrates on their experiences in the subfields of education, training, paid work and the welfare system. The reasons for this are fourfold. First, it allows me to give attention to a particular phase of youth that has been undergoing substantial social change. Traditional trajectories through this stage of the life course have been radically reformulated, more than for any other age stage; therefore it is appropriate that a book on social change concentres on this age period. Second, the focus on this age band is partly pragmatic in that it allows me to maintain a clear focus on the subject under review. There is always a danger in writing about youth that they are viewed as homogeneous, when in reality there are enormous differences across these age bands (let alone between different social groups). What it means to be a young person at 13 is very different from what it means to a 20-year-old. Third, the concentration on employment, education, work and welfare arises partly because of limits of space. I recognise that other aspects of young people's lives, including leisure and cultural activities, consumption patterns and family relationships are important, yet I suggest that how they experience 'being and becoming', is strongly influenced by their relationships with post-schooling structures and institutions that aim to manage their movement towards adulthood. For example, getting a job and earning a wage is still seen as a fundamental requirement for independent living. Finally, while there have been attempts to examine this period of the life course by looking at national trends (for example; Furlong and Cartmel, 2007 in the UK; Woodman and Wyn, 2014 in Australia; Andres, 2010 in Canada), cross-national analysis is more limited. While a number of good studies have involved international comparisons (Andres and Wyn, 2010 [Canada and Australia]; Roberts, 2009 [post-communist countries]; and Antonucci et al, 2014 [a European comparative analysis]), the analyses in these studies were mostly unable to explore the impact of the most recent economic crisis and great recession.

A key focus in this book is thus on exploring what I call the political ecological context of growing up. Such an approach recognises that 'the everyday "worlds" that young people engage in, and interact with, are a product of external "political" forces evident at a number of levels' (France et al, 2012, p.5). Influenced by Pierre Bourdieu's theory of social practice and power and Urie Bronfenbrenner's social ecology, this approach provides a framework for exploring the structuring processes of everyday life (France et al, 2012). In youth sociology, much recent attention has focused on exploring the meaning of agency and how young people make choices.[2] However, as I will argue in Chapter One, more attention needs to be focused on understanding the structures that are structuring the process of growing up. Detailed attention needs to be paid to these structures to see how they are shaping the lives and choices of the young.

A central feature of this analysis is its focus on the relationship between the economic and the political. In terms of the economic, this book charts how capital has been evolving, especially in relation to the crisis and the great recession that followed. The analysis shows how the world 'out there' is not natural but is instead strongly influenced by broader economic processes that have major shaping qualities (Harvey, 2010). Sometimes, surprisingly, in youth sociology we take this argument for granted. We expect our colleagues to recognise this is a part of the 'backdrop' to how the world is operating for the young, so we are not always forthcoming in illuminating how these processes operate at the macro level and how they shape the micro worlds of the young; especially how they may affect the range of choices available. This book examines these processes as its central task and aims to illustrate how the restructuring driven by economics is reconfiguring not only the future of the young but also their everyday experiences of institutional arrangements and architecture.

Of course, this book is not simply about how economic processes are structuring young people's lives. We also have to recognise the critical role of social policies in the structuring of everyday life. As Steven Ball suggests, 'Policies ... have a semantic and ontological force, they play their part in the construction of a social world of meanings, of causes and effects, of relationships, of imperatives and inevitabilities' (Ball, 2008, p.13). It is therefore critical that any analysis of social change includes a reflection on how policy is affecting both social and welfare reform (Hamilton, 2014, p.454). The approach taken here is strongly influenced by a critical discourse tradition that explores ideology and hegemonic politics in action (Marston, 2000). This method highlights the underlying ideological context embedded within policy that aims

---

[2]   See Coffey and Farrugia (2014) for a good review.

to determine what type of moral and political order should dominate in modern society. Such discourse, sometimes called 'moral economy', examines subject identities, social relationships and wider normative structures (Fairclough, 1992), helping to shape and create policy subjects and set a range of normative standards that structure social relationships, including the relationship between the state and the individual (Marston, 2000). As a result, this book also prioritises an analysis that recognises not only the key role played by the economic and the political but also the *interrelationship* that exists between them.

The key themes of the book are therefore:

- What has been happening, over the past thirty years, in young people's experience of growing up after leaving formal schooling and/or between the ages of 16 and 24?
- How have the 2007 economic crisis and the recession that followed affected these trends in countries from the advanced economies?
- What have been the key 'drivers' of social change and what role has youth social policy played in this process?
- What impact has social change had on the experiences and understandings of youth in contemporary society?

The use of multiple case studies

To understand the changes taking place in young people's lives this analysis has used a multiple case study approach (Yin, 2014). Case study research methods allow us to 'investigate a contemporary phenomenon and context within its real-life context, especially when the boundaries between phenomena and context are not clearly evident' (Yin, 2014, p.13). As a method of understanding social context, this approach can be used for exploratory, descriptive and explanatory purposes, helping us to understand the how and why questions (Lewis et al, 2009). It can help to explain the processes and examine linkages over time specific to certain historical, cultural and political events. Complex and in-depth case studies of social phenomena can also illuminate conditions and events that are pertinent to the matter under investigation (Yin, 2014). Case studies can be helpful for 'making analytical distinctions between the different layers of context' (Lewis et al, 2009, p.19) making them a useful tool for examining cross-national phenomena as well.

The use of multiple rather than single cases increases our ability to see interconnections, similarities and contradictions, and to compare across boundaries (Yin, 2014). Using multiple cases, attention can be paid to more than one unit of interest. Focusing on these subunits allows the investigation to determine the salient aspects of the cases. When they are brought together and combined they create a more holistic picture of events. In this analysis, the subunits have been the fields of education, work, and welfare, although, as we shall see in Chapter Nine, the impacts of changes in these areas are also affecting other parts of young people's lives. While a case study approach has been seen as lacking the ability to generalise, its strength lies in 'the richness of thick descriptions of a few cases that make it possible to extrapolate from single cases features that are transferable across time and space' (Lewis et al, 2009, p.19).

This method allows us to identify a wide range of similarities and trends across national borders. These may arise for many different reasons, but the task in this analysis is to move beyond mere description by exploring a number of core questions as outlined earlier. For example, as we will see in Chapter Five, precarious work for the young has become a widespread phenomenon. By investigating it through a case study approach we are able to identify what is driving this development in specific national contexts, how extensive it is and what might be mediating it. By using a number of case studies we can start to draw out trends and commonalities (and differences) that begin to illuminate some of the key drivers of social change. While this will not be a global picture, the intention is to show how and why recent changes in the advanced economies have taken place.

A wide range of evidence can be used in case study research, ranging from primary data (surveys, qualitative/ethnography interviewing) to secondary data analysis (existing reports and documents), which may be theoretically driven or 'grounded'. In this research, the focus has been on a range of primary and secondary data sources. First, I have drawn upon both primary and secondary data from sources such as the Organisation for Economic Co-operation and Development (OECD), the International Labour Organization (ILO) and national statistical units in the case study areas (for example, the Australian Bureau of Statistics [ABS] in Australia, and Statistics Canada). This has been supplemented by quantitative data reported by others doing research in the relevant areas, which, combined with the national material, has allowed me to gain a detailed understanding of national and international (and, where necessary, local) trends. The research also has a strong policy focus and, as a result, I have drawn upon policy documents and statements that have emerged from particular institutions responsible for developing and implementing policy. The approach taken follows the work of Dorothy Smith (2001) and others (Ball and Exley, 2010; Gerrard, 2013) that suggests 'texts mediate, regulate and authorize people's activities' and, by examining them in detail, 'it is possible to trace sequences of action through institutional paths, identifying where and how the institutional texts produce the standardized controls of everyday work activities' (Smith, 2001, p.161). The research has also drawn on a wide range of academic literature that has helped to develop many of the ideas discussed in this book.

The case study sample

The selection of case studies was theoretically driven, with a set of research questions to be explored and cover (Yin, 2014). How many cases should be used, and the extent of their divergence, is important. 'Cases need to be carefully selected so that they either produce similar results (literal replication) or produce contrasting results but for predictable reasons (theoretical replication)' (Rowley, 2002, p.19). As Yin suggests, 'Every case should serve a specific purpose within the overall scope of inquiry' (2014, p.45). Issues of social change and its impact on the lives of young people in advanced nations from different parts of the world are, as outlined earlier, central to the analysis, yet from the early scoping of the themes it became clear that a number of issues were dominant, and these needed investigating as a primary feature of the analysis. As a result it was reasonable to select a range of countries that were geographically separated, but seemed to be following a similar path. One way of doing this was to focus on countries from the Commonwealth. This not only allowed me to have at least one country from Europe (the UK), one from Australasia (Australia) and one from North America (Canada), but also countries that clearly had similar pathways into their development. While there were potential historical interconnections (as a result of the colonial past) that suggested a similar path of development, it also seemed that there were significant differences in how these three countries had evolved, for example, the federal systems in Australia and Canada, which would provide an interesting insight into how this contributed to the differences between these countries. It was also decided to include New Zealand alongside these three. The rationale for this related partly to a personal interest (it is now my country of residence) but also to a desire to examine a smaller nation that had, in its early development, created political systems and practice not too different from those in the UK, Australia and Canada. It offered an insight into how a small country 'cut loose' from its colonial past constructed policies towards its young people. It also provided a good comparison, in terms of size, to other countries to be included, as it has a similar population size to that of Norway.

Differences across nations also seemed to exist: it was clear that some nation states within the advanced economies have taken significantly different paths in their development. These tended to be strongly influenced by regional contexts and their own specific histories and culture. As a result it was necessary to include four other case study areas to try to capture this divergence and difference. The first was the inclusion of a nation from the Nordic states. These are recognised as having a distinctive approach, which in some circles is called the 'Nordic way'. This is strongly influenced by principles of social democracy and tripartite relationships between the state, unions and employers (Esping-Andersen, 1990). Of the possible options, Norway was selected, partly because it had weathered the worst of the 2007 economic crisis and had some interesting divergences in youth policy (Mydske et al, 2007), providing a contrast to the other countries. The second was the inclusion of a post-communist nation. A recent development in Europe has been the arrival of the newly emerging post-communist states. These states, known as the Central and Eastern European (CEE) countries, broke away and distanced themselves from the Soviet regime, eventually entering the European Union (EU). This gave an array of options for selection of a suitable country. I chose Poland, not only because it was one of the first to join the EU (being a major driver for the rest that followed), but also because it has an interesting history around migration and movement of young people to find work outside of their home country (Hardy, 2009). A third inclusion was a state from the South East Asian region. This region has a notably different historical context around the emergence of what has been called the 'development state' (Child Hill et al, 2012). Japan was chosen because it was a major influence in the growth of the development state model in this region and has also recently had a lengthy period of economic stagflation, prior to the 2007 crisis, that brought about changes to both economic and social policy (Tsukamoto, 2012). Japan also has a very interesting youth policy history that is closely tied to the way the state has evolved. It therefore gives a different dimension and comparison to the other cases selected. Finally, it was important to recognise the differences that exist across Europe especially in relation to the Southern European countries. These countries (Portugal, Italy, Greece and Spain, known as PIGS) are seen as having a distinctive set of features that set them apart from other European countries (Minas et al, 2014). A significant difference relates to the relationship of the family in the provision of welfare. It is claimed that the development of the welfare state in countries such as Spain is built upon cultural beliefs surrounding the role of the family (Allen, 2006). Including Spain provides another distinctive case study.

The strength of this sample is threefold. First, the case studies allow a detailed analysis to be undertaken of the state in different contexts. Not only does the sample provide us with insights into the policy regimes of the liberal democratic states in the UK, Australia, Canada and New Zealand but also a range of the other major national state configurations that exist across the advanced economies: the 'Nordic state', the developmental state, the newly emerging Eastern European state and the Southern European state. By including countries that have different histories and approaches we are able to capture the way that local context, especially around the operation of the state and its policies, can and does shape the lives of young people differently. Second, the variety of case studies also gives us access to different continents or areas of the world. So, for example, we have three countries from Europe, one from the Nordic region, one from South East Asia, one from North America and two from Australasia. Again, this offers us a way of capturing the global nature of policy and economics and the way that it can and does operate across a wide range of settings. Finally, the eight countries analysed here also provide substantial difference and diversity. They allow us to investigate how they have responded to both longer term developments and the 2007 crisis and great recession that followed. For example, as we shall see, the response to the crisis has varied across different countries. While some of this emerges because of the principles and practices (and access to resources) that drives policy in different countries, it is also about the cultural context of each nation state and how it sees the problem, and how it uses policy and practice to tackle the challenges young people both create and face.

Of course, there are also limitations to this approach. While it offers a way into a more international form of analysis, it is limited to those countries identified by the OECD as among the 'advanced economies'. As outlined earlier, it is not a global analysis and the case study countries do not capture those countries defined as 'developing'. The book cannot really claim the status of being a global analysis. But it is also the case that, while different countries illuminate a particular type of national state, significant differences can and do exist between countries in a particular region. For example, while Poland is a good example of one of the emerging Eastern European states, it was one of the first and its development compared to others is far more advanced and now in line with other European liberal economies (Hardy, 2009).

Similarly, Japan is seen as a very distinctive form of development state, being significantly different from other countries in the region that are seen as having a similar but different form of state (Child Hill et al, 2012). The same can be said about Norway. While it is a good example of the Nordic state, substantial divergences exist in policy and practice between Norway and countries such as Demark, Sweden and Finland (Berglund, 2010). We therefore have to be cautious about seeing individual countries within regions as too alike in the ways they have developed. That said, the model used here can, I believe, increase our understanding of the different types of experiences young people are having, especially since the 2007 economic crisis.

Book structure

In Chapter One, the discussion begins by exploring how youth sociology has historically theorised youth and the 'youth question'. It introduces an abridged history of the key arguments and ideas that have structured the disciplinary focus. The discussion proposes that, more recently, youth sociology has under-theorised the concept of 'structure'. As a result, I suggest we need to have an approach that recognises how the interplay between the economy, culture and the state (through social and economic policies) operates to structure the ecological environment that young people have to manage as a part of their everyday lives and trajectories towards adulthood. This then provides the theoretical framework for the discussion that follows.

In Chapter Two, the focus moves to the economic crisis of 2007 and recent policy initiatives introduced around austerity. Here it is suggested that we cannot understand either the 'causes' or the political responses that followed without recognising the growing influence of neoliberal philosophy and practice. Of course, neoliberalism is not new and what we have been witnessing over the last thirty years in a number of nation states is a roll out of neoliberalism as the way to manage not only the economy but also social life. In this chapter the analysis of this historical and contemporary process concentrates on events in the UK, Australia, Canada and New Zealand, where there is greater synergy, although, as we shall see, differences can and do exist, showing that its introduction and practice has not always been linear, smooth or without contradictions. The discussion also looks at the implications of these developments for young people and their citizenship. The final section examines in detail how these states have responded, over the past eight years to the crisis and the recession that followed.

In Chapters Three, Four, Five and Six, the focus is on the types of changes that have taken place in the lives of young people, not just since the 2007 crisis, but over the last thirty years. Again, the focus is on the UK, Australia, Canada and New Zealand. Through an in-depth analysis of developments in these four countries, we start to see a number of major trends and practices emerge that reflect a changing landscape for the young. How and why these developments have taken place is explored and analysed in detail, giving an opportunity to see, not only how the structures and pathways have been changing in these countries, but also what the drivers have been and how instrumental they have been in reconfiguring young people's opportunity structures and life worlds. For example, we see young people's participation in education and training going well beyond the traditional schooling years, requiring substantial cultural and financial investment by the young and their parents. Similarly, we see high levels of unemployment and the growth of precarious work, creating situations where insecure, non-standard conditions and low pay are normalised for a large number of young people. In this way, the 'promise' that increased qualifications and training would bring financial reward is being broken, especially for the most vulnerable. Alongside these developments we also start to see increased concerns about NEETs (those not in employment and education or training) and the expansion of welfare-to work strategies that target those who are seen as a financial burden and high risk to the state. As a result, new forms of regulation and control are being introduced that involve sanctions and penalties. This is both reducing costs to the state while also allowing great control of 'risky' populations.

In Chapter Seven, we turn our attention to the experiences in our other four countries to explore how far these major developments have been impacting elsewhere. The studies of Norway, Japan, Spain and Poland provide a contrast to the other four case study areas that were central to the analysis in the previous chapters. As discussed earlier, these countries add value because of their different histories, and the different cultural and political environments in which they have been operating. The chapter starts by outlining the ways that each of these countries have been encountering and engaging with neoliberalisation, and how neoliberal philosophy and practice has impacted on youth policies in these countries. It concludes by looking at the impact of the crisis and how the different countries have responded. As we shall see, over the past ten years all four countries have drawn upon neoliberal philosophy and principles in one way or another to shape youth policies. In the final part of this chapter we explore the experience of citizenship for young people in these four countries prior to the crisis.

In Chapter Eight we show how the core practices and experiences identified in the previous chapters have become a part of life in Norway, Poland, Spain and Japan. Questions such as: What has been happening to graduate employment, especially after the crisis? How has the state responded to the international unemployment question? How has work been evolving in these countries and is precariousness a dominant feature especially since the crisis? To what extent do these countries see themselves having a NEET problem? How have these countries developed active labour management policies (ALMPs) and have they followed the welfare-to-work models identified in the previous discussion, especially as the great recession had its impact? As we shall see, the answers to many of these questions offer insights and contrast, not only as to how these nation states have been responding to the 'youth question' following the 2007 crisis but also regarding the historical, cultural and political environments that can and do make the experience of growing up in these countries different from those in the other countries discussed earlier in the book. Of course we also start to see that there are areas of synergy and similarity that suggest neoliberalisation has been making substantial progress, especially since the crisis, even in states that traditionally rejected or were opposed to the core principles of neoliberalism.

In Chapter Nine we explore questions of mobility and movement as a way of understanding how the changes discussed in the previous six chapters have been impacting on the young. The chapter will focus on evidence from the eight case study areas as a way of recognising how the crisis and the great recession that followed has impacted on youth mobility. Exploring the concept of mobility is important. In late modernity there is growing evidence (and belief) that substantial changes have been taking place, with young people becoming more mobile as a way of managing their precarious situations. This chapter explores the issue of mobility in a number of diverse ways. First, it looks at mobility *within nation states*, and the question of *social mobility*. As we shall see, there is a growing body of evidence in a number of states that suggests not only that there is growing inequality between generations but also that, when inequality increases in a society, social mobility for the young is reduced and, as a result, we see a continuation of significant embedded forms of inequality, especially among the youth population. Second, mobility *out of the family home*, especially since 2007, will be discussed. Being able to leave home and move towards independent living is critical for the young. What we start to see is that some groups are able to be more mobile and create a 'yo-yo' relationship with the family home to help them gain their full independence, while others find themselves immobile and stuck. Finally, we examine the importance of *migration* for the young. Especially since the crisis, rates of migration have been increasing, with the young moving abroad in search of work or education. Evidence is starting to suggest that 'being internationally mobile' for the young is a new core requirement in neoliberal times.

The conclusion (Chapter Ten) then brings us back to the core questions that this book has addressed. It discusses the implications of the social changes identified and, in particular, the consequences of the 2007 crisis and its aftermath for what it means to be young in late modernity. This discussion suggests that we need to recognise not only the diverse ways that different groups are expected to be a citizen in this economic and political landscape of neoliberalism but also that the experience of citizenship for the young is shaped by class, gender and other inequalities. It is critical to remember that, within the field of practice, variations of experiences are strongly influenced by a young person's social space and access to economic, cultural and social capital. We need to acknowledge that citizenship will and does have different meanings for different groups in these neoliberal times.

ONE

A political ecology of youth

Introduction

The process of 'growing up' or 'becoming adult' is highly complex and is shaped and influenced by *ideas*, *relationships* and *events* in the local and national context (Heinz, 2009). Growing up is therefore experienced differently in different environments and settings. However, as will become clear in the discussions that follow in this book, there are similar patterns and outcomes that can create a collective experience of growing up, even across national boundaries. Making sense of how social context constructs and defines what it means to be young, especially in periods of social change, is important and has long been a central feature of the study of youth (White and Wyn, 2008; Jones, 2009a; MacDonald, 2011; Furlong, 2013). While the history of youth sociology is not straightforward, its theoretical development has shadowed that of sociology in general. However, the ability of existing approaches to make sense of the contemporary worlds of the young has been increasingly challenged by the limits of these models. Therefore I believe an approach that draws on broader sociological and other social science approaches is needed. In the first part of this chapter we will explore recent developments in youth sociology, highlighting a number of key debates and challenges that, despite producing important knowledge, have left us with gaps in our understanding about the structuring of young people's social, cultural and economic lives. In the second part of the chapter I will develop an alternative way of making sense of and conceptualising the social context of young people's lives, introducing a political ecological approach that aims to provide a framework for the rest of the book. In the third section the discussion will focus on the ecological role of 'policy,' showing how it has a critical role to play in structuring young people's experiences at a number of levels. It finishes with an exploration of how youth policy is formed, emphasising the forces and processes that underpin its construction.

Theorising youth

Theorising of youth in sociology has a long history, linked to the Chicago School and other early American critical sociologists in the 1930s and 1940s (France, 2007). Some of the most influential works in the modern era came from the American functionalist theorists Parsons (1942) and Eisenstadt (1956). Writing at a time when functionalist thinking was at the core of sociological theory, these writers proposed that youth was an institution with a core function in the reproduction and maintenance of social order. Eisenstadt argued that age was socially significant because its influence could be found in all societies, both primitive and advanced. It performed a vital social function through the allocation of social roles to individuals. He suggested that members of societies were more or less clear about the appropriate roles attributed to specific ages and thus age worked to define appropriate social relationships and so maintain the stability of a social order. Having clarity over such roles ensured that individuals were correctly socialised, and that young people in particular learned appropriate behaviour patterns. Different social roles attached to different ages taught young people how to obey authority, cooperate with equals and accept responsibility. It was through these different age-grades that an 'internalisation of the adult's "image"' (Eisenstadt, 1956, p.29) took place, whereby young people learned and acted out appropriate age-related roles. It also provided young people with clear definitions of the pathways into adulthood. Eisenstadt argued that 'age-grades' were the glue that ensured personal adherence to the maintenance and reproduction of the social system, because the age at which an individual became a full member of society was crucial in maintaining the correct ordering and distribution of rights and obligations.

Such theories have remained influential in shaping the way academics have explored and explained young people's relationship with the life course for over sixty years. For example, they led to the development of a body of work that gave focus first to the transitions from school to work (Carter, 1966; Ashton et al, 1990; Roberts, 1995) and then to more recent explorations of the transitions into 'adulthood' (Jones, 2002; Thomson et al, 2004). Yet such approaches had limits when it came to explaining the social context of growing up. Much of the early work was criticised for its close association with essentialist models of youth development (Allen, 1968; Cohen and Ainley, 2000; Wyn and Woodman, 2006), and while later work focused on opportunity structures and marginalised transitions, as opposed to psychological underpinnings (Furlong, 2013), this model had a strong emphasis on what Cohen and Ainley argue has led to:

> a limited research paradigm focused on 'transition' as a rite of passage between developmental stages of psychological maturity and immaturity, complemented by a sociological transition narrowly restricted to (vocational) maturity and (nuclear) family formation. (2000, p.80)

Others have broadened the focus, drawing upon more radical forms of analysis of transitions that show how normative timetables have undergone significant changes, creating diverse impacts on young people's movement into adulthood (Walther, 2006; du Bois-Reymond, 2009; McDonald, 2011; Moreno, 2012). Transitions have also more recently been seen as extended, fragmented and/or 'broken' (Jones, 2009b). Such a model has significant traction in youth sociology and frames much of the analysis of what it means to be young in contemporary times. But, as others have noted, this model may only be a partial picture of social life and seems to be unable to understand recent social changes (White and Wyn, 2008). It also tends to correspond to a functional integration model that problematises those young people who do not make normative transitions (Wyn and Woodman, 2006). Yet, as Roberts (2003), MacDonald (2011) and, more recently, France and Roberts (2015) suggest, we need to recognise the importance of transitions in the process of 'becoming' for the young and should not undervalue their significance. Transitions clearly remain a critical feature of young people's everyday experience and are a major contributor to social reproduction in late modern society (France and Roberts, 2015).

A second theoretical strand in youth sociology that emerged partly in response to the early failings of functionalism was influenced by Marxism. Again its influence corresponded with its growing impact on broader sociological debates (France, 2007). This approach has many strands, yet as a theory it is fundamentally concerned with explaining the relationship of the individual to economic processes and forces in capitalist societies, and with questions of class. Marxist influences in youth sociology first emerged through the work of the Centre for Contemporary Culture Studies (CCCS) at Birmingham University. CCCS took a political economy approach to analysing youth and proposed that a close relationship existed between economic and political power in defining and shaping the lives of the young (Hall and Jefferson, 1976; Hall et al, 1978). This approach, expanded by others both inside and outside the Birmingham School, tried to explain and explore social reproduction, looking at class and other social divisions in areas including school-to-work transitions (Hollands, 1990), training initiatives (Finn, 1987; Bates and Riseborough, 1993; Mizen, 1995) and the shaping of gender transitions (McRobbie, 1978; Griffin, 1985).

As sociology embraced post-structuralist ideas in the 1990s, the analytical approaches that had emerged from CCCS lost favour, but two significant developments evolved out of the work and remained influential. The first was the recognition of a need to acknowledge the political economy in youth sociology, and the importance of the relationship between capital and politics in shaping young people's lives. Stuart Hall (1985) developed the notion of 'authoritarian populism', in which the state was able to mobilise popular support from the electorate for right-wing economic and social policies that marginalised and problematised opposition and resistance. In this process, 'race' and youth were symbols of crisis and thus justified authoritarian policies and practices targeting these groups. This approach tended to find more favour with the newly emerging critical criminology that focused on Youth Justice Policy and practice (Muncie, 1984; Goldson, 1997; Scraton, 1997) than with mainstream youth sociology, although it later connected with the works of Foucault and other more post-structural writers who concentrated on the discourses of power and governance questions. More recently, there has been an attempt to reinvigorate a political economy approach to youth sociology. Côté (2014) argues for the importance of highlighting the interface between economics and political action in trying to understand the situation that young people find themselves in today, suggesting that there is a clear relationship between economic interests and political power in shaping their social world;

> In many societies, dominant political and economic power sources are closely aligned, and governments therefore have a tendency to develop policies favouring those with economic power, while ignoring those without economic power. (Côté, 2014, p.2)

The second development that came out of the work of CCCS was a growing interest in the cultural practices of the young. The expansion of this approach coincided with and influenced the emergence of the 'cultural turn' (Bennett, 2011), youth subcultural theory in sociology and also the introduction of postmodernist ideas on youth culture. The latter started with a critique of CCCS and led to the emergence of what has been called post-subcultural theory (Bennett, 2011) that challenged the class-based analysis of youth subcultural theory. Writers such as Bennett (1999), Malbon (1999) and Miles (2000) argued for a recognition that youth culture and youth identities in particular needed to be 'regarded as reflexively articulated lifestyle projects that appropriate and combine resources from both local, social-cultural environments and from global cultural industries' (Bennett, 2011, p.28). This saw an expansion and growth of youth research that explored the cultural activities of the young, such as 'clubbing' (Thornton, 1995) and music (Bennett, 1999), focusing on how culture was constructed, appropriated and used in the leisure and lifestyle activities of the young. While such a perspective has introduced new ways of looking at the cultural activities of the young, it has also moved away from a structural analysis within youth sociology (France, 2007) to one that sees culture as a 'fusion zone' (Bennett, 2011): an expression of innovation, creativity and agency in youth sociology. Concepts such as 'identity', ' agency' 'neo-tribes' 'and 'scenes' become the 'theoretical' tools of the cultural theorist (Bennett, 2011).

How useful this approach is in understanding the diversity of young people's social lives remains unclear. It is claimed that those using this approach tend to make large 'leaps of faith' by suggesting that club culture and other forms of popular culture are significant identify-forming sites for the young (Hollands, 2002). It emphasises culture over other important factors such as work and education when the evidence does not always support such claims. It also fails to recognise both the broader political context that shapes popular culture and the political economy of leisure (Hollands, 2002). It is not surprising that post-structuralists have little focus on these broader processes because they are not looking for these connections. They do not have a theoretical framework that allows them to explore and understand how youth might be differentiated by their economic, domestic and geographical positions, or by the focuses and power of the cultural and media industries (Cohen and Ainley, 2000).

Over time, therefore, we see a fragmentation of youth sociology into two camps: first, that of youth transitions with a focus on the political economy; and, second, cultural studies that emphasise the 'creativity' and diversity of youth through cultural practices. More recently, attempts have been made to try to reconcile these differences, to explore how these two strands can be better integrated (Furlong et al, 2011) and to 'bridge the gap' between these divisions (Woodman and Bennett, 2015). Some examples already exist. MacDonald (2011) shows how transitional studies bring a more cultural perspective to analysis, especially if we recognise that youth culture is broader than post-subcultural theory allows, where it is usually narrowly defined as being expressed in relation to consumption practices. Youth culture operates in a wide range of settings, including schools, neighbourhoods and peer relationships, and has a major impact in shaping participation in formal education and work. A recent example can be seen in Robert Hollands' (2015) analysis of night-time leisure in Newcastle. Here he highlights how the social and cultural practices of the young in the context of leisure show not only the changing social condition of youth in late modernity but also reveal and remind us that consumption 'like transitions, is not just subjective and freely chosen, but is structured and/or "disposed" by economic, political and social forces' (Hollands, 2015, p.75). Night-time leisure is becoming a context where social inequalities are maintained and displayed, reinforcing class differences and contributing to the diverse and different transitions of the young in contemporary times.

The challenge remains within youth sociology to find an approach that explores the 'doing' or 'being' of youth alongside the 'becoming' of their transitions (France, 2007). Theoretical distinctions that separate the material and political from the cultural and the social do not always do justice to young people's experiences of growing up. As Furlong suggests, the 'shifting metaphors [of youth] … represent changes in theoretical fashion amongst youth researchers which can be identified in social science more generally' (2013, p.8). Concepts such as functionalism and Marxism intersect and neat distinctions between one and the other are never easy to make. Other ideas, such as postmodernism and post-structuralism (McRobbie and Thornton, 1995) have been influential, yet such approaches can go in and out of fashion. However, it is important to recognise that the 'cultural turn' and the work that followed has brought a new dimension to our understanding of youth and the youth question (France, 2007). The challenge is to create a more holistic understanding of what it means to be young that includes both cultural and economic factors and explains both the 'being' and 'becoming' of the youth experience.

The 'structuring' of social life

A second major debate that has dogged the sociology of youth is discussion over the relationship between structure and agency (Coffey and Farrugia, 2014). This is not surprising, as it has been a central theme in sociology in general. The recent resurgence of attempts to understand 'agency' in youth sociology and to reclaim it from youth cultural studies has been valuable, yet little discussion has focused on what we mean by structure and the structuring qualities in social life. Our interest here focuses on this question and on how structures operate to influence the actions of young people. What is clear in these debates over agency is that the use of a dichotomy that suggests structure and agency are opposite ends of a spectrum is problematic (France et al, 2012). Therefore we need to recognise the 'duality of structure' (Giddens, 1991) and the embedded nature of structure in social practice (Bourdieu, 1998). This book is not directly about the interplay between structure and agency. It focuses on illuminating the structural ecology of youth suggesting that there needs to be a greater understanding in youth sociology of what the key macro- and/or micro-institutional processes are and how they operate in the structuring of decision making. For example, one of the major institutions that impacts on the lives of young people is the state. In many youth sociology studies there is an underlying set of assumptions, influenced by the ideas of critical theorists working in the area of political economy, that the state and youth policy operate as a backdrop to the experiences young people have, yet how this works in practice is never fully explored or theorised. It is usually claimed to be a force of control, regulation and surveillance, or governance (Goldson, 2002; Muncie, 2009). While there is clear evidence to suggest that the state, and government policy, do not always benefit the young (Mizen, 2004; McDonald and Marsh, 2005), and that the state targets the young as a social problem (France, 2007), much youth sociological research struggles to recognise how these relationships between the state, social policy and young people's trajectories operate. Youth sociology has a tendency to give limited attention to the diverse ways in which policies intersect with, shape and impact the daily lives of young people (France et al, 2010). What we need to recognise is how the state and social policy, as a set of institutional arrangements, operate at a number of levels in the lives of young people across time and place and with sometimes contradictory objectives and outcomes (France et al, 2012).

A similar problem exists when theorising the relationship between the 'economic', the state and youth policies. Again there is almost an implicit set of assumptions in much youth sociology that global capitalism and its institutions and practices exploit the young, and that the state is an extension of capital operating in favour of the privileged (Côté, 2014). This may be the case in many situations, but theorising in youth sociology tends to struggle to grasp the complexity of this relationship and fails to show how the state and corporate organisations may collaborate and/or be in conflict with each other at a number of levels. It also struggles to conceptualise how capital and its economic processes and practices may be impacting everyday areas of young people's lives, including family life, personal relationships, neighbourhoods, consumption and social spaces. When there are attempts to understand this relationship, the focus tends to be more on the 'dangerous, disadvantaged or spectacular' youth subcultures, giving limited attention to the 'missing middle' or ordinary youth (Roberts, 2011).

However, there are examples of studies that have tried to show how this relationship works. MacDonald and Marsh (2005) for example draw attention to the relationship of global capital and national youth policy in shaping the ecological environment of Teesside around work and unemployment for young people in the North of England, showing how it acted to exclude and marginalise the young. Similarly, Chatterton and Hollands (2003) also show how the 'nightlife economy' of Newcastle was constructed through the interplay of global corporate finance, national policy strategy on alcohol use, and local policies on policing and licencing, which then created a particular environment for youth leisure. From another viewpoint, Kelly (2000) explores how political discourses and practices around 'youth at risk' populations are used as a form of governing the young. These studies are the exception rather than the rule and in general the interplay between the state, youth policy, global capitalism and local practice is given limited attention in most studies of youth. Such 'structuring processes' are usually only acknowledged in the background when proposing an economic framework that is claimed to usually disadvantage the vulnerable or to marginalise the young as a collective group.

One final recent development that is important to our discussion of youth sociology has been the emergence of a potential new orthodoxy known as social generation theory (see Wyn and Woodman, 2006; Woodman and Wyn, 2014). Here it is argued that traditional methods of theorising and understanding youth have become of limited value and that a social generation approach, influenced by the work of Karl Mannheim (1952) offers a new way of understanding the lives of young people. Youth, it is argued, should be conceptualised and analysed through the notion of social generation:

> [Generation] locates young people within specific sets of economic, social, cultural and political conditions [and therefore] offers a way beyond seeing generations as a series of birth cohorts because age is no longer the defining feature. (Wyn and Woodman, 2006, p.499)

Generation theory is not about lineage or descent or about people sharing the same birth date within a given time frame. A 'social generation' is seen to exist as a specific collective identity with distinct new life patterns (relative to its predecessors). Each generation is seen to have its own script that 'will continue to shape their lives well into the future when they are no longer youth' (Wyn and Woodman, 2006, p.496-7). For Woodman and Wyn (2014), recent social changes, many of which we will explore in this book, have given rise to a new generation who are distinctively different from the previous one (the baby boomers). From this position, it is argued that it is membership of a generation that delivers a better understanding of sociological questions – both in terms of an individual's social position and their general orientations (Woodman and Wyn, 2014). Such a position has been criticised for its limited understanding of transitions research, its underdeveloped analysis of social change and its lack of attention to questions of social inequality (France and Roberts, 2015).

Towards an ecological understanding of young people's lives

So far I have suggested that most theorising in youth sociology, while raising important questions, has had limited success in conceptualising a more integrated way of understanding young people's lives. Issues of 'transitions versus culture' or 'structure versus agency' leave us with a partial picture of what it means to be young and with significant gaps in our understanding. Such an approach also tends to create 'camps' that position themselves against each other. I suggest that we need to develop new tools and ways of analysing the lives of young people and draw on the findings of other theorists working in the social sciences to help us understand how young people's lives are constructed in the present era.

One of the most significant sociological theorists of our time is Pierre Bourdieu, yet outside the sociology of education his influence in youth studies has remained marginal.[1] Bourdieu is useful for a number of reasons. First, he rejects dichotomous forms of analysis, seeing them as unhelpful, and aims to move us away from allowing such arguments to frame our analysis. Second, he provides a broad conceptual framework that recognises the importance of economic, cultural, social and political processes, highlighting how they are relationships of power.

---

[1]   Although more recently his influence has grown, see Threadgold and Nilan (2009), Coffey and Farrugia (2014), Woodman and Wyn (2014).

Third, he is keen to encourage interplay between the theoretical and the empirical world, suggesting that we need both to make sense of the social world. He also draws our attention to the importance of social spaces and the relationship they have with shaping and structuring social life and it is here that I propose our ecological analysis should start.

Bourdieu suggests that we need to recognise the important role of fields in locating the specific historical, local, national, international and relational contexts of individual social practice (Bourdieu, 1993). 'Fields denote arenas of production, circulation and appropriation of goods, services, knowledge, or status' (Swartz, 1997, p117). Bourdieu uses fields as an analytical tool to highlight the workings of areas of literary and cultural production (Bourdieu, 1993) and in examining the operation of philosophy and science (Bourdieu, 1975), although he also focuses on institutional settings, including schools (Bourdieu and Passeron, 1977) higher education (Bourdieu, 1988) and housing policy and practice (Bourdieu, 2005). Fields can be underpinned by institutional and legal arrangements, although Bourdieu is keen to emphasise them as sites with boundaries that are not fixed. They are sites of competition and struggle, usually over resources and definitions of practice and value. Fields are where an individual's capitals (social, economic and cultural) and habits can operate in structuring their lives (Bourdieu and Wacquant, 1992). Bourdieu sees them as hierarchical and embedded in dominant and subordinate positions, where unequal distribution of relevant capital produces different experiences of social reproduction of life chances (Bourdieu, 1990). A field is then:

> a structured social space, a field of forces, a force field. It contains people who dominate and people who are dominated. Constant, permanent relationships of inequality operate inside this space, which at the same time becomes a space in which various actors struggle for the transformation or preservation of the field. (Bourdieu, 1998, pp.40–1)

It is 'a separate universe governed by its own laws' (Bourdieu, 2005, p.5) where 'knowing the rules of the game' is critical to shaping individual outcomes. Fields can be multiple and intersecting, and individuals can be active in more than one field at a time. They have an 'exchange value', in that what happens in one field can have consequences in another. For example, what happens in the field of education can affect a person's future employment prospects and living arrangements.

Bourdieu wants to impress on us that fields are not simple systems (Bourdieu and Wacquant, 1992). Fields are fluid and dynamic and open to change, but we need to recognise that institutional systems and arrangements do operate within fields and are critical in shaping the landscape of a given social field. We therefore need to understand how these operate within and between the different fields of practice that are central to young people's lives. It is in this context that Bronfenbrenner's work (1979) on social ecology can help. He proposes a model of a 'nested ecology': one that constructs a systematic analysis of how the social environment is shaped and intersects with systems and wider ideas and practices. While he recognises the importance of microsystems and relationships for identity building (France et al, 2012), he is more concerned with identifying how the settings and social spaces (fields) in which young people participate are influential and structuring. He suggests, like Bourdieu, that it is the interconnections, ordering and social relationships embedded in these contexts that are important in structuring young people's everyday lives.

Youth exists and is constructed in a number of social spaces and settings, although the core fields of practice can be found in education (both secondary and tertiary), the family, neighbourhoods and in the workplace or through unemployment. Bronfenbrenner's model recognises the existence of mesosystems and exosystems that exist in and across these fields of practice. Mesosystems are critical institutional arrangements and relationships between settings that are central to the lived experiences of the young. They include relationships between families, schools, peer groups, neighbours, services and recreational spaces where young people spend their time and they may be legally defined. For example, legislation requires the young to go to school and social policy shapes their tertiary experience and pathways towards independence. Policing practices in neighbourhoods and the operation of youth justice systems locally are put in place to deal with 'problem youth'. The mesosystem may also include relationships in which young people do not directly participate, such as parents' interactions with their teachers and other professionals. However, these systems tend to bring young people into direct contact with the laws, policies and institutional arrangements of fields of practice through interactions with adults and professionals. Practices at the mesosystem level can also be culturally defined, shaped by local practice and young people's understandings of the 'rules of the game' and how the system works for or against them (France et al, 2012).

Bronfenbrenner (1979) also proposes that any analysis of young people's lives needs to recognise how systems can operate out of the direct experience of or contact with the young yet remain of significant consequence to the different fields of practice. He identifies what he calls exosystems that are extensions of meso structures and include settings that do not involve the developing person directly but directly affect their settings and so have an indirect but important influence (Bronfenbrenner, 1979). Bronfenbrenner includes the media, government agencies and services such as health and transport at this level. Exosystems, in a sense, carry various macro forces into immediate ecologies. The arrangement of public transport in a city and young people's access to it, the availability of local neighbourhood amenities, the structuring of commercial and public leisure facilities in areas where young people live, and the availability of work in a given area can all be influential in shaping the experiences young people have within the fields of practice. The organisation of schooling (the availability of private and public schools in a given area), the methods of monitoring a young person's progress and the allocation of school places can direct young people's pathways. Built into both mesosystems and exosystems are ecological transitions that can be institutionally organised and structured (such as moving from primary to secondary school) or may be cultural trajectories (Bottrell and France, 2015) that are locally specific and defined. These transitions cut across fields and operate to shape young people's movement into adulthood (Bottrell and France, 2015).

Finally, Bronfenbrenner's model of human ecology introduces the importance of recognising the broader macrosystems that exist at the level of belief systems or ideologies in a given society. This is what he calls the 'blueprint' for social life that provides the laws, rules and regulations and attitudes towards business, economic activity and social welfare. This blueprint has a significant part to play in shaping the exosystems and mesosystems of the everyday worlds of the young and directly affects the fields of practice, creating custom and practice in everyday life (Bronfenbrenner, 1977). It embeds core principles and political practice through the operation of public policy, and determines both how professionals operate in different fields and the priorities that are set in tackling social problems and societal challenges. It informs and prioritises how people understand concepts such as social mobility, inequality, crime, order and disorder, and even childhood and youth. Variations between nation states are shaped and influenced by their history, values and cultural beliefs about how life should be ordered:

> The systems blueprints differ for various socioeconomic, ethnic religious and other subcultural groups, reflecting contrasting belief systems and lifestyles, which in turn help

perpetuate the ecological environments specific to each group. (Bronfenbrenner, 1979, p.26)

Aspects of the blueprint of a society can then be traced in the ecologies of the fields of practice. These can intersect and cut across the mesosystems and exosystems and then structure the opportunities and practice of others operating in the fields of practice, shaping the everyday context of young people's decision making. The 'nesting' qualities of ecology are therefore critical for understanding the fields of practice.

Bronfenbrenner offers a more systematic way of understanding the ecological context of fields, although his approach lacks an understanding of how power operates throughout the process. It is here that Bourdieu's work on power is useful (Bourdieu and Passeron, 1977; Bourdieu, 1990). Two key concepts are relevant to this discussion: 'symbolic violence' and 'symbolic interests'. Bourdieu suggests that the principal mode of domination has shifted from overt coercion and the use of physical violence to forms of manipulation (Swartz, 1997). If privilege and advantage operates to advantage the disadvantaged, we should all be more equal than we are. For example, even though social inequality and poverty remain major social problems, this is legitimised by a system that sees them as inevitable outcomes of individual actions. Symbolic violence is a 'process whereby power relations are perceived not for what they are objectively but in a form which renders them legitimate in the eyes of the beholder' (Bourdieu and Passeron, 1977, p.xiii). Structures and policies are embedded with 'codes' that provide shared meanings and logical rationales to the dominant classes. Practices of symbolic violence also categorise and classify people in ways that reinforce and reproduce the existing social structure (for example, deserving and undeserving poor), giving reasons and justifications for particular forms of action. Symbolic interests operate beyond purely economic interests to maximise both 'material and symbolic profit' and give legitimacy to the privileged. Those in powerful and influential positions are able to suggest that there are 'natural' divisions, and hierarchical hegemonic social arrangements around certain professional groups, such as doctors, lawyers and academics, are seen to be 'natural' but in reality are driven by self-interest.

One final and important aspect of Bourdieu's theory of power can be found in his discussion on the dominant feature that he calls the 'field of power'. This cuts across all fields and is dominated by the economic and political interests of the elites (Bourdieu, 1998). The field of power operates to maintain and reinforce privilege and systems that perpetuate domination by one group over another in the economic and/or cultural spheres. Those groups that hold power are critical in constructing and shaping fields of practice as they hold both the economic and cultural capital to create the 'rules of the game'. An example that Bourdieu uses is the functioning of schools in France, where elitism operates at all levels to ensure privilege is maintained (Bourdieu, 1998). 'The patterned, regular and predictable practices within each field bear striking similarities, as do the kinds of social agents who are dominant in each field' (Thomson, 2008, p.70). In this context, the field of power is a 'mutual process of influence and on-going co-construction' (Thomson, 2008, p.71).

Policy as ecology

In understanding the structuring qualities of institutions within different fields, it is important not only to grasp the nested qualities of organisations and the way that power operates within and across certain contexts, but also to understand how institutions and organisations both within and outside of the state construct policy and social practice. In terms of understanding the structuring of social life, we need to recognise the important role that policy plays in this process and how it is ecological and embedded in power relationships (Ball, 2008). Of course our main understanding of policy usually relates to the 'big P' of policy that is formal and usually legislated in parliaments around the world (Evans et al, 2008). However, policy is created in many places and many 'little p' policies are formed and enacted in localities and institutions (Ball, 1997). In this context we need to recognise that policy is reproduced and reworked over time in many different settings and sites: it is dynamic and continually negotiated and reconfigured depending on circumstances. In other words, we have to acknowledge that policy is a process that can be unstable and open to interpretation

> Policies are contested, interpreted and enacted in a variety of arenas of practice and the rhetorics, texts and meanings of policy makers do not always translate directly and obviously into institutional practices. They are inflected, mediated, resisted and misunderstood, or in some cases simply prove unworkable. (Ball, 2008, p.7)

In this sense, policy is messy, confused and in many cases contradictory. It does not necessarily follow a linear pattern of development. For example, 'big P' policies may emerge and evolve as a set of values and ideological positions at the macro or 'blueprint' level, yet as they cascade through the mesosystem and exosystem levels to the ecological levels of micro interactions, they can be contested and acquire different interpretations and meanings that impact on social practice and outcomes (France et al, 2012). As Gerrard and Farrell suggest:

> 'policy implementation' is socio-culturally and politically deconstructed; in other words, policy practice comes to refer to the diverse ways in which people in local settings come to produce, read, interpret, act upon, ignore, dismiss, adapt, co-opt, reject, disseminate and perform formal policy directives. (2013, p.2)

While we need to recognise this in understanding the policy process, we also need to understand how power and dominant ideas shape the terrain of the fields of practice in which policy implementers operate. Smith (2005) shows in her work on institutional ethnography how the 'text' and documents of policy affect relationships of power. Similar to Bourdieu's concept of 'fields of power', she suggests that the policy texts, documentation and discourses around the meanings of policy are embedded in the 'ruling relations' that shape professional practice (Smith, 2005). These cannot be reduced to 'relations of dominance or hegemony' and are not 'monolithic or manipulated' (Smith, 1999, p.77) yet the concentration and emergence of policy 'texts' at macro, mesosystem and exosystem levels are able to shape everyday practice and institutional culture by reproducing relations of power and dominant ideas. This process can start at the macro level, involving government bureaucrats, politicians and political advisers who aim to influence and shape policy in particular ways by drawing on 'think tanks', the media, professional associations, interest groups and pressure groups (Ball and Exley, 2010). These processes then operate at the level of exosystems and mesosystems to 'ferment policy documentation, institutional cultures, knowledge and discourses [that] begin to be formalised and normative and thus prepare the cultural and epistemological conditions for policy implementation' (Gerrard and Farrell, 2013, p.4). It is through these dynamic processes that ruling relations within particular policy arenas become normalised in a wide range of communications to practitioners at the local level (via guidelines, emails, memos, forms and regulatory requirements). These are then reinforced by discussions in wider texts, such as in articles in professional journals, newspapers and textbooks that produce and invoke the need for a form of professional practice that replicates and reinforces ruling relations (Gerrard and Farrell, 2013).

Youth policy is therefore an important part of how we understand the ecological context of young people's lives (White and Wyn, 2008; Williamson, 2012). It operates as a 'field of practice' that has significant consequences for what it means to be young. A number of processes and discourses are influential in shaping youth policy and in the discussion that follows we will explore them in detail. First, it is important to recognise that how youth is defined and understood has particular impacts on how policy is constructed. Age is critical (Mizen, 2004): the age when a young person should be in education; the age of criminal responsibility; the age when young people can take up paid work and the types of work they can do; the age for being able to have a consenting sexual relationship; the age at which they can get married without consent from a parent; the age a young person can vote and participate in politics are all socially constructed categories that are built upon perceptions of what young people can and should be doing at a particular age. As Heinz (2009) suggests, these arrangements and perspectives construct and provide the framework for young people's life transitions and pathways towards adulthood. But this is a dynamic and evolving process, and one that has to recognise historical and cultural differences. Youth is a concept that has been 'discovered' and its meanings vary with social context and in response to social change: thus, like other life stages, youth emerges and re-emerges, is discovered and re-discovered time after time, becoming in turns a source of hopes and fears as the rhythm of social change increases. (Chisholm et al, 2011, p.14)

Youth has had different meanings at different stages in history, creating a wide range of contradictions regarding what youth might mean today (France, 2007). These processes have differed not only historically but also across national boundaries (Wallace and Kovatcheva, 1998). For example, in many Eastern European countries during the communist period, youth as a social category was strongly structured by the existence of three different youth organisations that were spread across the life course but were age-related:

> At the basic level of schooling, young people joined a junior youth organisation (given different names in different countries) and then from the age of 10 to 14 they joined 'Young Pioneers'. From then until the age of 28 they joined the official youth organisation, which was known in many

countries as the 'Komsomol'. (Wallace and Kovatcheva, 1998, p.41)

Young people were required to join these organisations and they were highly structured, with activities and routines including mass rallies and cultural activities. In this context, young people knew the pathways they had to take to become adult and everyone knew who the young were (Wallace and Kovatcheva, 1998). The level and type of state intervention in youth policy also varies across time and place (Hahn-Bleibtreu and Molgat, 2012). For example, in the south of Europe the family has been central to the institutionalisation of welfare systems. The welfare regimes in Mediterranean and Northern European countries differ in how they support young people. In Southern Europe a strong emphasis is placed on the family being responsible for the welfare of the young into early adulthood, while in the north responsibility rests more with the state.

This can bring diverse policies and legal contexts into the lives of young people in different nation states. For example, in Sudan, Pakistan and Singapore, the age of criminal responsibility is 7, in Australia, England and Wales it is 10, in Croatia it is 13, in Sweden it is 15, in Brazil and Peru it is 18, while in the United States it varies from state to state. Similar variations exist regarding the age at which a young person can consent to a sexual relationship: in Angola it is 12, in Japan, 13, in India 18 and in Tunisia it is 20. We also see other international variations in the age at which young people can vote, drive a car, get married or buy alcohol and cigarettes. As Mizen suggests, it is important to remember that 'age' and the roles attached or ascribed to it are political in nature: 'it is the political importance attached to age that in many respects shapes young people's lives' (2004, p.20). We should recognise the political nature of these processes in that the construction of youth around 'age' does not happen in a vacuum separate from political ideologies, motivations and economic developments: youth therefore is political in its nature (Cohen and Ainley, 2000; Kelly, 2001; Mizen, 2004; France et al, 2012)

A second important feature of youth policy is the sets of assumptions and understandings of youth and age that operate to 'problematise' young people. In many senses:

> the constructions of 'youth' during the modern age say as much about the builders as about their subjects, and the way that the concept of youth has been used clearly relates

very closely to historical conditions and the social concerns of the times. (Jones, 2009a, p.4)

In this context the construction of youth is shaped by the common-sense and dominant views of what it means to be young that exist in public perceptions, media representations and political discourses (France, 2007). These tend to rely upon a number of core assumptions strongly influenced by a psychological and developmentalist paradigm (Davis, 1990). Adolescence was 'discovered' in the 19th century by G. Stanley Hall (1904) and was seen as a set of individual dispositions with physical or psychological attributes (Springhall, 1986). These ideas first emerged in the Enlightenment period and were given a scientific basis via developments in psychology (France, 2007). This essentialist model is based upon beliefs and values implying that youthful behaviour is strongly influenced by the need to biologically reproduce. In this model, heterosexuality and Western Anglo-Saxon notions of 'normality' dominate (Wallace and Kovatcheva, 1998). This model of youth dominates discourses across the world. For example, Toivonen explains how psychiatric and medical discourses underpinned perspectives in Japan on 'the youth problem' and ultimately led to policy approaches that are 'coercive and punitive strategies, delivered, for instance, at correctional boarding schools or at hospitals for the mentally ill' (2013, p.35). He shows how, even in modern Japan, these ideas continue to remain central to how policy perceives and understands the causes of dysfunctional behaviour in the young. More recently, brain science and the development of new technology that measures and observes brain functioning has re-established genetics and biology as a powerful means of explaining the expanding time scales of the adolescent phase of life (Bessant, 2008; France, 2012; Kelly, 2012). It claims that the young brain does not mature until the person is in their late 20s, and therefore we need to recognise that the period of growth during adolescence may well be longer than previously assumed. While there remain serious concerns about the science and the causal relationships, these views have gained popularity around the world (Bassant, 2008; Choudhury, 2010; Kelly, 2012; France, 2012). We see a wide range of ideas and beliefs about what youth and age are and how they need to be managed underpinning the policy-making process. In many cases these beliefs reinforce the belief that youth is a problem that needs to be managed.

The ecology of youth policy, as a field of practice, is not shaped only by ideas and perceptions of youth and age; it is also shaped by the interplay between political ideology and policy delivery that is managed through the political machinery of policy making. Therefore the institutional arrangements that organise and deliver social policy are also instrumental in shaping the youth experience:

> The dimensions of historical time and place must be considered in order to understand the restructuring of the youth phase. The coordinates of this period of life vary according to the economy and the educational and social policy of the state ... Modern societies differ in their institutional arrangements concerning life transitions: education and training provisions, labour market regulations, exclusion mechanisms, social assistance rules, and to the extent to which there is an explicit youth policy. (Heinz, 2009, p.6)

Youth policy remains messy and complex (Ball, 2008) and has to be seen as dynamic and multidimensional (White and Wyn, 2008). Drawing on the concept of 'nested ecology' and Bronfenbrenner's concept of social ecology, we can see that youth policy operates over many levels and across a variety of social spaces and practices. The macro level is where 'big P' policy is made in government (Ball, 2008), usually resulting in legislation and a policy framework that shapes the exosystems, mesosystems and micro levels of social practice (France et al, 2012). How this policy is constructed and shaped is in itself an interesting question. Historically, youth policy has been highly political, in that it is strongly influenced by ideological interests (Pitts, 2001).

Youth policy can emerge from anxiety around social change or a recognition of perceived societal needs (White and Wyn, 2008; Williamson, 2012). As we shall see in the following chapters, recent policy initiatives in a wide range of countries around unemployment, training and pre-secondary education have emerged partly as a result of societal anxieties about social and economic changes and young people's abilities to respond. Modern societies need to respond to social change and find ways of supporting the young as they move towards adulthood (Williamson, 2012). However, these processes are not neutral and are entangled with power relationships (Ball, 2008) and 'ruling relations' (Smith, 1999). What the problem is and how to respond are usually defined by a political elite that operates in and through the state (Bourdieu, 1998; Wacquant, 2009), making macro policy highly political (France et al, 2012). In many cases youth policy is an evidence-free zone, where powerful political ideological interests of key stakeholders can shape what is to be done with young people

(Williamson, 2012, p.26). We will explore this further in the next chapter, when looking at the influence of neoliberal thinking on policy making, especially in relation to the recent economic crisis.

Youth policy is also a product of a wide range of institutional processes:

> 'Youth policy' as a concept is the *product* of (international), national, regional (provincial) and local political decisions made within a range of policy sectors (such as education, training, housing and health). It is concerned both with the general population of young people and with specific sub-groups within that general population (such as young women, offenders or ethnic minorities. It may even extend to highly focused initiatives directed towards sub-categories around specific policy themes (such as young mothers or ethnic minority unemployment). (Finland International Report on Youth Policy, quoted in Williamson, 2002, pp.35–6)

Who is responsible for constructing policy in government at the macro level is also complex. How countries organise themselves in terms of policy has a major impact on how policies are formed (Williamson, 2002). The institutional and structural arrangements of youth policy are usually fragmented across a number of internal departments. Some government departments are seen as being more about youth than others. Education departments are fundamentally about the needs of children and young people, as are youth justice and post-secondary education, but most other departments or ministries in government will make policies that have impacts on young people. Government departments responsible for health, employment (and unemployment), finance and housing are responsible for all age groups, and of course all their policies affect young people as a part of that general population. Attempts to achieve better coordination across policy domains can arise as a result of having a dedicated minister or ministry (such as a Department of Children and Young People or a Ministry for Youth), although its degree of influence, level of resources and areas of responsibility can determine how successful it is in making and implementing youth policy (Williamson, 2012).

Macro youth policy making has a major impact on the exosystem and mesosystem levels of institutions responsible for delivering and implementing youth policies. It provides the legislative framework, the legal context for professional social practice, and usually provides guidance and direction for local policy makers (Williamson, 2002). However, the ways in which these policies are interpreted and implemented (or resisted) are determined by those operating at the local level. Some policies will be 'non-negotiable' and fixed (usually around legal requirements), although the level and extent of this will be determined by the relationship the state has with local areas and those responsible for the delivery of policy (Williamson, 2002). This can differ significantly between nation states (Hahn-Bleibtreu and Molgat, 2012; Antonucci et al, 2015).

Youth policy can also be made at the exosystem and mesosystem level of social practice. At a local level, regional assemblies, local states, provinces and/or local councils can create youth policies that reflect local circumstances and the local use of resources (White and Wyn, 2008). Local areas have legal powers, legislative authority and mechanisms for delivering services and resources to the young. For example, Australia has six states, each with its own constitution, legislature, executive and judiciary, and each state is permitted to pass laws related to any matter not controlled by the Commonwealth under Section 51 of the Australian constitution. Australia also has three territories (Northern Territory, Australian Capital Territory and Norfolk Island). Legislation by the federal state is protected by the Australian constitution, although it only permitted to legislate on matters in the states outlined in this constitution, thus giving the states a strong legislative role in policy making. The territories are directly subject to the policies of the federal state, although the smaller territories have a degree of self-government. However, the Australian parliament can override laws in these areas. Each state, apart from Queensland, has a bicameral parliament (with an upper and lower house), with the major legislator being the lower house. Add to this the distribution of local councils and the system of youth policy making and practice becomes even more complex. For example, in the state of Western Australia there are 140 local government areas that provide services in cities, towns and shires. Similar diversity exists in Canada. Canada also has a federal government with states and territories, although these differ from Australia's system. The ten Canadian provinces have constituted powers while the three territories have powers delegated to them by the federal government. This means that the provinces are co-sovereign with their own Crown representative (a Lieutenant Governor who is appointed by the Queen in the UK). This gives them substantial autonomy in the policy-making process over areas such as health, education and welfare, although they receive transfer payments from the federal government, which can use these payments as a way of influencing policy direction. Each province then has a unique system of local government with municipal districts and regional municipalities and districts. These can also involve urban jurisdictions, such as cities, towns, villages and parishes. Cities in Quebec are further subdivided into *arrondissements* ('boroughs').

Youth policy making is also undertaken institutionally and located in the everyday lives of the young at the micro level. For example, local schools and workplaces have significant autonomy to develop their own policies and practices. While these are usually framed by national or provincial legislation, each institution can decide its own priorities and responses to local issues. Schools, for example, can have policies on bullying, on catchment areas, on teaching of the curriculum (for example, sex education or not) and on exclusion that are distinctly of their own making (Ball, 2008; White and Wyn, 2008).

Who delivers youth policy is also an important question. While the state (in all its guises) may have a core responsibility for constructing and developing youth policy, the way it is interpreted and delivered is also important (Williamson, 2002; White and Wyn, 2008). Again, this is a complex issue and can vary according to domain area and the different emphases of national and local states. Historically, youth policy and practice has always been delivered through a wide range of organisations and institutions (France, 2007). For example, in terms of youth justice in the UK, the voluntary sector had a critical role to play in the late 19th century in providing care responses to those in trouble (Muncie, 2009). Similarly, education has always involved a mix of providers such as private, independent and public schools (Ball, 2008). We also see a strong, lengthy and illustrious history of voluntary organisations such as Barnardos, the Children's Society, the Salvation Army, local churches and other community organisations providing locally based youth services (Davies, 1999). This mix of providers between the state, non-government organisations (NGOs) and the private sector has been a central feature of the delivery model used in the field of youth policy. As we shall see in the chapters that follow, this relationship is ongoing and has become more diverse (Williamson, 2008).

The development and construction of 'youth policy' is thus shaped by a wide range of ideological and structural features. As with the challenges posed by the discourses on youth, tensions and contradictions also exist at the level of structural development of youth policy. The underlying values and focuses of youth policy in government circles are dynamic and diverse. But who provides the driving force behind a particular youth policy and who 'owns' a policy can create conflicts between departments or organisations:

> ministerial portfolios are invariably, understandably, stubborn in defending their particular domains of policy in which young people may often figure relatively marginally. (Williamson, 2012, p.25)

Questions of siloing and interdepartmental conflicts have been rife in recent debates over youth policy (White and Wyn, 2008; Williamson, 2012). Such differences create problems in coherence and delivery (Williamson, 2008). Historically, the aims and purpose of youth policies have differed depending on the governing political party. Williamson (2012) reminds us that there is no single youth policy operating in any nation state: policy aims can vary not only over time but between and even within domains. For example, education can be seen as both providing opportunities for social mobility and as creating a system that reproduces the status quo (Ball, 2008). Youth justice policies can navigate between care and control, aiming not only to protect but also to regulate and govern young people's behaviour (Muncie, 2009). Other policies can aim to be protective and supportive while having unintended consequences that lead to exclusion or marginalisation (Ellis and France, 2012). Similarly, tensions and contradictions can also exist over who should have the core influence in shaping policy. Issues surrounding the relationship between state and local control have been at the heart of conflicts over provision (Williamson, 2012). What the relationship should be regarding the delivery of services between the state, civil organisations, NGOs and the market can also vary between nation states, creating a range of tensions over both resources and values (Williamson, 2012). In this context we therefore need to recognise not only the ecological dimension of youth policy but also its political nature.

These processes of policy formation and delivery cut across many sites and age categories. As we know, youth is a social construct: who is included and who is excluded from the coverage of 'youth policy' is a political decision. Our interest, in the chapters that follow, centres on the group aged between 16 and 24, who are seen as 'post-school' but neither adults nor children (France, 2008a). As a field of practice it includes a range of subfields that are shaped by certain policy institutions and practices. This age group, as we shall see in in the discussion that follows, is of significant political interest because major changes are taking place that bring the youth question into sharper focus in this group. Our core focus will be on a number of major changes that have been taking place in dominant policy areas for this group, including education (that is, tertiary/vocational), employment/unemployment and welfare policies. We will also examine the impact of these on other parts of young people's lives, such as leaving home and gaining financial independence, but the primary focus will be on the restructuring of the school-to-work transition for those aged between 16 and 24.

Conclusion

This chapter has set out the core theoretical framework underpinning the discussion that follows. I have suggested that the dominant theories in youth sociology have both limits and gaps. The focus on the historical division between transitions and cultural studies, and limited engagement with the social context of young people's decision making and social action creates only a partial picture of what it means to be young. In tackling this I suggest an ecological approach can be more beneficial in that it includes a more holistic understanding of the structuring processes of institutions and social practices that determine how young people experience the everyday. In this analysis I suggest that we also need to understand how youth policy is both political and important in constructing the ecology of young people's lives. Not only is it normally underpinned by common-sense (but often incorrect) perceptions of youth and age but it also relies on scientific constructions of developmentalism that tend to problematise the young. This approach, mixed with ideological and structural economic forces, shapes policy in particular ways and creates a complex environment for 'being' and 'becoming'. In the next chapter, we will explore the broader political and economic issues that have been taking place, particularly around the recent economic crisis, that we must understand if we are to see how the youth policy programmes discussed in the rest of this book are being shaped.

TWO

The global crisis and the 'age of austerity'

Introduction

We are all familiar with the economic crisis of 2007. This was the 'mother of all crises' (Harvey, 2010, p.6) yet, as history shows, economic crises are not unusual in the history of capitalism. Evidence suggests there have been hundreds of crises around the world since the 1970s: it is suggested there have been 146 banking crises, 218 currency crises, and 66 episodes of sovereign debt crisis (Laeven and Valencia, 2012). Even the *Financial Times*, discussing an International Monetary Fund (IMF) report, suggested that there had been 132 countries that had experienced 'macroeconomic or financial crisis' between 1980 and 1996 (Bevins and Cappitt, 2009).

Not all of these crises have been global, although what constitutes a 'global crisis' remains unclear in the literature. It is suggested that a global crisis, while having its epicentre in national economies, will have a wider impact on a number of other economies. How far they reach into the 'global' and how much impact they have remain problematic in any definition, although it has been suggested that between the 1970s and the recent 2007 crisis there were in fact four major crises that had a global impact (Tapia, 2013). These are: the 1970s oil crises; the 1980s US monetary crisis; the 1990s collapse of the USSR economy; and the multiple crises in South East Asia and South America in 2000 (Tapia, 2013). Again, how far these were truly global can be debated: as we shall see in the discussion that follows, the 2007 crisis far exceeded the global impact and reach of all these other crises. It is clear that the 2007 crisis touched every economy worldwide and, while some have been more affected than others, it can be seen as truly global in its reach. It is in this context that the 2007 crisis is usually compared with the other major economic crisis that caused the great depression of the 1930s. As a result, what followed after the 2007 crisis is now called 'the great recession'.

This chapter will provide an understanding of the political ecological framework that has been shaping the 'youth question' over the last twenty years. It will provide an overview of the landscape not only of the crisis and great recession that followed, but also of the policy frameworks that were operating in the UK, Australia, Canada and New Zealand prior to the crisis. It will first discuss the causes of the 2007 crisis, noting that we need to recognise the core role played by both long-term capital development and more contemporary neoliberal social and economic policies. The focus will be on showing how the crisis can only be understood through exploring this historical relationship. To understand the 2007 crisis we need to recognise the interrelationship between the state and markets. The chapter also sets the scene for subsequent chapters by giving an historical analysis of this relationship of state and capital within these four case study areas, showing how these processes positioned states prior to the crisis and drawing out the core trends and influences that were in operation when the crisis emerged. This political ecology, as we shall see, had already established for the young in our case study areas a reconfiguration of their citizenship in which neoliberalism was being constructed as the core of social practice (Kelly, 2006). To conclude the discussion the chapter will explore how 'austerity' has been constructed in recent academic and political debates and how it has been used as a means of dealing with the great recession that followed the crisis of 2007, suggesting that in fact it has accelerated the neoliberal agenda. This will provide a framework for the discussions that continue in the following chapters.

Economic crisis and neoliberalism

To understand the crisis of 2007 it is essential to have an historical perspective of the major economic and political changes that have been taking place across the globe in the last forty years (Harvey, 2010). As we shall see, while the 'trigger' for this crisis was the collapse of the US subprime mortgage market and the associated banking crisis, the major causes were problems within capitalism itself (Harvey, 2010). While the key problem emerged through the crisis in capital accumulation, it can only be understood in relation to the role that neoliberalism played in framing the ecological landscape of different nation states. As a way of managing economic affairs, the concept of neoliberalism has gained enormous credence in a wide range of circles and has, since the 1970s, dominated national planning in a number of major economies (Harvey, 2010). Neoliberalist approaches have also been widely accepted as an economic strategy by organisations such as the World Bank, the IMF, the General Agreement on Tariffs and Trade (GATT), and the

World Trade Organisation, ensuring neoliberal approaches have had significant impact across the globe in terms of how to run capitalism efficiently (Harvey, 2010; Wacquant, 2011). We see crises arising out of the architecture and contradictions embedded within the neoliberal economic and political strategies used by national governments to help manage capital accumulation and increase profit (Harvey, 2010; Duménil and Lévy, 2011; Peck and Theodore, 2012).

So what is neoliberalism? Harvey suggests that neoliberalism is:

> in the first instance a theory of political and economic practices that proposes that human wellbeing can best be advanced by liberating individual and entrepreneurial freedoms and skills within an institutional framework characterised by strong property rights, free markets, and free trade. The role of the state is to create and preserve an institutional framework appropriate to such practices ... (Harvey, 2005, p.2)

Neoliberalism is fundamentally a set of principles and ideas about how the economy should be run. As an ideology, neoliberalism is informed by the neoclassical economic theory of 'free markets' where there is a 'freeing up' and deregulation of markets in favour of capital or business interests, not just at the national level but also internationally (Brenner and Theodore, 2002). In this process, those drawing on neoliberal principles will side with business, aiming to create an investment climate. It always favours the 'integrity of the financial system and the solvency of financial institutions over the well-being of the population or environmental quality' (Harvey, 2005, p.71). Neoliberalism is traditionally seen as having an intolerance of state intervention (other than to 'free up' markets) and is anti-trade union, viewing the Keynesian policies and 'social consensus' of the post-war years as detrimental to individual freedom and economic growth (see Hayek, 1944; Friedman and Friedman, 1980). Claims regarding the withering away of the state or small government have therefore become synonymous with neoliberalism (Cahill, 2010). It is suggested that neoliberalism is in fact an 'historic victory of capital over labour' (Berger, 1999, p.453), leading to claims that it is a class-based process (Duménil and Lévy, 2005; Harvey, 2005).

As a set of policies and practices neoliberalism has a range of approaches that national governments can draw upon. For example, it can argue for an aggressive downsizing of the state and of public spending in areas such as health and welfare benefits while also reducing taxation, especially for the rich. It is usually in favour of privatisation of public services such as education, state housing and building programmes, and is strongly in favour of de-nationalisation and asset sales of public goods and services such as railways and utilities such as electricity, gas and water suppliers. As Cahill suggests, it is keen to see 'an expansion of the sphere of commodification, by deregulation and the opening up of former state-monopolised services to profit-making enterprise' (2010, p.303)

The history of neoliberalism can be traced back to the 1930s although it emerged more strongly and its influence grew in the 1970s (Harvey, 2005; Peck, 2010). It is claimed that it grew in influence as the Keynesian project, established after the Second World War, was fragmenting and entering a period of decline (Harvey, 2005). While it seemed to have its roots in the UK and the US, led by Margaret Thatcher and Ronald Reagan, it clearly had a major impact in the 1980s in states such as Canada, New Zealand, Germany, the Netherlands, France, Italy and even Sweden (Brenner and Theodore, 2002). Its emergence was seen as a result of reaction to the excesses of previous phases and a re-embedding of markets and marketised governance into community and strategic planning (Craig and Porter, 2006). 'Faced with the declining profitability of traditional mass production industries and the crisis of Keynesian welfare policies … national and local states … started to mobilize a range of policies intended to extend market discipline' (Branner and Theodore, 2002, p.350). While the welfare capitalism of Keynesian economics delivered high rates of economic growth in the 1950s and 1960s, by the 1970s there were major problems, with a number of large domestic economies moving into stagflation, suggesting that Keynesian policies were no longer working. What became clear was that there was a growing crisis in capital accumulation alongside a growing demand from labour for more resources (Harvey, 2005) and this brought major political threats to the economic elites and ruling classes in many advanced capitalist countries. Neoliberalism then became 'a political project to re-establish the conditions for capital accumulation and to restore the power to economic elites' (Harvey, 2005, p.19).

Since the 1970s, this form of financialisation has expanded across the globe. Capital and money and neoliberal ideas about them have not only become more mobile and influential but also entrenched in key thinking. This was defined as the 'Washington Consensus' (Williamson, 1990), which was seen a strongly neoliberal perspective among senior policy advisers and politicians about how national economies should be run. The list of recommended policies included the avoidance of national deficit budgets; tax reforms to reduce the burden on finance; the use of interest rates as a way of managing the market; the creation of competitive currency rates; trade liberalisation; and deregulation policies (Williamson, 1990). Neoliberalist policies and practices have therefore become more central, not only at a national level but also in the global economy, suggesting that neoliberalism is the new orthodoxy, not just in nation states but also internationally, thus creating a new hegemony and world order for capital. As Peck and Tickell suggest, 'neoliberalism has provided a kind of operating framework or "ideological software" for competitive globalisation' (2002, p.380).

The 2007 crisis

It is important to recognise, first, that the economic crisis of 2007 was in fact a crisis in neoliberalism and is connected to problems of capital accumulation (Harvey, 2010; Duménil and Lévy, 2011; King et al, 2012) and, second, that in fact we need to talk about not one crisis but two (Ortiz and Cummins, 2012; Konzelmann, 2014), with the second being driven by the use of austerity as a policy response to the great recession. In terms of the 2007 crisis, a number of contradictions driven by neoliberal politics converged simultaneously to create a crisis not just in one sector of the economy but in many. First, over the previous decades neoliberalism had driven, shaped and influenced US policy by freeing up many of the financial organisations, such as banks and investment companies, from national and international regulation. Neoliberal focused governments created the 'New Financial Architecture' (NFA), shaped by the financial deregulation that had been emerging since the 1970s:

> The NFA is based on light regulation of commercial banks, even lighter regulation of investment banks and little, if any, regulation of the 'shadow banking system' – hedge and private equity funds and bank-created Special Investment Vehicles (SIVs). (Crotty, 2009, p.564)

It also embedded in the structure 'perverse incentives that induced key personnel in virtually all important financial institutions … to take excessive risks when markets were buoyant' (2009, p.565). Similarly, in the banking sector individuals were encouraged to take risks without accountability and banks were allowed to become more concentrated, allowing for wider diversity in investments, especially in higher risk areas (Morgan, 2009; Tregenna, 2009). This created an environment where the searching out of high profits by the financial sector created a moral hazard (Harvey, 2010), allowing banks and bankers to act irresponsibly and not have to face the consequences of their high-risk behaviour. The quest for greater profits was led by a politically influential class within the financial sector that was already earning and generating great swathes of wealth. The high earners and the wealthy class increased their share of income and wealth throughout this period (Duménil and Lévy, 2011), and the NFA of neoliberalisation created opportunities for their share to grow further. This does not seem like a problem of capital accumulation, but the second development that had been evolving since the end of the 20th century located profit accumulation within a culture of indebtedness (Duménil and Lévy, 2011). While those already on high incomes were able to push their incomes even higher, the growing financialisation of the market place enabled both governments and US households to increase the use of debt while wages were kept low (Harvey, 2010). Thus a gap was created between what labour was earning and what it was able to spend, leading to the freeing of credit markets by governments and the increased use of debt by households. For example, between 1980 and 2007 household debt almost quadrupled in the US; mortgages became easier to get and credit card spending increased substantially. By the late 1990s the market among the middle class was saturated with debt so new ways of bringing in those on lower incomes were needed (Harvey, 2010). As a result 'financial institutions, awash with credit, began to debt-finance people who had no steady incomes' (Harvey, 2010, p.17). This was a critical feature of the 'spark' for the crisis, in that the subprime market collapsed and debt could not be collected. National governments had also got themselves into high levels of debt. The collapse came when borrowers defaulted in large numbers, especially in the subprime market. These risks had been shared across international borders in the form of property stocks, or what became seen as 'toxic debt'. The financialisation and liberalisation of the global market place that had been taking place under neoliberalisation since the 1990s meant that this hit a number of international banks and national economies, leading from a financial crisis to an economic crisis for large sections of the world (Farnsworth and Irving, 2012). Major problems in liquidity appeared in the banking sector and banks started to collapse.

The ripple effect was colossal, affecting almost every nation state. In a report for Eurostat (Moulton, 2014), the impact of the great recession on gross domestic product (GDP) was outlined. Between the first quarter of 2008 and the first quarter in 2009, GDP across the Organisation for Economic Co-operation and Development (OECD) countries dropped, on average, by 4.9%. The initial impact was mild but by the last quarter of 2008 it had greatly increased. In the USA GDP declined 4.3%. In Europe the impact was greater, with the average drop being 5.7%, although some countries, such as the UK (7.2%) and Italy (7.2%) suffered more. Internationally, some countries were hit even harder. In Japan GDP dropped 9.2% in one year. In Estonia GDP dropped 20% and in Ireland, where three of the largest banks collapsed, GDP dropped 12.8%. A number of countries experienced more limited impact: in Australia the drop was only 0.9%, in New Zealand 2.6% and in Norway 3.4%. There was also a massive drop in consumer demand of 2.7% on average across OECD countries, although this hides national variations. The downturns were concentrated in manufacturing, with a fall of 16.3% between 2007 and 2009 in Europe and 11.5% in the US.

'Actually existing neoliberalism'

While it is clear that neoliberalism has grown in influence worldwide and played a major role in the 2007 economic crisis, we also have to recognise that significant geographical differences exist in how it is operating (Peck and Tickell, 2002; Harvey, 2005). Harvey, for example, shows that many nation states have only partially taken the 'neoliberal turn' (2005, p.87). We therefore need to resist the idea that neoliberalism is universally applied and instead recognise the processes that neoliberalisation draws upon to become embedded within the infrastructure of everyday life. Peck and Tickell suggest an emphasis on:

> ...walking a line of sorts between producing, on the one hand, overgeneralized accounts of a monolithic and omnipresent neoliberalism, which tend to be insufficiently sensitive to its local variability and complex internal constitution, and on the other hand, excessively concrete and contingent analyses of (local) neoliberal strategies, which are inadequately attentive to the substantial connections and necessary characteristics of neoliberalism as an extralocal project. (Peck and Tickell, 2002, pp.381–2)

The neoliberalism discourse presents itself as 'naturalised', with tendencies towards 'homogenization, levelling out and convergence' creating a sense of the 'all-encompassing politics of neoliberalism' (Peck and Tickell, 2002, p.383). Yet this approach does not recognise the diversity of neoliberalism as a process and one where the state regularly puts regulations in place. We need to acknowledge the dynamics of the process, rejecting the concept of neoliberalism as 'static' and monolithic, and incorporating shifts in logic and patterns over time, showing how neoliberalism both exists and changes in different social and economic contexts. Understanding the process of neoliberalisation is important, recognising that in reality there is not one single form of neoliberalism but many versions (Larner, 2003).

Such an approach acknowledges how neoliberalism operates in different contexts at different times in history. For example, it is sometimes assumed that in neoliberal ideology market forces operate according to specific laws and rules, but the reality of social, economic and political practice is very different. Therefore neoliberalism can only be understood in its specific context, as influenced by a range of factors at the national and local levels. It is important to recognise in the variety of neoliberal approaches their 'politico-ideological foundations ... their multifarious institutional forms ... developmental tendencies, their diverse socio-political effects and their multiple contradictions' (Peck and Tickell, 2002, p.353). We also need to acknowledge the interplay between the state and markets and realise that while the 'model' of neoliberalism suggests 'one size fits all', we need to recognise the 'extraordinary variations that arise as neoliberal reform initiatives are imposed within contextually specific institutional landscapes and policy environments' (Peck and Tickell, 2002, p.353). Capitalist relations and forms of state regulation have to be understood in both their historical and geographical contexts.

The state, markets and citizenship

The process of neoliberalisation (or actually existing neoliberalism) creates a situation where different countries are at different stages of development of the neoliberal approach. The movement towards a fully operational neoliberal state is therefore never linear or smooth and, at certain times in history, under certain circumstances and conditions, it may retreat or become reconfigured (Peck and Tickell, 2002). The state is seen as having a distinctive role in creating the right economic environment for markets, yet this is rather a narrow view that fails to grasp the complex relationship the state has in managing the neoliberalisation of society. While recognising the centrality of the state in this process, Wacquant (2009, 2010, 2012) proposes that it is critical to recognise that neoliberalisation is also a political project, not just an economic one, that involves not only dismantling the state but also using it to engineer itself into a particular form. For Wacquant, most studies of neoliberalism concentrate on the 'thin side', that is, the economic conception of the approach, giving little attention to the 'thick side' of the 'institutional machinery involved in the establishment of market dominance and its operant impact on effective social membership' (2012, p.71). He suggests that while there may be many forms of neoliberalism there remains an:

> '...institutional core that makes it distinct and recognisable. This core consists of an articulation of *state, market and citizenship* that harnesses the first to impose the stamp of the second onto the third. So all three of these institutions must be brought into our analytical ambit. (2012, p.71)

Wacquant draws on Bourdieu's theory of the 'bureaucratic field' to show that some of the most pivotal political struggles are not always the most visible ones or those between external forces and the state, but are internal battles in 'public bureaucracies that compete to socialize, medicalize or penalize urban marginality and its correlates' (2012, p.218). It is here that organisations of the state monopolise the definition of the 'public good' and reinforce the notion that the state is 'not a monolith, a coherent actor or a single lever' but:

> a space of forces and struggles over the very perimeter, prerogatives and priorities of public authority, and in particular over what 'social problems' deserve its attention and how they are to be treated. (Wacquant, 2012, p.73)

The internal battles are between the 'right hand' of the state, the 'high-state nobility' who are strongly committed to neoliberalism and fostering marketisation, and the 'left hand' of the state that forms the 'social wing' that aims to protect its citizens from the worst ravages of neoliberalism. For example, since the 1970s, US society has shifted its priorities and actions from the left to the right hand, 'from the protective pole to the disciplinary pole of the bureaucratic field' (Wacquant, 2009, p.73). This shift has seen the convergence of welfare and penal policies, creating a double regulation in welfare and criminal justice policies and practices, and the penalisation of poverty which sees the '"iron fist" of the penal state mating with the "invisible hand" of the market in conjunction with the fraying of the social safety net' (2009, p.67). The success of this project can be seen not only in the US but also in parts of Europe and in other advanced economies where such strategies have been driven not by neoliberal right-wing governments but by the 'third way' politics of the left. In this context the 'neo' aspect of neoliberalism can best be understood by recognising that it is the:

> remaking and redeployment of the state as the core agency that actively fabricates the subjectivities, social relations and collective representations suited to making the fiction of markets real and consequential. (Wacquant, 2009, p.68)

Wacquant does not deny the centrality of marketisation within the ethos of the state, or its critical role in promoting and deregulating capital and the freeing of markets; what he proposes is that we need to recognise and understand how the bureaucratic field functions not only to aid the embedding of neoliberalism but also to normalise neoliberal ideas within the everyday discourses about how society should be run. This happens through a number of processes. First, the state and its agencies have a growing role in the 'devolution, retraction and re-composition' of social welfare. It has a core function in getting resistant individuals to accept de-socialised wage labour through the practice of workfare programmes (Wacquant, 2010, p.213). The reclassification of the subject as the 'client' and the commodification of individuals as responsible citizens undertaking their obligations becomes a central function. Second, the state builds a large and intrusive penal apparatus that operates to 'contain the disorders and disarray generated by diffusing social insecurity and deepening inequality' (Wacquant, 2010, p.213). It also operates to legitimise the state and the officials who run it. Finally, it has a critical role in promoting the concept of individual responsibility, which 'invades all spheres of life and creates legitimacy for non-state action' (2010, p.213). In this context, the state not only creates the framework for neoliberalism to flourish but also provides resources and legitimacy, while promoting a form of citizenship that is imbued with the importance of 'individual responsibility'.

Neoliberalism 'in practice'

In the following discussion, the history and context of how neoliberalism has unfolded in the UK, Australia, Canada and New Zealand is outlined and reviewed. The aim is to show how neoliberalism was operating in a different context until 2007, and to illustrate both the drivers and the points of resistance that created the versions of neoliberalism that now exist in our different states following the crisis. This helps us understand the discussions in the chapters that follow as it contextualises the different strategies of governments in dealing with the youth question before and after the crisis.

The United Kingdom

Since the 1980s government of Margaret Thatcher, UK politics has embraced neoliberalism as a core strategy for running the country (Jessop, 2002). What we see is a range of social and economic policies that embraced Thatcher's 'authoritarian populist hegemonic project, a centralizing "strong state" project and a neoliberal accumulation strategy' (Jessop, 2002, p.3). This incorporated four key approaches: monetarist economic policies aimed at reducing government spending and taxes while freeing the market; a social policy aimed at revitalising entrepreneurship and competition in the private sector (including breaking down trade union power); a form of redistributive welfare that aimed at breaking the dependency culture of social benefits; and, finally, an administrative policy that aimed at improving the effectiveness, responsiveness and accountability of public services by means of decentralisation, internal competition and further privatisation. This strategy aimed at liberalising and promoting the free market, deregulating and privatising the state, increasing capital accumulation and internationalising the economy (Jessop, 2002).

After the fall of Thatcher, her approach was continued by the John Major government, which consolidated 'Thatcherism' as a core way of 'doing business'. The government continued to oversee the financialisation of the economy and processes of deregulation that were aimed at curbing trade union power and continued the privatisation of the state. In 1997, we saw the arrival of Tony Blair's New Labour government with its strong commitment to 'third way' politics, which stayed in power until 2010. This was seen as a more compassionate and 'modern' approach that drew on both left- and right-wing policies (Ferguson, 2004). Stuart Hall suggested that New Labour was distinct from the previous Thatcher-inspired governments in that it was a 'hybrid regime' (Hall, 2003, p.19), a 'social democratic variant of neo-liberalism' (2003, p.22) that 'modified the anti-statist stance of American-style neo-liberalism by a "reinvention of active government"' (Hall, 2003, p.19). However, it also continued the neoliberal approach of being committed to market fundamentals, whereby the state is seen as inefficient and the market as efficient. Throughout its time in power, New Labour embraced the market and this was seen as a key driving force in its economic and social policy programmes. We saw policies that created internal markets and increased forms of financialisation of public policy. For example, in the National Health Service (NHS) and higher education we saw the expansion of 'quasi markets' and competition, and the introduction of public finance initiatives (PFI)[1] in the building of schools and hospitals. We also saw greater deregulation of the financial sector and the movement of the Bank of England to independent status in order to deregulate and free up international markets. Welfare policies, such as the New Deal programme, aimed to tackle the so called dependency culture and those who were unwilling to take responsibility for themselves (Lister, 2010), along with antisocial behaviour orders tackling those who were seen as problematic (France, 2009). Its 'soft side' was a focus on community, social inclusion and social democratic politics that aimed to protect individuals from the worst aspects of the market while enabling them to take responsibility for themselves and their families. This also included increased government spending on childcare support, education, and the NHS.

Australia

In Australia the neoliberal agenda has its origins in the 1970s but was accelerated by the Hawke government (1983–91) and then by the Howard administration in 1996 (Deeming, 2014). Successive governments drew on neoliberal principles in constructing national and regional economic policies that embedded core principles into a wide range of policy areas (Western et al, 2007). The first signs of neoliberalism emerged as a response to the 1970s oil crisis. The newly elected conservative government introduced what was called the 'death of a thousand cuts' (Starke, 2013, p.658), in which cutting health and welfare benefits, and a focus on inflation and deficit budgets, became core to federal policy making. While other governments that followed were more reluctant to take on free market ideas, the changing economic climate throughout the 1980s and 1990s saw the financialisation of Australian policy and practice become normalised (Cahill, 2010). For example, over this twenty-year period, we saw deregulation of the telecommunications market and the airline industry. The privatisation of Telstar, Qantas and the utilities, alongside the use of 'markets' in health care and child care, and the contracting out of states' services, all contributed to increased financialisation of Australian society. We have also seen, over the last forty years, the erosion of trade union rights (Western et al, 2007), with reforms such as the

---

[1] PFI is a public/private funding partnership that sees public infrastructure projects funded with private capital.

'Workchoices' legislation introduced by the Howard coalition putting major restrictions on trade unionism in the workplace (Ellem, 2006). In contrast, Australia has also retained 'big government' with a major role in maintaining economic stability. For example, state spending as a proportion of GDP increased from 18% to 24% between 1974 and 2007, showing that neoliberal states do not 'wither away' but need to maintain high spending levels (Cahill, 2010). In 1996, the conservative-led Howard government took power. While reasonably liberal in its thinking, Howard's government introduced a number of major reforms that clearly helped to embed neoliberalism into Australian society (Deeming, 2014). By the beginning of the 21st century, the Australian economy was growing at one of its fastest rates ever as a result of the mining boom, with the Howard government delivering six budget surpluses in a row. Unemployment was at its lowest and government revenue at its highest for over 33 years. While government spending increased across a wide range of sectors throughout this period, the Howard government introduced major tax reforms that provided massive benefits to high earners in Australia: 'of the AU$169 billion in tax cuts, 42% of them or $71 billion, went to the top ten earners' (Grudnoff, 2014, quoted in the Saturday paper, *Australia*, 20 December 2014). The Howard government was also strongly influenced in its approach to social policy by US conservative thinkers Charles Murray and Lawrence Mead (O'Connor et al, 2001), and it is at this time that welfare to work programmes began to emerge in Australia as a way of instilling a sense of obligations and responsibilities into 'dependent' benefit claimants and reducing 'undesirable incentives' in the form of benefits (Savelsberg, 2010).

Canada

Similar to the UK and Australia, the watershed for neoliberalism in Canada arrived in the 1980s, and by 2006 it was well entrenched and normalised. As the Keynesian welfare state reached a point of crisis, commitments to full employment in Canada were eroded and monetary economic policy took hold (Stanford, 2014). The conservative Mulroney took office in 1984 and neoliberal strategy of the roll back of the state was introduced (Carroll and Little, 2001). The government's engagement with neoliberal reform was incremental and could be seen as an erosion rather than an outright dismantling (Banting, 1987) but, as McBride and McNutt suggested: 'it appears that instrumentalism and "stealth" over a protracted period produced fundamental change' (2007, p.186). This was a period when monetarist economic policies such as the deregulation of the labour market, privatisation of public services and the introduction of a regressive tax system alongside a commitment to free trade (especially with the US) took hold and became a core part of the policy-making agenda in Canada (Carroll and Little, 2001; Stanford, 2014). Throughout the 1980s and into the 1990s a major reconfiguration of social programmes was undertaken, although 'the means of implementing changes in social programmes were initially cautious and incremental' (McBride and McNutt, 2007). These involved 'transforming universal to selective social benefits, tightening eligibility requirements, imposing ceilings on programme costs, making programmes self-funding and "claw backs" on certain benefits' (McBride and McNutt, 2007, p.186). This saw massive changes in benefits paid out, with some programmes saving millions of dollars (MacDonald, 1999). McBride (2005) suggests that these changes, alongside major free market reforms, were core aspects of the growth of a corporate state. McBride (2005) further suggested that, by the early part of the 21st century, Canada was normalising neoliberalism as a way to do business.

One of the most significant changes made in the 1995 budget was the introduction of the Canada Health and Social Transfer (CHST), which reduced Canada's social wage dramatically and created conditions that demanded greater flexibility of the workforce (McBride and McNutt, 2007). This had an impact in the form of reductions in budgets to provinces and reduced commitments to social insurance schemes by the federal state. Alongside this, there was a prohibition on workfare programmes being abolished, allowing new schemes to be developed and run in the provinces. As McBride and McNutt suggest:

> we can see the end of the full employment commitment, the gradual erosion of the social policy network during the 1980s and, after 1995, sharp cuts to social programmes and the abandonment of Federal conditions that had, for example, prevented Provinces implementing workfare programmes. (2007, p.187)

What we start to see is neoliberalism being impacted upon by its uneven development in different countries (Peck and Tickell, 2002). Provinces, under the new arrangements of the CHST, had no legal requirement to match expenditure allocated by the federal government, thus giving them more autonomy in their spending. Canada's main provinces then began to take a central role in 'rolling out' neoliberalism (McBride and McNutt, 2007). For example, Young (2008) shows how British

Columbia acted as a key driver of neoliberal reform in Canada by bringing in social and economic reforms, including changes such as cutting personal tax contributions by up to 25%, raising premiums for medical insurance, increasing fees for tertiary education and reducing child care subsidies (MacPhail and Bowles, 2008). Neoliberalisation was then increased at the local level by the policies of the provinces. Stephen Harper, a strong advocate of neoliberalism, was elected in 2006 and as a result the neoliberal 'roll out' has continued at the federal level (Stanford, 2014).

New Zealand

> Of all the countries involved in the OECD, New Zealand
> has embraced neoliberalism with the most enthusiasm.
> (Larner, 1996, p.32)

New Zealand has been seen as one of the leaders in the 'rush for neoliberalism', offering a 'textbook' example of 'good practice' that others were encouraged to emulate (Kelsey, 1993; Larner, 1996). In the 1990s it had undertaken a successful (though painful) restructuring of all walks of life. Neoliberal ideas reshaped policies in the economy, in social policy, in education, in health and even in the political system itself. The watershed period for New Zealand was seen as 1984. Not only were the ripples of economic crisis impacting on the economy but its economic problems were exacerbated by Britain joining the European common market. This in effect destroyed a major export industry in New Zealand almost overnight (Jesson, 1992; Kelsey, 1993), bringing massive public debt, inflation as high as 15% and extreme levels of unemployment (Larner, 1996). Led by Roger Douglas, the incoming Labour government introduced what is now defined as 'Rogernomics', a neoliberal, market-oriented approach to government (Larner, 1996). In its first year, the Labour government passed more legislation than any previous New Zealand government. It opened up its financial markets to outside investors, floated the dollar, created an independent Reserve Bank, removed large financial assistance programmes for agriculture and introduced a wide range of policies deregulating the business environment for manufacturing. This increased financialisation of the economy, opened up New Zealand to the internationalisation of the economy and led to foreign capital not only investing in New Zealand but also making substantial profits from its resources (Larner, 1996). It also split the state into funder and provider (Craig and Cotterell, 2007). Thirty state agencies were 'corporatised' and reconfigured as commercial enterprises, acting to contract out public services to the private sector and installing private sector principles (Larner, 1996). In this period New Zealand also sold off large sections of its nationalised industry, such as telecommunications, the railways and electricity. Such a dismantling of the state had never taken place anywhere else in the world.

In the 1990s, neoliberal policies remained and grew in influence (Humpage and Craig, 2008). Throughout the decade, social benefits were cut, with the abolition of universal family benefits shifting the focus towards targeted benefits, self-reliance and individual responsibility. Targeted work-activation programmes were introduced, which framed 'joblessness as the personal responsibility of the unemployed' (Humpage, 2011, p.6). Major trade union reforms removed collective bargaining as a right and replaced it with individual and local bargaining (Boston et al, 1999). Health services were radically reconfigured, with the costs of health being reframed as individual responsibilities. New Zealand was 'transformed along commercial lines through radical decentralisation, cost efficiencies and user-pays charges for all but the neediest' (Humpage, 2011, p.6). By 2000, a Labour government led by Helen Clarke was elected, and while it operated to 'soften' market forces (influenced by the 'third way politics of New Labour in the UK), it continued to support a neoliberal agenda. First, it is important to note that during this period the Labour Party did little to reverse the structural changes that had been imposed over the previous years. Their approach was to 'tinker' and limit the impact. For example, they extended a number of 'welfare to work' regimes and situated work as the first arm of welfare (Humpage, 2011), while also undertaking tax cuts in 2008.

There are a number of conclusions we can and should draw from this analysis of our case studies' relationships with neoliberalism. First, it is reasonable to say that, by 2007, neoliberalism was affecting the development of ideas and policies in all four of our case study areas discussed here in a significant way, although its development was not always linear or without points of resistance. Each country had its own timetable, using different approaches from the neoliberal 'toolbox' at different times, yet it is reasonably safe to say that neoliberalism remained an ongoing influence on policy making in all these countries. Second, at a national level, the ideology and practice of neoliberalism was not the sole preserve of the political right; the political left not only accepted the philosophy of neoliberalism but also enacted it in policy. When they were returned to office they tinkered with the system, offering stronger social welfare support, but the core principles of neoliberalism remained intact. Third, all forms of policy began to be about embedding markets. Policy was not to be simply about stopping the worst impacts of market forces. Markets were seen as important and good and the main way to do business. For example, it can be seen that 'third way politics' have been influential in all the countries. Such an approach introduced 'softer' versions of markets where the state had a more central role in running and regulating them, yet it is correct to say that it also normalised the use of markets as a way (the only way?) of distributing resources and providing services in all walks of life. Particular practices were thus embedded into the architecture and structures of the delivery of services. The use of markets in areas such as social policy and welfare services is now accepted policy in the four case study countries discussed. Neoliberalism's breadth of influence ranges across most public policy areas, shaping how services and welfare are delivered. For example, in Australia, employment services were contracted out so that now they are provided by the private sector and the third sector. Similar developments are taking place in the UK and Canada, and in New Zealand this has been a core policy for over thirty years. Fourth, neoliberalism is not just an economic project: it has a strong moralising component that is reshaping how we see social problems. Through its notions of tackling the 'dependency culture' of benefit claimants or tackling worklessness, the underclass are now seen as a necessary focus of all social and public policy and across all our case study areas the re-moralising agenda (especially of the poor) has been a central feature of political practice. Tony Blair's 'respect' agenda[2] is a good example of how a moral agenda supplements and supports the neoliberalisation of society. Finally, it is important to recognise that diversity does exist across these four case study areas, not only in the timing of the roll back of the state, or the roll out of neoliberalism, but also in different states/territories in Australia and different provinces in Canada. For example, in Canada the provinces shape the way that neoliberalism is developed and delivered, and it may be more appropriate to suggest that there are many 'neoliberalisms' that operate across the provinces. Similar issues arise in how neoliberalism is implemented in the different states of Australia, and in the UK with respect to the operation of social policy in Scotland, where substantial autonomy exists in setting and delivering policy.

---

[2]   In 2005 Tony Blair argued that there was a problem of disrespect in society and he formed a Respect Task Force with an action plan (Respect Action Plan). It built on the initiatives concerning 'anti-social behaviour' and was to be cross-departmental in its focus.

Youth, citizenship and neoliberalism

One of the major consequences of the 'neoliberal turn' has been a shift in the relationship that the young have with the state and with citizenship (France, 1996). As we shall see in the chapters that follow, young people's experience of 'belonging' and 'becoming' (France, 2008a) has undergone significant reconfiguration since the 1980s. The experience of growing up in late modern society is a combination of changes in international capital and national state policies that reinforce the economic imperative and the value of market forces. In this context, traditional models of youth transition (from school to work) have been radically altered and resituated (Woodman and Wyn, 2014). Young people across the globe now continue in education, in a variety of ways, well into their early 20s, with unprecedented numbers involved in higher education (OECD, 2014a). The development of human capital and the need for more qualifications has now become a dominant feature of most societies (Brown et al, 2011). Paid work is also harder to get and it takes longer for the young to achieve the careers they desire (Cuervo et al, 2013). Early experiences of work are, for many, precarious and uncertain, resulting in financial insecurity and lack of opportunities, especially for those who are vulnerable or want to leave home (Standing, 2011). State welfare regimes and support networks have also been strongly influenced by active labour market policies that see getting the young into work as the only way of ensuring their future wellbeing (Bonoli, 2010).

After the Second World War, there was an expansion of welfarism across the advanced economies such as the UK, Australia, Canada and New Zealand that embedded within both social and youth policy a notion of collective security that aimed to provide social solidarity through a form of welfare citizenship (France, 1996). Risks and uncertainty were to be managed through universal rights; benefits and welfare services that were to be provided by the state (Rose, 1996). In late modernity we have seen a reconfiguration of the temporal and spatial parameters of social and economic life (Leccardi, 2005; Wacquant, 2012) as collective rights have been eroded and individualisation, as a core aspect of policy and institutional arrangements, has re-emerged (Kelly, 2006). In this context, young people are required to think of themselves as 'flexible, creative, and not to blame failure on structural conditions but to see this as a result of their own underdeveloped entrepreneurial spirit' (Woodman and Wyn, 2014, p.47). In this new environment 'choice biographies' are seen as a core aspect of youth social policy, where the young have to take responsibility for managing their own lives (Beck, 1992). As a result, what we have started to see throughout youth policy is the emergence of a new form of citizenship that emphasises the 'entrepreneurial self' (Kelly, 2006); one that requires individual young people to be 'rational, autonomous, responsible ... and [having] dispositions of a free, prudent active subject', who are engaged in the process of 'reflexivity, continuously, endlessly for the term of [their] natural life' (Kelly, 2006, p.18). In this sense, we are seeing a form of neoliberal citizenship embedded in policy and institutional arrangements that advocates for a person to be responsible for themselves 'in the business of life, as an enterprise, a project or a work in progress' (Kelly, 2006, p.18). Similar to the discussions on the roll out of neoliberalism, this project or form of citizenship is at different stages in different countries. We cannot see it as complete or accepted by young people. It is important to recognise that this relationship is dynamic, evolving and consistently under negotiation and review. We will return to this point when considering what has happened to young people since the recession.

The 'great recession'

So far we have explored the cause of the crisis and outlined the relationship each of our case study areas has had with neoliberalism. But what happened after the 2007 crash? The detail of this in terms of youth policy will be discussed throughout the following chapters, but it is important to have a general picture of its impact on both the global economy and individual countries. The initial response worldwide was to act swiftly and to develop a number of national and international economic stimuli (Farnsworth and Irving, 2012). In late 2007, the European Union (EU) and the G8 countries met in order to develop a coordinated response. A number of high-level international agreements were made that involved multi-billion-dollar cash injections into the banking market by countries such as the US, the UK, Canada and Japan, as well as the EU, leading to claims that a new multilateralism was being formed and that the Washington Consensus was over (Farnsworth and Irving, 2012). In fact, some went so far as to say that neoliberalism was dead (Konzelmann, 2014). The growing consensus across a range of states was to increase spending. For example, in the UK, Alistair Darling, the Labour Chancellor of the Exchequer, wrote that 'much of what Keynes wrote makes sense ... You will see us switching our spending priorities to areas that make a difference ... we can allow borrowing to rise' (quoted in Konzelmann, 2014, p.24). It was claimed that, 'for a short period of time in 2009 and 2010, there was a "Keynesian moment" when all governments implemented fiscal stimulus packages' (Seccareccia, 2012, p.64). By 2011 this had changed and 'austerity' had become the dominant paradigm with respect to how to respond to the crisis (King et al, 2012; Ortiz and Cummins, 2012; Konzelmann, 2014). A number of factors came into play. First, there remained an 'ideological war' over how best to tackle the growing crisis (Clarke and Newman, 2012), in which neoliberal advocates constructed the problem as a problem of 'public debt':

> The current dominant image of its locus has been moved from the private to the public sector (from the financial services industry to public spending). It has been transformed from a financial crisis to a fiscal crisis (centred on government debt). (Clarke and Newman, 2012, p.300)

This 'shape changing' (2012, p.300) approach relocated the problem, ensuring that the debate concentrated on cutting public spending and moving towards 'surplus budgets' rather than drawing on fiscal stimulus. This ideological position was also reinforced by the IMF and others, such as the European Bank, through loan programmes (Clarke and Newman, 2012). This ideological positioning towards the crisis and the need for policies of austerity was also reinforced by the work of Reinhart and Rogoff (2009). They gave academic credibility to the rationale of tackling debt as a key priority. Their study of the relationship between GDP and debt claimed that the 'threshold' at which economic growth contracts is when the ratio of debt to GDP is 90%. This argument was then used by a range of influential political advisers and leading policy makers to argue for the introduction of austerity policies (Konzelmann, 2014). Even though the article has since been discredited (Herndon et al, 2014), its impact was to reinforce the hegemonic positioning of 'austerity' across a number of significant economies (Theodoropoulou and Watt, 2011), creating what Ortiz and Cummins (2012) claim is a second economic crisis, caused by the reduction of public and consumer spending.

Austerity policies have a long history (see Konzelmann, 2014, for a historical perspective), yet in reality, in these contemporary times, they have a strong association with neoliberal ideology and practice. The types of options open to governments include cutting back government spending, reducing public debt and reducing the tax burden on individuals, allowing them to have extra money for consumption (King et al, 2012). These strategies can be seen as neoliberal and reflect the ideological positioning of freeing up markets and tackling the excesses of the state (Konzelmann, 2014). However, the evidence for austerity remains weak in that the proposition that high levels of public debt impact on economic growth is unproven. In fact, as Taylor et al (2012) have shown, over the last fifty years, fiscal expansion and the use of public debt has repeatedly increased economic growth across the USA. So why continue with an austerity programme given it is an unproven strategy? First, a number of states have used the great recession as a way of either re-establishing or accelerating the implementation of core neoliberal principles. For example, nation states such as the UK, Australia, Canada and New Zealand introduced austerity policies by choice: other options were open to them but by 2010 the governments in these countries were persuaded by the idea of austerity measures, ensuring such ideas dominated the way the problem was understood and responded to (Farnsworth and Irving, 2012). As a strategy, austerity aims to drive down costs to businesses and free up labour, ensuring that capital accumulation can be increased (Labonté, 2012; Levitas, 2012). Second, those who benefit from austerity are those who hold significant power and influence. This is not new, in that the history of austerity shows us that it is class-based, creating and shaping divisions between different social groups. Much economic policy has been driven by narrow private sector interests consisting of financial and industrial elites supported by a neoliberal state that is willing to bail them out and cover the costs of the crisis (Konzelmann, 2014). Economic policy is therefore 'dictated ... by financial market traders, with their own interests at heart and very little loyalty to any national social or political economy' (2014, p.35). As we have seen, between 2000 and 2007 the deregulation of financial markets worldwide has meant that the levers government previously had were removed and the economies become 'prey to hostile speculation' (Konzelmann, 2014, p.34). Therefore nation states have limited influence. Austerity measures can then be imposed because the 'votes of the speculators in financial markets carry more weight in determining economic and employment policy and outcomes than do those of the electorate' (Konzelmann, 2014, p.34).

Ortiz and Cummins (2012) undertook a major review of how national economies were engaging with the austerity agenda. They found that that by 2012, 133 countries had reduced their annual expenditure: 93 of these countries were from the advanced economies and 39 countries were undergoing excessive contraction. This included 73 countries where wage bills or caps were being imposed, 55 countries that were rationalising social protection schemes, including the reform of pensions and welfare benefits, and another 73 countries where subsidies on food and transport were being removed. Similarly, Theodoropoulou and Watt (2011) investigated the use of austerity measures in 17 European countries and found that all of them had planned programmes between 2012 and 2016. It was estimated that this would save or generate over €500 billion across the region. Types of programmes include cutting the minimum wage; reduction in welfare programmes; reduction in pensions and other social benefits; job losses in public administration; and increased indirect taxes.

Austerity 'in practice'

The details regarding youth policy and austerity will be the focus of the next six chapters but it is important to recognise that, across our case study areas, the implementation of austerity measures has varied. In Australia, Canada, the UK and New Zealand we see them gaining influence, with conservative governments having substantial influence throughout the crisis and the great recession. For example, in the UK the coalition government, led by the Conservatives, was elected in 2010 followed by the election of a purely Conservative government in 2014, while in Australia the Liberals were elected in 2013. In Canada a centre-right government had been elected in 2006 and was re-elected in 2010, and in New Zealand a National (conservative) government has been in power since 2008. By 2013, all four of these governments had ensured a focus on reducing the deficit and the use of extensive austerity measures. This has not been a smooth or linear process in that, similar to other parts of the world, the initial response had been to use economic stimulus. For example, in Australia the newly elected Labor government in 2008 responded to the potential economic crisis by setting a major stimulus budget as it still had a healthy economy driven by mining revenue and resources. The stimulus included the direct transfer of money to pensioners (AU$1,400) and families on means tested benefits got AU$1,000 per child. Each person also got a AU$900 tax bonus. Overall, from 2007 to 2009, the Rudd government approved AU$95 billion in spending. But by 2012 the Labor government, led by Julia Gillard, had shifted its focus and embarked on a programme of austerity measures even though its economy had 'weathered the storm' and was still one of the strongest in the world. This prepared the way for the Abbott government, elected in 2013, which was determined to introduce austerity measures, even though Australia was not in a recession. His government has a strong commitment to neoliberal principles and has cut welfare benefits and state services. Similarly, in the UK the Labour government initially responded to the economic crisis by making huge bailout payments to the banks, including re-nationalising Northern Rock. Its bailout was the equivalent of 12% of GDP (Gough, 2011). In 2010, the election produced no clear result, leading to the formation of a Conservative-led coalition, which aimed to bring the UK economy into surplus by 2015. This saw austerity become central to the language and policy of government, and again, at its heart were neoliberal reforms that attacked the 'dependency culture' of welfare, reduced taxes and reduced the role of the state. In 2012, further cuts were proposed, and in 2014 the austerity programme was extended, with over £12 billion of cuts being planned to be implemented between 2015 and 2017. In Canada, the initial response to the economic crisis in 2007 was also to propose a stimulus budget. This increased investment in skills training and education (CA$8.3 billion), house building (CA$7.8 billion) and infrastructure development (CA$12 billion), but by 2010 the focus had shifted to austerity measures that brought in substantial cuts in government spending. This programme became more extensive in 2012, with plans to have a balanced budget in place by 2015.It was to be partly financed by job losses in government and the freezing of government operating costs. In New Zealand, the incoming conservative government inherited a healthy economy that had a deficit of only 20% of GDP. It was in a strong position to avoid the worst effects of the global economic crisis. While the new government had a strong neoliberal interest its first budget increased spending to over NZ$16 billion for five years as a way of avoiding economic fallout from the great recession. By 2010 a shift had taken place and the deficit had become a central focus of policy. This saw tax cuts and proposed reductions in public spending. In 2011, the earthquake in Christchurch required substantial investment and, as a result, the government increased its austerity programme to help balance the books. In 2014 the National Party was elected for a third time.

Conclusion

This chapter has introduced the broader macro developments that are shaping the ecological landscape in which young people now have to exist. It sets the scene for the discussions that follow. What is clear is that, over the last twenty years, neoliberalism has made substantial inroads in reshaping the political and policy arena across the four case study countries discussed here. Since the 1980s its economic and social doctrines have become normalised and embedded, not just at the level of ideas but also within the architecture of the infrastructure of public and social policy. It is also clear that neoliberalisation has been accelerated as a result of the 2007 economic crisis and the great recession. Austerity measures are fundamentally neoliberal practices that encourage states to prioritise the 'economic imperative' and market principles as the core of economic recovery. Of course, the emergence of a form of citizenship for the young, strongly shaped by neoliberal politics and policies, has its roots in the 1990s. The growing demands by the state for 'self-actualisation' and 'personal responsibility' among the young have long been in place, but, as the following discussion will show, the economic crisis and great recession is driving the political project of the 'entrepreneurial self' as the norm of what it means to be a citizen in the 21st century.

THREE

Education and training: the broken promise

Introduction

Over the last thirty years we have seen more young people worldwide participate in education than ever before. This increase has accelerated in the early 21st century. In 2000 less than one-fifth of those aged 18 to 24 in Organisation for Economic Co-operation and Development (OECD) countries were engaged in some form of post-16 education or training (OECD, 2014a). Between 1999 and 2012, post-16 education and training enrolment among those aged 16 to 25 grew by 45 million to 138 million, with Brazil, China, India, Nigeria, Cuba and South Korea showing the greatest gains. By 2012, across all OECD countries, 82% of 15–19-year-olds and 38% of 20–24-year-olds were participating in some form of full-time education[1] (OECD, 2014a). By 2012, in most industrialised and developed countries, higher education (university-based) enrolments reached approximately half of the age group (18–24-year-olds) with rates exceeding two-thirds in some parts of North America and Western Europe and three-fifths in parts of Oceania (OECD, 2014a).

The post-16 domain in education and training has now become a central field of practice for the young. School-to-work transitions, where the majority of young people left school and went straight into work, have become a distant memory and have been replaced by new transitional arrangements that have strong connections to training and education (Brown et al, 2011; Woodman and Wyn, 2014). Participating in education and training after leaving compulsory schooling has now become more normalised for the young. In fact, as we will see in Chapter Six, some countries are now making it compulsory to be in education or training for those aged 16 to 18. Even in countries where it is not compulsory we also see high levels of engagement for this age group, as they recognise that 'qualifications' are essential cultural capital if they are to get work in the future. While those aged over 20

---

[1]   This figure includes all types of education and training.

have historically always been less involved in education and training, we have now started to see increased numbers, suggesting they have an extended relationship with education and training that may continue well into their mid 20s. Understanding how the expansion of this subfield of the post-16 experience has taken place and what the key drivers are, is important to our discussion.

In this chapter we start by outlining international trends in the growth of education and training, followed by a review of how this growth has affected our case study countries. This analysis shows that these trends are not new (having their beginnings back in the 1990s) but also indicates that, after the economic crisis, the level of engagement in education and training has remained stable and in some cases has grown. In the second part of the discussion we will see how social policies in the UK, Australia, Canada and New Zealand have contributed to this process and also, through a range of 'third way' strategies, how they have aimed to widen participation for groups that historically struggled to take part in post-16 education and training. In the final section we will examine the impact of these approaches on the 'skills revolution,' suggesting the promise that the new era would produce jobs that need high skills has been broken and what have become available are actually more low-skilled and low-paid jobs. In the next chapter we will continue this discussion by exploring how these changes and developments impacted on the structure of education and training, and the impact on young people's relationship with, and participation in education and training.

Participation in education and training

This increase in young people (aged 16 to 25 years) enrolling in post-school institutions has been one of the major developments in the advanced economies for over thirty years. This is not a new phenomenon, although its pace has been increasing since 2000 (OECD, 2014a). For example, in the UK by the end of the 1990s, 55% of 16–18-year-olds were in some form of education programme and the number of young people entering university had increased from one in five to one in three of all 18–19-year-olds between the years of 1991 and 1998 (Mizen, 2004). These figures have continued to grow until the UK now has the highest ever numbers of 18- and 19-year-olds entering university (HEFC, 2014). Not only has there been substantial growth in participation in education but we also see young people increasing the level and quality of their qualifications (OECD, 2014a). This is not just a growth in university degree qualifications: the young have been increasing their levels and types of qualifications at all stages of their education. For example, upper secondary graduation[2] rates have increased on average, across all OECD countries, by 8% (OECD, 2014a). Over their lifetimes, 84% of people in the OECD will have completed this level of qualification. This is now seen as a minimum level for successful entry into the labour market (OECD, 2014a). Growth in vocational education and training (VET) graduations at upper secondary level is also increasing by an average of 3% per annum across the OECD countries (OECD, 2014a). Graduate rates of completion differ. In 2012 it was identified that, over their lifetime, more women than men will now have this level of qualification (87% of women compared to 81% of men). Gender differences also exist in VET courses at this level, although they tend to be reversed in that more men are graduating with a VET qualification (50%) than young women (46%). The major growth area has been in Tertiary A,[3] with an increase from 20% to 36% between 1995 and 2005. Since then it has remained reasonably stable at 38% across all OECD countries. One of the major consequences of this expansion has been more young women entering universities and increasing their qualification levels. For example, 16% more women are now likely to have a type 'A' qualification compared to young men (47% compared with 31%). In terms of Tertiary B type[4] qualifications, the level and numbers of young people gaining these has remained stable throughout this period (11%) although there have been some significant variations within countries. For example, Spain has seen an increase from 2% to 20%, while New Zealand has seen levels increase by 15% (OECD, 2014a). Slight gender differences also exist in type B qualifications, in that 12% of all young women – compared to 10% of young men – are likely to gain this qualification over their lifetime (OECD, 2014a).

---

[2] That is, students who are typically expected to have completed nine years of education and are generally 15 or 16 years old.

[3] These are defined as 'Programmes, typically offered by universities [that] are largely theory based designed to provide qualifications for entry into advanced research programmes and professions with high requirements in knowledge and skills' (OECD, 2014a, p.76).

[4] These are defined as 'Programmes that are classified at the same academic level as theory-based programmes but are shorter in duration (two to three years). They are not intended to lead to further university level degrees but rather equip individuals with skills that can be used directly in the labour market and also respond to employers' needs for specialised skills' (OECD, 2014a, p.76).

What we have been seeing is a skills revolution where the young are increasing their levels of qualification. As a recent OECD report showed:

> In most OECD countries, younger adults (25 to 34 year-olds) have attained higher levels of education than older adults (55 to 64 year-olds). On average, 82% of younger adults have attained at least upper secondary education compared to 64% of older adults. Younger adults also have higher tertiary attainment rates than older adults by about 15 percentage points. In some countries, the difference between generations is significant. (OECD, 2014a, p.31)

This trend is clearly reflected in our case study countries. In Table 3.1 we see that the level of educational attainment (including both type A and type B qualifications) has been increasing since 2000.

Table 3.1 Percentages of the population aged 25 to 34 years with post-secondary educational attainments (type A and B qualifications) in 2000 and 2011*

Country	2000	2011
Australia	68	85
Canada	88	93
New Zealand	69	80
United Kingdom	67	83
Norway**	94	84
Spain	55	64
Japan	94	100
Poland	89	94

*This is a combination of upper secondary/post-secondary, Tertiary 'A' and Tertiary 'B' qualifications. Data analysed from OECD Factbook (http://www.oecd-ilibrary.org/economics/oecd-factbook-2013_factbook-2013-en).

** Norway reclassified in 2005 in line with other nation states.

It is also the case that since the 2007 economic crisis, participation in education across the OECD countries has continued to increase (OECD, 2014a). The proportion of those attending all educational institutions increased from 62% of the 15–24-year-old age group in 2005 to 65% in 2011 (OECD, 2014a). As we can see in Figure 3.1 and Figure 3.2, this pattern is reasonably consistent across the seven countries and across age bands. Poland's high level of participation of 15–19-year-olds can be explained by the fact that education was

Figure 3.1 Percentage of 15–19-year-olds in education 2005–11

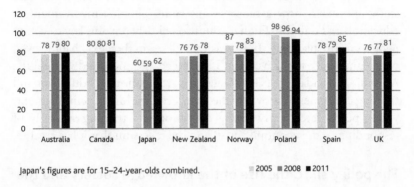

Japan's figures are for 15–24-year-olds combined. 2005 2008 2011

Source: OECD (2014a)

Figure 3.2 Percentage of 20–24-year-olds in education 2005–11

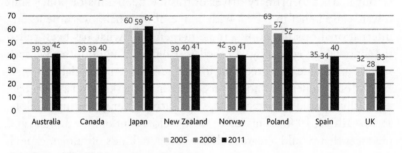

Japan figures are for 15-24 year olds combined

Source: OECD (2014a).

made compulsory for all 15–18-year-olds in the late 1990s. The drop in level of participation of 20–24-year-olds arises due to fewer young people taking university degrees (OECD, 2013a). In Norway there has always been a strong post-16 commitment to education. We do see a decline in young people's participation in education in 2005, but this is as a result of more young people moving into work (an increase of 7% between 2005 and 2011; OECD, 2014a). A similar picture also emerges for the 20–24-year-olds. Employment for this group expands between 2005 and 2011 (from 49% to 54% in work). It is not until 2011 that employment of this group drops in Norway (to 49%) and more young people return to education (OECD, 2014a). In Spain, expansion of education is significant, with 15–19-year-old engagement increasing from 79% to 85% between 2008 and 2011, and 35% to 40% for 20–24-year-olds. But even when there are signs of a dip in education participation, as in 2008 when the crisis hit, by 2011 all of our case study countries show a recovery in young people's involvement in education and training. Higher education clearly remains key to young people's future planning. In fact, as we will see in the next chapter, even when university fees have been introduced and increased in the UK, Australia, Canada and New Zealand, participation in education and training continues to grow. As the crisis brought high unemployment, young people are clearly seeing education and training as a way of responding to the economic crisis and the recession that it has created.

The policy shift: the rise of the knowledge society and the 'skills revolution'

It is clear from this evidence that young people themselves are seeing education as a strategy for improving their future position in the labour market. A primary driver of this has been a major policy shift towards and belief in – by a wide range of national governments and international organisations – the emergence of what has been called the 'knowledge economy'. In the late 1990s, throughout the Western world, it became accepted that in the new 'post-industrial' or 'post-Fordist' era, modern economies required different skills and knowledge, especially around new technology, science and engineering (Delors, 1996; OECD, 1996). This led to the development of new policies and practices that would 'create and draw on new kinds of human capital, requiring ever-increasing higher levels of education' (Wyn, 2013, pp.105). It was argued that young people would need to get a wide range of new skills not only to be competitive in the labour market but also to help maintain economic growth (OECD, 1996). From the 1990s onwards national governments, especially within the advanced economies, advocated the growth of training and skills relevant to a new type of workforce, believing it would bring economic prosperity. Such a strategy was argued for by a range of international organisations. For example, the OECD encouraged this approach, claiming that the shift in European policy to meet the challenges of the knowledge economy had 'set the goal for Europe to become the number one knowledge economy … with a radical transformation of its economy and modernized social education systems' (OECD, 2005, p.3). Such a position was taken up by all of our case study countries. Canada, for example, saw this as a major policy goal early in the 21st century;

countries that succeed in the 21st century will be those with citizens who are creative, adaptable and skilled. The so called 'new' economy is demanding new things from us. The need for ingenuity, creativity and hard work has not changed. How we do our work has. (Government of Canada, 2002, pp.5–6)

Tony Blair in the UK also saw this as a core policy development, suggesting in a speech the production of a new form of human capital, as 'education is our best economic policy … this country will succeed or fail on the basis of how it changes itself and gears up to this new economy, based on knowledge' (Blair, 2005). Similar arguments also underpinned the 'third way' politics of the 2008 Australian Labor government (Hinton-Smith, 2012) and the Labour government between 2000–2008 in New Zealand (Larner and LeHeron, 2005). As a result we see, from the middle of the 1990s, a massive investment by all four of the case study countries in developing educational programmes for those aged 16 to 25 that aimed to increase their active participation in acquiring new skills so that they could compete for jobs and contribute to the new economic challenges of the 21st century (Brown et al, 2011).

Expanding the post-16 education and training sector

At the heart of the 'skills revolution' has been the expansion of university education. This was seen as a key area for investment in human capital, where many of the new high-level technical skills could be gained. As a result, massive resources were diverted to this expansion in our main case study countries, and policies were developed that aimed to encourage and support the young to get more skills at university. But governmental concerns about this expansion also focused on those who did not seem to participate in higher education and, as a result, there was a desire to encourage this group and widen opportunities for all in the university sector. This approach was a key aspect of the 'third way' politics of the political left and became popular in all four of our countries (Southgate and Bennett, 2014). As a part of this model, governments also wanted to address questions of social justice. Therefore aiming to increase opportunities for all by widening participation at university was seen as a desirable outcome that operated to soften the harshness of neoliberalism. For example, in the UK it was claimed that such an approach would 'help to combine equity and social justice with competitiveness and market policies …

suggesting a clear continuity with the right-of-centre and neoliberal policies pursued by the Conservatives over the previous government' (Lunt, 2010, p.103). While the expansion of the university sector has been driven by the desire to have a well-educated and highly skilled workforce that is able to compete, there has also been a focus on policies of equity and fairness through the widening participation policy agenda in universities. How effective this has been remains a point of contention and is something we will explore in the next chapter, but as we shall see, education is now being seen as the best way to encourage social mobility (Lunt, 2010). We will also see, in the discussion that follows, that governments have recognised the need to increase vocational skills and thus expand the training sector. Again, there has been increasing use of neoliberal models of delivery and, while this sector has not been as well funded or given such central attention in policy terms, it has also been expanding across our four case study areas. Since 2008, a core area of development has been the introduction of government-funded apprenticeships and 'on the job' training. However, concerns remain over who participates in this sector and what opportunities it really creates for social mobility.

The United Kingdom

Tony Blair's governments in the UK placed higher education policies at the centre of his strategy for change. "Education, education, education" became his mantra and what was seen as a defining feature of his time in office (Walford, 2010). On winning the election in 1997, New Labour was confronted by the Dearing Report (1997). This focused on how the expansion of higher education could be funded. As a solution, New Labour introduced student fees for the first time in the history of UK higher education policy (Brown, 2005). This strategy set out the rationale for the 'user pays' orientation in tertiary study, which has now become normalised in the UK (Lunt, 2010). By 2004, a new bill was being introduced that set out the long-term vision of the Blair government for developing higher education in the UK (Department for Education and Skills, 2004). It had a number of critical implications for the expansion and marketisation of post-16 education (Lunt, 2010), but it also gave universities a bigger role to play in providing the core high-tech skills and new knowledge that would be needed for the UK to compete on the global stage (Brown, 2005). At the same time, New Labour expanded the 16 to 18 education sector (further education sector) through a wide range of initiatives, targeting resources to expand vocational training between the ages of 14 and 19 (Pring, 2010). This brought with it a wide range of reforms of qualifications, aimed at increasing the value and usage of vocational education for the private and business sectors. For example, it introduced diplomas that aimed in the longer term to replace traditional 'A' level/academic qualifications (Pring, 2010). In terms of widening participation, energy was focused on the higher education sector. A 10-year target was set, of having at least 50% of all 18–30-year-olds entering university, which would include increased participation by some of the most disadvantaged. In trying to achieve this, while introducing fees, New Labour provided access to a system of loans. It also insisted that universities use a proportion of their new income from tuition fees to create a substantial stream of bursaries to guarantee funding opportunities for access for lower socioeconomic status (SES) groups (Harrison and Hatt, 2012). This process was then to be monitored through the establishment of the Office of Fair Access (Lunt, 2010).

By the end of 2010, the new coalition government had overseen major changes in higher education policy that aimed to increase the marketisation of higher education. One of the most significant shifts was in the funding arrangements which included:

- any university or college being able to charge a fee of up to £6,000, or, if they meet conditions on widening participation and fair access, being able to charge up to £9,000;
- universities being able to decide individually what they will charge, including whether different levels of charges will apply for different courses;
- the phasing out of teaching grants, with the limited remaining income focused on priority areas where tuition fees alone may not meet all costs;
- graduates not making a contribution towards repaying tuition costs until they are earning at least £21,000 (gross per year), with this threshold uprated in line with earnings from April 2016;
- repayments to be 9% of income above £21,000, and all outstanding repayments written off after 30 years;
- a real rate of interest to be charged on loan repayments for graduates earning above £21,000, a tapered rate for graduates earning between £21,000 and £41,000, up to a maximum of RPI [retail price index] plus 3%. Graduates earning above £41,000 to be charged the maximum real rate of interest, rate of RPI plus 3%.

The reforms took effect for the intake of new students in the 2012–13 academic year at institutions in England, but there were variations in

Scotland, Wales and Northern Ireland. For example, Scottish students still did not have to pay fees if they went to Scottish universities.

Participation numbers in higher education continued on an upward trajectory from 2007 to 2010, when they dropped by over 50,000 students. A small recovery was followed by another drop in 2011, but then there was another gradual recovery and participation has now returned to 2010 levels (HEFC, 2014). At the same time, the 18–19-year-old population in the UK decreased, which meant that while actual numbers have not increased greatly, 30% of this age group now go to university; the highest participation rate ever recorded (HEFC, 2014).

There have been other interesting changes: there has been an increase of 37% in the delivery of degree courses at further education colleges and a decline in universities delivering foundation and HND (higher national diploma) courses, so the degree has become the core qualification available at university. The removal of non-degree courses is thought to have been a result of new funding arrangements introduced by the government (HEFC, 2014). However, there has been an increase in local degrees being delivered at further education colleges, which is seen as a result of increasing demand from students who want to live at home to study (HEFC, 2014). One other key development is the dramatic decline in students studying part-time. This figure almost halved between 2010 and 2013, with a drop of 46% (HEFC, 2014). The reasons for this include factors such as reduced funding for non-credit courses, the removal of access to loans for those studying less than 25 hours per week, reduced opportunities for funding from other sources (such as employers) and the challenging economic conditions caused by the financial crisis (HEFC, 2014).

In other areas of post-16 education we see a decrease in funded training in further education colleges and a drop of nearly 500,000 young people undertaking training between 2010 and 2013 (Department of Business, Innovation and Skills, 2014). This has to a certain degree been offset by a gradual growth in apprenticeships between 2005 and 2009/10, from 175,000 to 240,000. Between 2011/12 and 2013, government-funded apprenticeships increased to over 500,000 a year, but then dipped to 444,000 in 2014 (Department of Business, Innovation and Skills, 2014). This expansion was not in traditional areas of manufacturing and engineering but in business, administration and law, health and public services, and retail. This development has seen more young women taking up apprenticeships than ever before (Department of Business, Innovation and Skills 2014). However, part of the growth in apprenticeships arose as a result of funding being released to expand opportunities for those over 25 years of age to take part. The government funded over 100,000 new apprenticeships in this age group between 2011 and 2013 (Department of Business, Innovation and Skills, 2014). To illustrate, in 2007/8, 40% of all apprenticeships were for 16–18-year-olds, 46% for 19–24-year-olds and 14% for those aged 25 and above. In 2012/13 the distribution had shifted to the older age group, with 22% being for 16–18-year-olds, 32% for 19–24-year-olds and 44% involving those 25 years of age or more (Department of Business, Innovation and Skills, 2014).

Australia

A similar programme that aimed to increase human capital and new skills was also instigated in Australia. The national government had seen the necessity of expanding post-16 education during the 1990s, showing a strong focus on increasing numbers attending higher education institutions (James, et al, 2008; Gale and Tranter, 2011). For example, the 1998 review of higher education policy established not only the central role that universities should play in the newly emerging 'high skills economy' but also the importance of 'life-long learning' and equity (James et al, 2008). However, as we shall see later, it was not until the election of the Labor Party in 2008 that such an approach was provided, with increased resources, and that it became a core part of federal policy and practice. Principles of social justice failed to impact on social mobility (James et al, 2008). Again, similar to the UK, Labor adopted a 'third way' approach that continued market practices in higher education while aiming to address inequalities and social injustice.

Central to this was the 2008 Bradley review (Bradley et al, 2008). This influenced the policy agenda of the incoming Labor government in Australia by helping to provide the rationale for reshaping the policy regarding expansion of skills training in Australia. At its heart – as in the UK – was a desire to prioritise the widening participation agenda in higher education (Hinton-Smith, 2012) although, as we shall see in the next chapter, major neoliberal reforms remained unchanged. The Bradley review recommended a range of targets, including increasing the attainment rate of degrees for domestic students to 40% of all 25–34-year-olds, increasing the proportion of low SES (socioeconomic status) students in universities to 20% and increasing the levels of participation of indigenous students from 15% to 20% over ten years (Bradley et al, 2008), arguing that government should put aspiration to attend university 'firmly on the "radar screen" of potential higher education participants while they are still at school' (2008, p.40). The Australian government supported this proposal and allocated over AU$1 billion to outreach programmes of Australian universities. These funds were to be distributed on the basis of universities reaching targets that showed they had increased participation of low SES groups and increased their levels of partnership working with local communities (Peacock et al, 2014).

Major changes also took place in vocational skills training for the post-16 age group. This is usually provided in Australia by TAFE (Technical and Further Education) based institutions. The TAFE sector saw the development of the ANTA (Australian National Training Authority) in the mid 1990s, which took on the role of coordinating the VET sector and ensuring quality control. It had a key role not only in stabilising VET training but also in implementing neoliberal reforms:

> The ANTA period saw the implementation of a wide range of programs and substantial progress on its foundational objectives of a competency-based system, greater use of quasi-market mechanisms, and a formalised qualifications and recognition framework. It introduced a number of productive programs in equity and diversity, professional development, research and VET in Schools. It also navigated a shift from funding growth to funding restraint. (Ryan, 2011, p.15)

By 2006 major problems had been identified with the VET system, in that confusion existed over its purpose. Conflict also existed between ANTA and the local states; it remained unclear who had the primary responsibility for programme delivery. By 2006 it was claimed that the sector was not efficient and therefore ANTA was abolished and replaced by 24 regional colleges and a VET in Schools programme (Ryan, 2011). By 2009 the newly elected government had developed a new national body with the aim of improving the skill levels of VET trainees. This received more resources and recognition in the Bradley review (Bradley et al, 2008) of its role in developing a highly skilled workforce while developing quasi-market delivery methods (Ryan, 2011).

Higher education reform has remained at the forefront of federal government policy and there has been continued year-on-year growth in student numbers. For example, enrolment in university increased by 15% between 2003 and 2008 but between 2008 and 2013 it increased 23%, with over 247,000 students entering university. Of these, 30% were studying part-time, while 25% of all enrolments were international and overseas students. Part of this growth arose due to New Labour adopting recommendations from the Bradley review. First, in 2009 the Labor government removed the cap on the number of students that universities could recruit. This saw the introduction of a demand-driven system where increased student numbers would bring in extra revenue to universities. Full implementation was not due until 2012, with the first two years being transitional. Alongside this the government also announced AU$436 million to help increase low SES participation across the university sector. This was distributed in the form of scholarships, bursaries and resources for funding partnerships in the community. The Labor government also pushed forward the New Public Management reforms with the introduction of performance indicators that had over AU$500 million worth of funding attached. These were to be linked to national priorities and required universities to prove they were delivering in key areas. But by 2012 the Labor government had started to make a U-turn and was announcing financial cuts of AU$2.3 billion to be implemented over four years. It also introduced a number of 'efficiency savings', including students having to pay back 'start up' scholarships and the removal of the 10% discount that had been given to students for paying their fees upfront.

The full impact of these cuts was not felt as the new incoming Liberal government proposed to introduce its own reforms. The government was strongly in favour of increasing the use of markets within higher education and of students being more responsible for paying their own way. The major changes advocated the removal of the financial caps to courses in universities, although at the time of writing this had not managed to get past the Australian Parliament. Abbott's government aims to create unfettered freedom for universities to set their own levels of fees, therefore increasing the cost of a degree. It also intends that:

- government contributions to the cost of a degree will decline by 20%;
- student loans will need to be paid back faster;
- interest on loans will be linked to the government bond rate rather than inflation – seeing it increase from 2.9% to 6%.

As in the UK, the TAFE sector also expanded after 2008, with new courses and qualifications becoming available. In 2006 over 1.8 million people took vocational training courses across Australia and this continued to grow year on year until 2010 (Australian Social Trends, 2012). It then dropped by 3.4% (NCVER, 2014). Variations existed between the states and territories, with a drop of 16% in enrolments in

Queensland and 5% in New South Wales and the Northern Territory, while an increase of 16% was identified in South Australia (NCVER, 2014). In 2013, 41.5% of all participants were aged 15 to 24, although more young men than women participated (NCVER, 2014). Again, as in the UK, the major growth area in vocational training has been in apprenticeships. These grew by 28% between 2004 and 2012 then dropped dramatically in 2013 by 26% (NCVER, 2014). Of these, 53% were undertaken by young people aged 16 to 24 and 61% of all participants were men (NCVER, 2014). A key part of this gender imbalance (unlike in the UK) was that the traditional male trade areas of engineering and construction dominated the expansion of apprenticeships. The growth of this sector was clearly seen as key to the new government elected in 2013 in that it has also expanded financing opportunities to students attending TAFE courses starting in 2015.

Canada

Canada has had a similar 'skills revolution' to those that occurred in the UK and Australia although there are a number of significant differences. First, the provision of higher education policy and VET policy is, as we have seen in the previous chapter, dominated and led by the provinces (Jones, 2009b). Post-16 education, at both the vocational and degree level, is designed and delivered at the local level (Jones, 2009b). A paradox exists over the way that post-16 education is delivered and constructed in Canada, which 'stems from the fact that Provinces have the constitutionally derived responsibility for social welfare, health and education while concerns of national interest [and] equality … [are] a Federal responsibility' (Fisher et al, 2009, p.551). No government department is tasked with responsibility for higher education at the federal level, but more recently the federal government has been attempting to drive the skills-based revolution, recognising that in the new economy Canada needs to increase the skill base of Canadian youth (Jones, 2009b; Kirby, 2011). This has been undertaken by the use of funding controls. Separation within post-16 education also exists between VET and higher education institutions, with VET being delivered traditionally in locally based community colleges (Jones, 2009b), although the distinction between community colleges and universities is becoming more blurred as community colleges are gaining the authority to confer degrees (Jones, 2009b).

As neoliberal ideas have infiltrated Canada, it has become important to recognise the mediating (or accelerating) role of the provinces in this process. While neoliberalism is a driving force at the national level, different provinces' ideological positions towards neoliberalism influence what approach is taken towards skills development (Fisher et al, 2009). For example, Quebec holds a more social democratic approach and has resisted the worst of the neoliberal ideology, while Ontario has pursued a more neoliberal model of market-driven policies in higher education and vocational training. This has had an impact on the level of engagement provinces have had with expanding and widening participation (Fisher et al, 2009).

Six of the ten provinces recently undertook reviews of their policies and systems relating to higher education. Similarities could be identified in that each:

> tended to emphasize an economic-utilitarian outlook on higher education's raison d'être. This included positioning higher education as an instrument of economic development with an integral role in fostering innovation and meeting the shifting educational and labour force development requirements of the 'knowledge economy'. (Kirby, 2011, p.270)

This has seen the increased usage of quasi markets at the local level in the delivery of post–16 education across Canada, driven by a neoliberal ideology (Kirby, 2011). Similar to Australia and the UK, questions of widening access, especially to university, have become important. Between 2004 and 2008 Ontario, Newfoundland and Labrador, Alberta, British Columbia and others have been emphasising not only economic necessity but also social justice as reasons for widening access (Kirby, 2011; Jones, 2012). As a result, we see a wide range of local initiatives being implemented (Jones, 2012). Central to this have been concerns over the participation of First Nation students (Kirby, 2011). In its 2007 Action Plan the federal government set out a number of key objectives for the provinces to meet as a way of trying to increase the participation of Native Canadians in higher education. This was monitored by a ministry steering group that aimed to provide guidance and advice as well as monitoring progress (Jones, 2009b). Recently, eight of the ten Canadian provinces also introduced performance funding of higher education institutions around the question of access, with the key aim of increasing participation, especially for those traditionally under-represented (Lang, 2013). Funding for these initiatives came from both the federal government and the provinces. For example, in the 2008 budget the federal government announced it would provide over CA$550 million by 2011/12 to the Canadian Student Grant

Program to provide support to over 245,000 low- and middle-income students across Canada, while the province of Saskatchewan provided a number of local grants to complement this system (Kirby, 2011). Similarly Ontario's 'access to opportunities strategy' provided CA$55 million to colleges and universities to undertake outreach work with under-represented groups. A number of other examples can be seen in British Columbia and New Brunswick (Kirby, 2011). In this context, not only has the allocation of funding for low- and middle-income and indigenous students increased since the beginning of the 21st century but we also see an increased usage of the quasi market place of the college and university sector to deliver increased access (Kirby, 2011).

In Canada, similar to the UK and Australia, growth in enrolments continued in higher education throughout the economic crisis. Participation almost doubled between 1985 and 2010 and, apart from a period of levelling off in 2008/9, growth continued (AUCC, 2011). However, what we start to see is a decline in federal spending on higher education reform and a reduction in spending by the provinces as a proportion of student numbers. As a way of addressing the shortfall, we see increased tuition fees in all of the provinces (Shaker and MacDonald, 2013).

Throughout this period, vocational skills development also expanded in Canada, especially at the local level. Again, one of the critical growth areas and key policy areas in VET was in terms of apprenticeships. Between 2008 and 2012, the number enrolled increased by over 54,000, although this enrolment growth was mainly in the 25+ age category. As a percentage, the number of young people aged between 16 and 24 declined from 38% of the total in 2008 to 33% in 2012 (Statistics Canada, 2014a). Growth in vocational skills training continues to be supported by the federal government. For example, in the 2014 budget it announced it was:

- reallocating CA$4 million over three years to work with provinces and territories to increase opportunities for apprentices;
- introducing measures that would support the use of apprentices through federal construction and maintenance contracts, investments in affordable housing and infrastructure projects receiving federal funding; and
- reducing barriers to apprenticeship accreditation, including examining the use of practical tests as a method of assessment for apprentices.

Apprenticeships remained gendered opportunities, with 88% (in 2008) and 86% (in 2012) of those enrolled being male (Statistics Canada, 2014a). As in Australia, the gendered nature of apprenticeships remained embedded in the delivery of these programmes.

New Zealand

One important feature of the New Zealand system is the unique way the tertiary sector is integrated. In 1992 and 1997, Acts of Parliament created a single sector that integrated universities and VET organisations. As Mahoney notes, 'NZ is currently unique in that no other country has clustered its community, vocational and academic education together this way' (2003, p.2). This brought together a wide range of public and private organisations to deliver post-secondary education and training (Grey and Scott, 2012).

The growth and expansion of the sector and the increased participation had its roots in the 1980s reforms. The Labour government of 1984–90 aimed to increase participation in tertiary education (Abbott, 2004) by enshrining in the 1989 Education Act principles of open access (Healey and Gunby, 2012). This had a major impact on university education in that it gave domestic students a right to enter university if they reached minimum standards and if they could afford it. It also gave a right of access to anyone over the age of 20, regardless of whether they have minimum entry requirements.[5] This saw a massive expansion of young people entering university in the 1990s (Mahoney, 2003). While the participation rate for Maori and Pacific students grew, this masked the fact that they were five times more likely to enrol in remedial and vocational schemes, and three times less likely to enrol in university, compared to Pakeha students (Ministry of Education, 2002). By the 21st century it also became clear that one of the implications of this massification of higher education was that attrition rates were high. In fact, while New Zealand had one of the highest levels of participation across the OECD countries, it also had the highest non–completion rates (Healey and Gunby, 2012)

By 2003, major reforms were being made by the Labour government. Again greatly influenced by the 'third way' politics of New Labour in the UK, the government advocated significant changes to higher education (Grey and Scott, 2012). Not only did it take a stronger steering role, it also wanted to make the system 'more efficient' and move the system

---

5   Universities could restrict access to courses where there were demonstrable capacity constraints, for example, medicine.

closer to meeting the needs of the economy. Participation remained important but other priorities emerged. While wanting to maintain increased participation, policy was strongly influenced by the need for young people to have the 'new' skills for the knowledge economy (Grey and Scott, 2012). New neoliberal reforms were being rolled out in New Zealand and significant changes took place in how the university sector was to be managed and run (Larner and LeHeron, 2005). Efficiency, for example, became an essential factor in university funding and New Zealand saw 'a modified funding regime introduced ... where instead of funding being demand-driven ... universities moved to a pre-determined enrolment cap' (Healy and Gunby, 2012). Penalties were introduced as a way of ensuring that universities kept to agreed levels of student enrolments. This increased the competition for students but has also resulted in a gradual decline in the numbers participating in university education (Healy and Gunby, 2012). Throughout this period, governments in New Zealand attempted to find ways of increasing the participation of Maori and Pacific students. A number of initiatives have developed over time to provide funding resources, institutional change and support. For example, universities are set targets for these groups in terms of set proportions of the main student body and if they do not achieve it they can be financially penalised, (Strathdee and Engler, 2012). Universities have also introduced targeted admission programmes that allow for entry below the usual minimum standards, alongside Maori and Pacific scholarships that provide financial support, and community-based work with schools. However, less focus is given to supporting students from low SES backgrounds (Strathdee and Engler, 2012).

Since 2008 the National Party government has continued to prioritise post-secondary education, seeing this as critical to the future competitiveness and productivity of the New Zealand economy. Caps on numbers in universities have remained, although those areas defined as critical for the economy have received increased funding. For example, in 2012 the government increased funding in engineering and related subjects by 8.8% and science by 2%, while other subjects received no extra funding. This was therefore a NZ$42 million increase in funding yet some areas benefited over others.

In 2012 the government also released its new Tertiary Strategy (Ministry of Education, 2014), which increased its focus on business-led research for commercial purposes; as a result, more places were made available in apprenticeships and vocational training (the modern apprenticeships). The needs of the economy became even more significant in New Zealand's social policy for education. Despite this, enrolled numbers in tertiary education actually declined between 2008 and 2013, although a slight improvement took place in 2013. Expansion is planned to increase further over the coming years. Degree enrolment remained reasonably stable apart from between 2008 and 2013. Trends changed in 2013, with enrolments for those over 25 dropping, while enrolments for 18–19-year-olds and international students increased (Ministry of Education, 2014). Maori continued to be under-represented in degree programmes and were more likely to participate in non-degree qualifications or lower level qualifications in the university sector (Ministry of Education, 2014). The largest drop in tertiary education was in non-degree enrolments and workplace study courses. Until 2008, the number in training courses and apprenticeships had increased year on year since 1995, but in 2008 it dropped dramatically (Ministry of Education, 2014). The biggest drops were in industry-based apprenticeships, while the modern apprenticeships dropped gradually. In 2012 numbers started to increase again as the National Party government put resources into funding these areas, but numbers rose only to levels just above the 2008 total. These apprenticeships remained gendered in that both modern apprenticeship and traditional apprenticeship enrolments were 88% young men, on average. The Industry Training programme had a smaller gender gap being 60–40 in favour of young men (Ministry of Education, 2014).

Graduate underemployment: the broken promise

What we have seen across the UK, Australia, Canada and New Zealand has been a massive skills revolution, which has seen resources being targeted on the expansion of higher education and, in many cases, VET. While this has been seen as essential, the growth of such a strategy is built upon the promise of a high-tech future of highly paid knowledge workers and, as we shall see in later chapters, the state and private industry have not kept their side of the bargain (Brown et al, 2011). A skills revolution is 'pivotal to the creation of a neoliberal opportunity bargain … [that has] … left individuals responsible for their employability through education and career development' (Brown et al, 2011, p.23). As a result, the state is limited to 'improving educational standards, expanding access to higher education and creating flexible job markets that reward talent, ambition and enterprise' (2011, p.23). It does not guarantee jobs; that is for the market and the private sector. But young people's failure to get a quality job and be successful in this environment is then seen as a problem of the individual (Mizen, 2004; France, 2007; Nairn et al, 2012). Not having got the right skills, being overqualified or not being flexible enough create a perception that the problem is with the attributes of individuals, not with market failure in providing jobs. Much of the rhetoric around the creation of high-tech skills and a knowledge economy is built upon claims that the future will require young people who are flexible, creative and able to adapt to new conditions, bringing their 'new' knowledge to bear to ensure success for nation states (Brown et al, 2011). Across Western advanced economies the primary ambition has been to create a highly skilled workforce for the future, yet what has become clear is that the highly skilled (and highly waged) jobs promised to the young have yet to materialise. Brown et al (2011) suggest that a proposed 'global auction' of high skills, while fuelling the explosion of higher education across the world, has only provided major problems with underemployment. Young people clearly continue to have a strong commitment to education, believing it will still help them in their career paths to successful employment (Cuervo et al, 2013). But does it?

Getting into permanent full-time employment and having a 'good' or 'standard' job that provides security, an element of control and a long-term future is becoming increasingly difficult for young people (ILO, 2013). But it is important that we recognise 'the predicted mismatch between the supply of workers with high-level skills and qualifications, such as graduates, and the demand for such workers from employers' (MacDonald, 2013). Evidence suggests that the real problem is not in the levels of unemployment but in the levels of underemployment caused by the lack of jobs available to the young, especially those who have been investing in gathering high-level skills, such as graduates (MacDonald, 2013). There are different definitions of underemployment. For example, some see it as those who are working part-time but would prefer to be working more hours (IPPR, 2010). Alternatively it can include the unemployed and economically inactive people as well as those working part-time (Aldridge et al, 2012). In the UK, underemployment is seen as a major problem; it is claimed over 2,460,000 are underemployed, with 424,000 not working to their potential, 762,000 not working enough and 1,274,000 not working but wanting to work (Gardiner, 2014).

In reality, the skills revolution has been less about the need for high skills and more about low skills (Ainley and Allen, 2010; Brown et al, 2011; Brinkley et al, 2013). As we will see in Chapter Five, the growth in employment is not in 'high skill' occupations, but in occupations that require 'low' or 'soft' skills (ILO, 2013). For example, in the UK, even though the number of unqualified employees will drop significantly by 2020, the number of jobs requiring no qualifications will remain high (MacDonald, 2013). Similarly, it is recognised that job growth in the UK is not only in the area of part-time and temporary work but also in those occupations that require low levels of skills (Sissons, 2011). This is leading to a situation where there is 'polarisation between "lousy" and "lovely" jobs ... with jobs in the middle of the employment structure being hollowed out' (MacDonald, 2013, p.3). These trends have a long history and are clearly evident in the UK, Australia, Canada and New Zealand. As we shall see, recent evidence suggests they have been expanding since 2007.

Underemployment and social mobility

A critical feature of discussions about underemployment is how it is affecting those who have been gathering higher skills and qualifications (MacDonald, 2013). One of the most influential features of this process is that many of the changes we have seen taking place are not just affecting the most vulnerable or the unskilled. In fact vulnerability and risk are now affecting the middle classes. For example, in Canada young people with post-secondary degrees are more likely to be unemployed than older educated workers (Foster, 2012). Similarly, in the UK, graduate unemployment remains a serious problem that has increased substantially since the 2007 economic crisis (Thomson and Bekhradnia, 2010). But it is more than just about getting a job. Young graduates are finding themselves struggling to find a 'good' or relevant job for their skill set and are having to take low-skilled work, far below their level of training or qualifications (Gardiner, 2014). These trends are not simply a result of the recent crisis: the evidence suggests that graduate underemployment is becoming more persistent and may not be a short-term phenomenon (Mosca and Wright, 2011). As Ainley and Allen suggest, what we are seeing is a shift taking place – not one that has increased the number of high-skilled occupations and jobs, but one that has taken us 'from jobs without education to education without jobs' (2010, p.13).

Getting a degree and other high-level qualifications does increase young people's chance of employment (Cuervo et al, 2013), but this relationship seems weaker than it was for past generations. Getting a job of choice after completing a degree now takes longer (between 5 and 10 years) and can also require young people to take on part-time and insecure work or to return to education for a number of years. And getting your job of choice is also heavily dependent on what university you attend. For example, those in the UK who were awarded a first class honours degree from a Russell Group University were more likely to have relevant employment six months after leaving university (Mosca and Wright, 2011). These graduates are more likely to be students from middle-class and more privileged backgrounds. Graduate recruitment agencies tend to target a small number of elite universities that are also the most selective in the country (Milburn, 2012). Universities such as Cambridge and Oxford, alongside the London School of Economics (LSE), University College London (UCL) and Manchester tend to provide the bulk of graduates for graduate employment and most of these will be from middle-class backgrounds (Milburn, 2012). This suggests that social class still matters in the new higher educational transitions that are being constructed, especially in the environment brought about by the 2007 economic crisis. While the transition into good jobs with high pay is being delayed for all, those from the higher SES groups eventually tend to get into occupations that provide good pay and interesting careers and maintain their middle-class status (Milburn, 2012). We shall return to this point in the next chapter when looking at the impact of the widening participation agenda in higher education.

VET and the low skills 'revolution'

The drive to meet the needs of the newly emerging knowledge society has also had major implications at the other end of the spectrum. As we have seen, governments have been keen to target programmes of skill development in the VET sectors of our main case study countries. Since the early part of the 21st century there has been continued growth of new training programmes (especially the reintroduction of apprenticeships and 'on the job' training), and a 'revolution' in new forms of training courses and qualifications targeted especially at the 15 to 24 age group. The key changes outlined in our case study countries claim to provide new qualifications in the form of diplomas and certificates that are supposed to be relevant to local labour markets and meet the needs of business and the economy. These non-academic qualifications are claimed to be more relevant in these tough economic times in that they will not only help the unemployed into work but will also increase the productivity of the economy (Wheelahan, 2008; Grey and Scott, 2012). However, while governments have focused on skills development, very little attention has been given to the types and quality of jobs that young people are now able to access as a result of gaining these new skills. As we shall see in Chapter Five, a large proportion of the 'new jobs' being created are in low-skill and low-paid areas (MacDonald, 2013), yet governments' economic strategies in the advanced economies, under neoliberal influence, are less concerned about what types of jobs young people get or the quality and income potential of those jobs. The key focus is on getting young people to find work and to ensure they do not create a financial burden on the state (Ainley and Allen, 2010; Standing, 2011; Tomlinson, 2013).

This approach has seen a raft of programmes being developed across our case study areas that aim to increase either the basic skills of the unemployed (and underemployed) or to upskill and reskill the employed (Wheelahan, 2008; Ainley and Allen, 2010; Tomlinson, 2013). We have started to see vocational training programmes that are creating low skills especially for certain groups of young people (Tomlinson, 2013). These programmes tend to focus on enhancing skills concerned with 'employability' (France, 2007), with much of the training concentrating on how to get work, how to be 'job ready', and how to manage the risk and uncertainty that now exists in the labour market (Tomlinson, 2013). In the late 1990s and early 21st century we have seen a growth in 'education for employability' (Ainley and Allen, 2010, p.41), where knowledge becomes replaced by a narrow focus on job skills and life skills such as team-building. These low-level skills are usually seen by employers as more useful in the workplace, but in reality they have little to do with getting well-paid jobs (Ainley and Allen, 2010). The language of VET concentrates on concepts such as 'competency training' and 'learning outcomes', which then bring about a radical change in educational curricula that shift the emphasis in outcomes towards 'employability' skills.

Such language has infiltrated secondary schools, especially those schools with low attainment levels, along with further education colleges that take the academically 'unsuccessful' and those institutions that target poor or problematic populations (Allais, 2012). Proposals to embed employability within a wide range of educational institutions have now become 'normalised' in youth policy and practice. This form of vocationalism continues to grow as a central part of the educational curriculum and has not only widened its reach (from 16–18-year-olds to 14–25-year-olds) but has also increased its activity and funding base. For example, in Australia, TAFE and the post-secondary sector now have over 5,000 registered training organisations and cost the Commonwealth government over AU$4 billion a year (Australian Social Trends, 2012). Those who use the vocational training route in Australia tend to be from low SES groups or indigenous populations. These patterns are stark, appearing in all four of the case study countries discussed here, yet this phenomenon is not new. Historically these pathways and routes have always operated to socially reproduce class, gender and racialised pathways that limit social mobility (France, 2007). The new skills revolution in the VET sector seems therefore to be continuing a process of social reproduction that has helped maintain levels of social inequality and seemingly has changed little over time.

While continued skill acquisition is now seen as a necessity for all young people, we start to see further education colleges, TAFE institutes, community colleges and other VET providers become involved in programmes offering basic skills training that are actually operating to 'warehouse' many of the unemployed. We are seeing a 'churning' of young people going through different vocational courses that may be increasing their qualifications but are not helping them get secure and well-paid work (Ainley and Allen, 2010; Tomlinson, 2013). In this context, involving the young unemployed in many of the vocational initiatives is less about them 'getting new skills' than the absence of alternatives (Ainley, 1997; Mizen, 2004). This has seen the creation of a system that is largely about managing the unemployed in an environment where work remains scarce (Ainley and Allen, 2010). VET courses then 'fill the vacuum left by the decline in youth jobs and traditional industrial apprenticeships that arise as a result of the post-industrial changes' (2010, p.41). This is an historical feature of how youth policies have managed the growth of underemployment of the young. Such policies are not generated just by recent changes and economic crises. For example, in the 1960s in the UK a quarter of a million young people entered apprenticeships and over a third found work in manufacturing, but by the 1980s youth unemployment had become a major structural problem for the state (Mizen, 2004) and, with the insecure service industries providing the majority of jobs for the young, training programmes were focused less on new skills and more on keeping the unemployed occupied and helping them manage the new landscape (Mizen, 2004). Such a pattern is not only continuing but is now expanding as jobs become even more scarce (Ainley and Allen, 2010).

Conclusion

This chapter has concentrated on showing how and why education and training has expanded across OECD countries and, in particular, across the four main case study countries discussed. It has shown how, over the last thirty years, education and training have become a central part of young people's lives and how neoliberal policies have not only reshaped the environment of education and training but also structured the types of policies to be used. For the young, negotiating their way from school to work has changed dramatically over the last three decades. The option of leaving school and getting a job has virtually disappeared, as students find it necessary to add to their qualifications as a way of maximising their future opportunities. These trends have clearly expanded throughout the crisis and the great recession that followed, and we see more and more young people regarding qualifications as central cultural capital to help them into the labour market. The chase to get the right skills or qualifications has been driven by the ideological arguments of neoliberal governments that claim the future will need those young people with high-level skills and qualifications. Improving the quality of 'human capital' was therefore seen as a necessity but, as we have seen in the discussion here, the promise of a 'good life' for those who succeed has been broken. In fact, as we saw, those with low-level skills are likely to be in more demand, while opportunities for secure employment that is well paid may well still be unattainable. The long-term effects on social mobility remain unclear, but indications suggest that those from low SES groups are more likely to lose out as the small number of good graduate jobs remains more easily accessed by those from the middle classes. In addition, those who take the vocational route to success continually find themselves with limited opportunities for social mobility. In fact, the types of skills they are gaining tend to be more focused on employability, reinforcing the view that failure is of their own making. We will come back to these issues in Chapter Four. For now, though, it is important to recognise that young people are clearly finding that the qualifications they are accumulating do not always guarantee them the future they are seeking.

FOUR

Education and training: from public good to private responsibility

Introduction

In the previous chapter we explored the expansion of education and training, showing how it has become a central feature of young people's lives. Our case study analysis drew attention to the political processes that have shaped this area, highlighting how 'third way' politics has had a major impact on determining what was to be achieved. We explored the implications of the failure of the graduate promise alongside the limited opportunities provided by vocationalism and the implications for social mobility. This chapter continues this analysis. First, we will explore in more detail the way neoliberalism has changed the field of practice in post-16 education and training. While 'third way' politics brought a commitment to questions of social justice, neoliberalism was hugely influential in reshaping the way that universities and vocational education and training (VET) providers were to operate. This process has increased since the 2007 crisis as a result of austerity measures being implemented. Second, a major change brought about by neoliberal principles was the 'user pays' philosophy. While this approach has a long history in some countries, by the 21st century it was fully established in the post-16 educational and training sector and, as we shall see, since the crisis it has had substantial impacts on levels of student debt. The final section of this chapter will return us to the question of the widening participation agenda, where we will examine how effective it has been in the UK, Australia, Canada and New Zealand in bringing different social groups into the education and training field.

Neoliberalism and the commodification of education and training

At the heart of the recent reforms in post-16 education and training has been the roll out and implementation of neoliberal approaches. These have had a significant impact on the educational experience of young people in Australia, Canada, New Zealand and the UK. When talking about higher education, 'under neoliberalism, markets have become a new technology by which control can be effected and performance enhanced, in the public sector' (Olssen and Peters, 2005, p.316). While these practices in the delivery of higher education can be seen in most advanced economies, the level and intensity of these processes varies by country and in some places by region (Marginson, 2013). As we saw in Chapter Two, neoliberalism does not constitute either a universal body of practice or a standardised model that all countries adopt (Marginson, 2013). Issues such as the role of resistance in federal states or structural differences in how higher education has historically been delivered, alongside ideological divergences, can all influence the approaches and practices undertaken by national governments. In post-16 education, two major trends can be identified: first, the introduction and roll out of 'quasi markets' or the 'neoliberal market model' in the way public services are to be delivered and, second, the implementation of what has been called the new public management (NPM) approach, which introduces private sector management strategies into public services (Marginson, 2013)

The use of the market model in education has been well recognised (Ball, 2008). In the post-16 education and training sector it usually operates through a range of 'quasi-market' arrangements that aim to reform the public sector while also creating new income sources for capital and business (Ball, 2008). As Ball suggests, this approach offers 'solutions to the "problems" of public sector reform' and is 'a new (and relatively safe) profit opportunity for capital (large and small) ... Public service markets involve huge expenditures, and governments are usually reliable payers' (Ball, 2008, p.229). Quasi markets are processes that involve 'partnership' between the public and private sector in delivery of a product (education in this case) and 'one of the major objectives of the reforms in higher education ... [is] to install relations of competition as a way of increasing productivity, accountability and control' (Olssen and Peters, 2005, p.326). In this process the use of quasi markets also aims to increase student 'choice' and create an internal market that will improve the delivery of higher education while reducing the cost to the state (Lunt, 2010). But they remain 'quasi' because the public sector and public finance still have a major role to play. For example, in Canada public universities remain important because they still receive significant funds from the federal and provincial government to finance higher education (Kirby, 2011). However, what we see are a whole range of market-focused practices being introduced into the delivery of higher education. For example, processes such as linking funding directly to recruitment encourages competition between universities for students (Grey and Scott, 2012).

Competition has also been introduced *within* universities by creating funding regimes where money follows the student, thus increasing competition between departments, programmes and faculties (Larner and Le Heron, 2005).

What we also see in the use of the quasi market is the introduction of private providers. These are evident in a wide range of areas across the post-16 education and training field of practice. In Canada and Australia, for example, we have seen an expansion of private universities (Fisher et al, 2009), while in New Zealand we have seen over 800 providers from both the 'not-for-profit' and 'for-profit' training sectors enter the market place, which can now access public funds to deliver vocational training (Grey and Scott, 2012). Similar developments and growth have taken place in the expansion of vocational training in Australia (Wheelahan, 2008), Canada (Fisher et al, 2009) and the UK (Pring, 2010).

A second and connected development has been the introduction and expansion of NPM into the post-16 education and training sector. This approach to managing public resources combines both business models and market principles, aiming to increase and improve the delivery of a service to customers (students in this case). These management techniques include the use of league tables to assess success, the setting of performance indicators and targets, the introduction of auditing and monitoring processes (Grey and Scott, 2012), and the use of benchmarking between universities (Larner and Le Heron, 2005), It moves universities into corporate-style management with the CEO (chief executive office, that is, the Vice Chancellor) being output- and goal-driven (Marginson, 2013). Concepts such as 'value for money', 'efficiency', 'customer satisfaction' and 'performance management' are now seen as a way of conceptualising and constructing higher education. These practices are now well established and are seen as how 'top' universities in particular should operate.

This combination of 'quasi markets' and NPM in the post-16 field is having a significant impact on young people's experience of the education process. A fundamental development is that these processes are reconfiguring education from a 'public good' to a 'private good':

> the new public management in applying quasi market or private sector microtechniques to the management of public sector organizations has replaced the 'public service ethic' whereby organizations were governed according to norms and values derived from assumptions about the 'common

good' or 'public interest' with a new set of contractualist norms and rules. (Olssen and Peters, 2005, p.324)

While education will always have an element of both (Marginson, 2013), the balance between public and private sectors has been shifted by the growing implementation of neoliberal practices and ideologies in post-16 education (Grey and Scott, 2012). In this process education is being commodified: knowledge is converted into a product that can be packaged, presented and sold to the customer (Naidoo and Jamieson, 2007). Olssen and Peters (2005) call this the growth of 'knowledge capitalism', which has intrinsic value as a way of helping students find work in times of scarcity, yet such an approach devalues traditional liberal educational experiences, giving emphasis to market principles and questions of employability. Around the world we have seen the liberal arts, humanities and social sciences under attack and criticised for their limited value in helping students get work or for providing them with the 'wrong sort of skills' for the knowledge economy and future employment (Rhoades and Torres, 2006). This approach is also influencing the curricula of universities, shaping what is taught and what subjects are prioritised (Olssen and Peters, 2005; Lunt, 2010; Grey and Scott, 2012) while also driving a strong vocational agenda in both the VET sector and universities (Olssen and Peters, 2005; Fisher et al, 2009; Kirby, 2011). In this new environment the student has become the 'customer' and 'purchaser' of their own education. For example, in the UK the national government linked the notion of 'student as consumer' to the key performance indicators of universities (Naidoo et al, 2011) and similar process can be seen in Australia (Naidoo et al, 2011) and Canada (Kirby, 2011). Choice is a fundamental aspect of universities' strategic planning and therefore understanding the desires and wants of students is seen as paramount to the educational process. Student satisfaction surveys and course evaluations drive the process, ensuring that the 'customer' is getting the product they want. We see a number of levers being used to increase the production of a consumerist approach: 'these include mechanisms for greater choice and flexibility, information on academic courses through performance indicators, league tables and student satisfaction surveys, and the institutionalisation of complaints mechanisms' (Naidoo et al, 2011, p.1145) As Lunt suggests, this is commodifying the educational process:

> the changed relationship between students ('the purchasers') and universities ('providers') has led to a change in the student orientation to learning and knowledge, and a

'commodification' of knowledge (or 'services') ... (2010, p.107)

Evidence suggests that when students are encouraged to see themselves as consumers, 'they are more likely to see the act of learning as a commercial transaction' (Naidoo and Jamieson, 2005, p.272). It also creates a 'culture of entitlement' where students see success in education as a right and where learning is perceived as 'neatly packaged bytes of information' (Naidoo and Jamieson, 2005, p.272). This type of education can lead to a banking model, where information is merely memorised and regurgitated (Grisoni and Wilkinson, 2005).

There also remain substantial problems with the operation of the concept of the 'student as consumer' making 'rational choices'. For example, in the complex world of marketing, where universities are proactive in creating an institutional reputation, students with extensive social, cultural and economic capital are fully aware of the need to score their university highly in student evaluations to ensure it remains seen as a top-class institution (Naidoo et al, 2011). Those from middle-class or more privileged backgrounds are also in a stronger position to be active consumers, having both the knowledge and the economic resources to make choices (Naidoo et al, 2011). The idea of the rational and informed consumer who makes choices on the information available does not recognise the complex way that privilege operates to maintain the status quo through seemingly rational action (Goldthorpe, 1998). The status exchange becomes even more important in a competitive environment. Top universities want the best students and top (privileged) students and their families want their children to attend the leading universities. The leading universities are significantly (if not intentionally) concerned with social reproduction of the middle class through the networks that attendance at elite universities gives access to. The idea of 'rational choice' is certainly rational for the middle class in that it is operating to secure privilege. However, the marketisation of higher education is providing new challenges even to the middle class as fees and competition for the top places become increasingly intense. At the other end of the scale, making choices in terms of what vocational courses to take, young people from working-class backgrounds also act rationally in that they tend to draw upon a wide range of external influences in making decisions. In many cases these are related more to personal interest: subjects they thought they were good at and activities that made them happy. Few base their decisions on courses that might provide them with jobs or guaranteed careers (Batterham and Levesley, 2011). Evidence also shows that those from working-class backgrounds make choices of degree and university based on their habitus and the need to fit in rather than long-term objectives (Raey et al, 2005). In this context, young people, regardless of their class, are choosing university careers or vocational directions by acting rationally in relation to their own social situation. As we shall see in the discussion on widening participation, this has implications for social mobility.

Paying for post-16 education and training

The expansion of post-16 education and training is reflected in the year-on-year levels of education expenditure in Organisation for Economic Co-operation and Development (OECD) countries. On average, expenditure per student in education increased nearly 60% between 1995 and 2011. The largest increase was between 1995 and 2005 but, even though spending has recently slowed, it continued to grow throughout the great recession (OECD, 2014a). Investment in all levels of education saw an increase in public investment of 7% between 2008 and 2011, although the level of investment dropped between 2008 and 2010. Between 2008 and 2011 only six countries cut public investment (in real terms) on educational institutions. These were Estonia (10%), Hungary (12%), Iceland (11%), Italy (11%), the Russian Federation (5%) and the US (3%). In these countries, this translated into a decrease in expenditure on educational institutions as a percentage of gross domestic product (GDP; either because the decrease in expenditure was larger than the decrease in GDP or because GDP increased at the same time). In all other countries, public expenditure on educational institutions increased even as GDP decreased in a

Table 4.1 Percentage of GDP spent on educational institutions 2000–10

Country	2000	2010
Australia	5.2	6.1
Canada	5.9	6.6
Japan	5	5.1
Spain	4.8	5.6
New Zealand	NA	7.3
Norway	6.8	7.6
Poland	5.6	5.8
United Kingdom	4.9	6.5

Source: OECD (2014a).

number of them. As a result, the share of GDP targeted to education continued to increase across the OECD countries between 2008 and 2011. As we can see in Table 4.1, investment in education has not only been maintained in our case study countries but in most cases it increased over the 10-year period from 2000 to 2010.

An exception to this trend was in Poland, 'where GDP increased at a faster rate than public expenditure on educational institutions, resulting in a decrease of public expenditure on educational institution as a percentage of GDP' (OECD, 2014a, p.227). But by 2010 this had recovered slightly to reach percentages similar to those of 2000. Education remained a key area of investment throughout the first phase of the economic crisis.

However, the way in which this funding is distributed across sectors has changed. For example, the level of funding allocated by national governments to the expansion of higher education has decreased year on year (OECD, 2014a). The share of public funding for the tertiary sector fell from 74% to 68% between 2000 and 2011, while there was an increased usage of private funding sources in three-quarters of OECD[1] countries (OECD, 2014a). The major contributor to these 'private funding' sources has been the increased use of tuition fees. This shift to 'user pays' has become central to national government policy across the four case study countries discussed here. Up until the late 1980s, post-school education was free in most liberal states, but with the massive growth of higher education and training, fundamental questions emerged over who, in the time of neoliberal economic reforms, was going to pay for it (Lunt, 2010). As a result major economies introduced tuition fees as a way of addressing the increased costs being incurred. This shift can be clearly seen in how the expansion of higher education is now being funded. For example, in the UK the government teaching grant was £4.6 billion in 2009 and has been decreasing every year, with the aim of it being reduced to £2 billion by 2015/16. In 2012/13, tuition fee income in the UK accounted for 42% of total income for universities (compared with 34% in 2010/11) and funding body grants provided a reduced income of 23% of total income (compared with 31% in 2010/11). In Canada, the fees contribution to university income has doubled as a percentage of total revenue for universities and colleges. On average, fees contribution rose from 10% to 21% while funding from government fell from 72% to 55% between 1989 and 2009 (Jones, 2012). In New Zealand, private income is now more than 30% of the funding source for universities

---

[1]   Data only available in 20 countries (OECD, 2014a).

(Grey and Scott, 2012). Along with the increased fees students pay, this has increased the competition for students as a way of maintaining the funding base of universities.

Tuition fees at university level have emerged incrementally over the last twenty years. In the UK the Labour government of 1998 introduced fees in 1999, when each student paid £1,000. This increased to £3,000 in 2005 and £9,000 in 2010. In Canada, the median domestic undergraduate fee was CA$1,545 a year in 1990: this increased 25% within five years and has continued to grow, even though there have been periods of freeze (Andres and Wyn, 2010). In 2012 tuition fees were on average CA$6,348 per year, which means they have more than tripled since 1990 when they were first introduced. Costs vary by province; in Ontario fees are over CA$8,000 a year, while in Newfoundland fees are just under CA$3,000. In Australia, having previously abolished fees, the government of the day reinstated them in 1988, arguing that those who benefit from education should pay for it. It introduced variable fees in 1996, creating a three-tier system based on 'perceived value', so that different subject areas cost different amounts. Those courses thought to generate higher incomes in later life (for example, law and medicine) should, it was argued, cost more than those with lower potential (for example, arts and nursing). In 2005 the government deregulated university fees, permitting universities to increase fees by a maximum of 25%. As a result, the cost of a law or medicine degree is on average AU$9,790 a year while a humanities or social science degree is AU$5,800 per year. In 2013, a medical degree could cost students over AU$64,000, while a social science degree would average AU$18,000. Similar patterns can be seen in New Zealand, with different fees being charged for different courses. In 1990, following recommendations made by the Hawke Committee (Hawke, 1988), the government introduced a flat tuition fee of NZ$1,250 for full-time study, but in 1992 responsibility for setting the level of fees was devolved to universities, which saw tuition fees become variable and increase by an average of 13% per year until 1999. University students were then paying an average of about NZ$3,600 for their courses. In the years 2000–3, tertiary institutions had an agreement to freeze tuition fees in exchange for an increase in government funding. This freeze was lifted in 2003 and tertiary institutions were allowed thereafter to increase fees by a maximum of 5% per year (Strathdee and Engler, 2012). This arrangement has remained in place under the National Party government following its election in 2008. As in Australia, different degrees cost different amounts and, as a result, if a student chooses to take a medical degree, there will be substantial extra costs.

As we have seen in the previous chapter, all governments in our main case study areas have developed mechanisms for providing financial support so students can take part in post-16 education. The major policy has been the introduction of student loans and finance that aim to ensure those who cannot pay upfront have a mechanism to support themselves while engaging in education or training. Most of these programmes have built into them delays in repayments, so repayments only become active when the student reaches a certain level of income. They also tend to have lower rates of interest than normal bank loans although, as we have seen, in Australia and the UK this is changing. Student loans are now seen as a normal part of the post-16 education sector. As the Minister of Education in New Zealand stated when introducing student loans in 1992:

> The student loan scheme is a good one. It improves access into university by providing a vehicle by which students can afford to pay the fees. They get the loan, the fees are paid. They get their education, go out into the workforce, and earn money. From those earnings they repay their loan over a 15 year period on average. That is very defensible. (Parliamentary Debates 15/12/1992 vol. 532, 13234, quoted in Higgins, 2002, p.48)

In New Zealand, the government established StudyLink, while Australia has the HELP scheme, in the UK it is the Student Loan Company and Canada has the CANLearn programme. All aim to help students to access student loans and resources while also overseeing collection of repayments. This is not just for students entering higher education institutions but also for other post-school activities that help young people develop important employment skills, including vocational courses. For example, in New Zealand 55% of loans go to students studying in a university, 31% to those at institutes of technology, 15% to those attending private training establishments and 2% to those studying at Wananga[2] (Ministry of Education, 2013). The central aim is to give students access to funding for a range of post-16 study opportunities and to remove disincentives to participate in education and training after leaving school. The level of borrowing

---

[2]   These figures will not add up to 100 per cent as students studying at more than one provider have been counted twice.

from such schemes reflects not only the growing numbers of young people entering post-16 education and training but also the increased costs of courses and being in education.

As we have seen in the previous chapter, widening participation has been a central feature of the expansion of the new education and training opportunities. As a result, in our four case study countries, national (and state and provincial) governments have introduced financial support systems that reduce the cost for the poorest students. All of these countries now have a wide range of scholarships and bursaries that are made available to the 'most disadvantaged' groups, with the intention of widening participation (James et al, 2008; Harrison, 2011). How effective these are will be discussed later.

From public benefit to private responsibility

What we are seeing is a fundamental shift in which responsibility for the cost of education is moving from the state to the individual. As Wyn suggests, 'Consistent with neoliberal philosophies education is being framed as a personal investment' (2012, p.106). Education was traditionally seen as a 'public good', which thus justified large investments by the state, but under the recent changes driven by the neoliberalisation of our main case study countries we see it being reconfigured as a 'personal responsibility' and a 'private cost' for young people and their families. Attached to this, the idea of student debt as a way of taking personal responsibility is now embedded and normalised as the way that education and training of the young is to be paid for. Paying for post-16 education and training is clearly being seen by politicians and legislators in the advanced economies as bringing private benefits, and therefore the cost of it should either be borne by the individual or, at the very least, a large proportion of the cost should be carried by those who benefit most. In this sense, it reinforces the idea that post-16 education and training is a commodity that is bought or paid for on the way to getting work (Higgins, 2002). It also helps the 'purchaser' of education see themselves as the customer who has a right to receive a certain type of service. Of course politicians and legislators still recognise that post-16 education and training has a key public role, although, as we saw in Chapter Three, much of this is being reconfigured around its economic contribution and getting people into work.

But of course the private cost of getting educated, especially at the post-16 level, goes beyond simply paying course fees. What we have to recognise is the 'added costs' that exist in the post-16 educational process that can have a major impact on students' participation and their longer term future. In the UK, living costs for an average year (not including tuition fees) as a full-time student at a university are estimated to be between £12,056 and £13,388 depending on location[3] (NUS, 2014[4]). This includes rent, food, insurance and transport spread over a 40-week year. If a student is living at home, this will be reduced by £4,000 and £6,000, as parents will not usually charge their child for rent or food. In Canada, living costs vary between CA$12,500 and CA$20,000 a year, depending on the province.[5] Again, living at home can reduce this, although over 65% of Canadian students move away from home to study (Berger et al, 2009). In Australia, where students tend to study in their home city, an average cost for a student who is living at home is AU$11,000 a year. Paying rent can add anything between AU$4,000 and AU$12,000 extra, depending on location. In New Zealand there is less variability by location, although if a student lives in Auckland the costs are likely to be higher as rents are well above the national average. Living costs for a full-time student living at home will be on average NZ$4,700 over the 40-week period, but if they live away from home it will average NZ$14,708 in private rented accommodation in Auckland, rising to NZ$15,500 if they live in university halls. We can see that going to university is expensive in all of our four countries. For example, students in Australia are having to find amounts between AU$52,000 (for a three-year nursing degree) and AU$238,000 (for a medical degree) to get a university-based qualification. This is increased substantially if they live at in university halls over this period. In England, a three-year degree for a student living away from home can cost anywhere between £63,128 and £67,164. Similar costs apply in Canada and New Zealand. So how are the young covering these costs?

First, as identified earlier, all the governments in the UK, Australia, Canada and New Zealand have been providing a range of loan packages that are aimed at helping the young to pay for their own education. How much is available varies by country (and by province in Canada). In the UK, for example, students have access to a loan each year that will cover their fees (£9,000). There is also an option of claiming a maintenance allowance if they are living away from home (up to £5,500). The government also provides a maintenance grant that does

---

[3]   London is the most expensive place to live and is at the top end of the cost range.

[4]   http://www.nus.org.uk/en/advice/money-and-funding/average-costs-of-living-and-study/

[5]   Toronto city is the most expensive area in Canada.

not have to be repaid but is means tested (based on parental income). Depending on circumstances this can be as much as £3,250 a year, although the average pay-out is £934. New Zealand loans full costs for fees and provides a living allowance of up to NZ$7,000 a year. It also provides a means-tested option that can be accessed only if a student is planning to live away from home. Australia has the HELP loans system through which a student can borrow the full amount of their contribution to fees (the Commonwealth government pays the other proportion). In terms of living allowances, students can claim Youth Allowance, which is a means-tested benefit. Parental income affects whether a student can receive this and how much it is. Those whose parents have an income of under AU$50,000 can claim the full amount. Students can receive between AU$116 a week and AU$213 (depending on whether they are living at home or not). Those eligible must be aged between 16 and 24 (depending on their reason for claiming). Funding is also available for those taking a range of technical and further education (TAFE) courses, apprenticeships and other courses available from approved providers. Canada has a similar system to Australia in that it provides a student loan and a system of student grants, with eligibility defined by a means-testing system. It can be used to fund study at university or vocational courses at local community colleges. However, the amount a student can claim through loans and grants is determined by a combination of funding from the federal state and the individual provinces (Berger et al, 2009).

A range of systems are being used in the four countries discussed here with the aim of providing resources to enable young people to continue into post-16 education and training. A combination of loans and means-tested grants are available (some are easier than others to access) and students are able to access a range of resources that can help them through the process. However, what is clear is that the amount available is usually not enough to cover the full range of costs, and in fact what we see is a large number of students generating huge debts that need to be repaid after study is completed.

The amount of student debt varies and in many cases is hard to measure, but what is clear is that over the last ten years students have been increasing their debt as a result of study (Bexley et al, 2013). For example, in the US, outstanding student debt almost doubled between 1989 and 2010 and 40% of households headed by someone younger than 35 owed student debt. The level and amount of debt increased significantly between 2007 and 2010 from US$23,343 to US$26,682 (Fry, 2012). Those with the most debt tend to be in the lowest socioeconomic status (SES) groups and have the lowest incomes

(Fry, 2012; Bexley et al, 2013; Crawford and Jin, 2014). This expansion of student debt can be seen in all of our case study areas, although its level is variable due to the different types of systems being used by national and regional government to support students as they study.

The fastest-growing debt levels seem to be in the UK and, with new legislation introduced in 2012, the level of debt is likely to increase; the time frames for repayment are also increasing. For example, the increases in tuition fees in 2010 combined with the changes to loan interest in 2012 mean that the average debt for students leaving university in 2015 will be almost double that for those leaving in 2013 (increasing on average from £24,000 to £44,000). The amount to be repaid will also increase dramatically from £32,000 to over £66,000. Previously, half of the debt would have been paid off by the age of 40, but under the new system only 5% will have paid it off at this age; in fact it is estimated that most will continue paying off the debt well into their 50s (Crawford and Jin, 2014). Similar patterns are emerging in Australia. For example when students were asked how much debt they expected to have on leaving university the average had risen from AU$28,800 in 2006 to AU$37,000 in 2012 (Bexley et al, 2013). The average debt for low SES students has increased from AU$45,397 to AU$54,938, and for indigenous students from AU$49,768 to AU$65,583 (Bexley et al, 2013). This is seen as potentially worsening as new arrangements to restructure the terms of the student loan repayment system have led to criticism that they will increase student debt even further (Sharrock, 2014). The evidence shows this will continue to have a disproportionate impact on future low earners (Chapman and Higgins, 2014). For example, those with AU$60,000 of debt will have to repay over AU$105,000 while higher earners will only pay AU$75,000 (Sharrock, 2014) as they pay it off faster. As in the UK, this process will also extend the repayment period substantially in most cases it will take 16 to 24 years for students to clear the debt (Ryan, 2014). Differences are also projected between genders, in that women will end up paying back more (as their incomes are always lower than men's) and it will take them nearly 24 years to pay off the full amount, raising the risk that they will default on payments (Ryan, 2014). In Canada, it is now estimated that over 50% of students leave college and university with debts of around CA$28,000. One growth area in debt management used by students has been the increased use of private banking (as opposed to government loans). Those using this route are acquiring higher than average debt and are taking longer to pay it off (on average 14 years) (Ferguson and Wang, 2014). Again, as in the UK and Australia, the impact of debt is affecting those on low incomes most severely, and is thus disproportionately hitting low SES groups and indigenous populations (Berger et al, 2009)

Second, students are having to rely on other resources, such as paid work and/or receiving parental financial support. For example, students are combining study with work. Historically, some students have always worked through their studies, but more recently the level and amount of work has increased substantially. In the Australian Life Patterns Longitudinal Survey (Wierenga et al, 2013), 82% of respondents said that they funded study through a mix of methods. This included 23% working full time, 21% using work and loans, 26% using savings and other sources (that is, parents) and 16% undertaking part-time work. Only 18% said they did nothing but study (Wierenga et al, 2013). A national study in Australia showed that over 80% of all students in full-time education were working and, while there was a small decline from 2006, the number of hours students were working within a semester increased (Bexley et al, 2013). Part of the decline could be attributed to the great recession and the decline in job availability. Similarly, in Canada working and being a student has become the norm for most. It is estimated that 62% of all undergraduate students were working an average of 18 hours a week during their course. Over 70% also worked during summer recess. Average earnings were approximately AU$3,775, with 25% of them earning between AU$2,000 and AU$7,000. Since the recession began, the number of students working during the summer has declined, although it is now slowly increasing (Berger et al, 2009).

One final point to make about financial support relates to the growing use by governments of bursaries and scholarships. Over the last twenty years there has been an expansion and roll out of bursaries and scholarships as a way of trying to widen participation by targeting the 'hard-to-reach groups'. In all countries this tends to mean low SES groups, although a wide range of criteria can be used, including geographic, group-based (that is, low SES/indigenous), and academic (most able). They can also be means tested (Harrison and Hatt, 2012). How they have been operationalised and used reflects the 'market' model being used in higher education and reinforces competition for resources. Again, such support does not necessarily help those groups that it claims to be aiming to help. In 2004 in the UK, the Labour government recognised that the widening participation agenda ran the risk of leaving behind those groups who traditionally did not attend university. As a result, it aimed to narrow this gap by requiring universities to spend a proportion of their new-found income from tuition fees to fund bursaries and scholarships. This saw a 'dazzling "market" ... in bursaries being made available ... with each university administering at least one such scheme' (Harrison and Hatt, 2012, p.697). Between 300 and 350 such schemes were put into place. This expansion was, then:

> conceived of and operationalised in the language of consumer choice and 'the market'. The government assumed that they would form part of the decision-making processes of prospective students, with students seeking to maximise their income within their choice envelope of subject area and entry qualifications. (Harrison and Hatt, 2012, p.699)

One major issue is that this new market is difficult to understand. Institutions are continually changing their criteria and also using available funds more as a marketing or branding tool (Harrison and Hatt, 2012). As a result, many young people from disadvantaged groups struggle to apply or gain access to funds in time (Harrison, 2011) What has happened is that a pseudo-market has arisen in which elite universities are able to provide large bursaries (small in number) that attract limited competition from those students most in need as students from low SES groups feel they are not for them (Callender et al, 2009). In fact evidence shows that it is the 'advantaged' groups who are gaining access to the larger bursaries, with disadvantaged students only accessing small amounts (Corver, 2010). Allocation is also still being made more to the 'most able' students rather than those in most financial need, leading to a situation where a large number of students from the low SES groups do not get access. Alongside this, evidence suggests that the most eligible students from the low SES groups are deciding to stay at home to go to university, thus limiting their access to the whole market of bursaries available. It is therefore 'only the most academically able and the most socially and geographically mobile students who are able (or feel able) to compete for the largest bursaries offered by the top universities' (Harrison and Hatt, 2012, p.704). All the evidence suggests that bursaries are having little impact on increasing the success of the groups that are supposedly being targeted in the widening participation agenda, and evidence shows they do not increase the completion rates of the students who have them (Office of Fair Access, 2014; Social Mobility and Poverty Commission, 2013).

Who benefits from widening participation?

The widening participation agendas in Australia, Canada, New Zealand and the UK have had limited impact in increasing the participation of 'disadvantaged groups'. Across these four countries a number of trends remain consistent, regardless of how widening participation has been implemented. While there are always problems of measurement (Gorard, 2008), the patterns and problems are consistent and highlight the entrenched inequality of access and participation for certain groups.

First, it is important to recognise that the expansion of higher education across our case study areas has had a bigger impact on the middle classes than on any other group. It has been shown that over the last fifteen years it is the middle classes who have benefited significantly from the expansion of higher education in the UK (Furlong and Cartmel, 2009; Elias and Purcell, 2012). This is unsurprising in that the middle classes have been quick to recognise that having a degree will bring added value to their search for a job (Elias and Purcell, 2012). Second, while low SES groups have been a key target group across all of the four countries discussed here, there has been little improvement or increase in levels of participation. There have been some minor changes and improvements over the last twenty years but they have had limited impact on social mobility for some of the poorest students. For example, in Australia the participation rate of low SES groups has remained at approximately 15% of the total share of higher education places since 1993. Even through the period of expansion (post–2000) this number hardly moved. The engagement of low SES students has remained 'virtually unchanged for the past decade despite the expansion in the total number of domestic students in higher education' (James et al, 2008, p.23). Some universities were more successful than others, but this related to regional positioning, in that local students would go to local universities, especially in rural areas (Bradley et al, 2008; James et al, 2008). Evidence showed that those from low SES groups are almost three times more likely to go to regional universities, with 9.6% at G08 universities[6] compared to 28.7% at regional universities (Gale and Parker, 2013). There was also a significant under-representation of low SES students in courses such as medicine, law and economics. Despite the introduction of the reforms in 2008 they continue to be almost entirely missing from courses that potentially offer greater income generation in the longer term (Gale and Parker, 2013). Retention and attrition rates are also different for the low SES groups, in that more

---

[6]   G08 universities are those defined as the top universities in Australia.

are likely to fail to complete their degree and more are likely to have very high levels of debt (Gale and Parker, 2013). Students from low SES backgrounds are also more likely to go into professional training VET courses rather than university and, although pathways exist into higher education, limited movement takes place between TAFE and the university sector (Wheelahan, 2008).

A similar pattern exists in the UK, although the involvement of those in low SES groups in higher education has increased (especially between 2004 and 2008). The engagement of these students in the UK has been slowly growing since the 1990s, increasing by 6% between 1995 and 2008 (Naidoo et al, 2011). However, this group remained a major concern in that the numbers involved do not represent the proportion of the population eligible. Although changes after the 2004 higher education bill had some impact, the main growth, as in Australia, was in lower-ranked universities (Harrison, 2011). There remains little movement, and in some cases a decline, in students from low SES groups being recruited into the top universities (Harrison, 2011). For example, in a recent report on the impact of widening participation in the UK on social mobility, three key findings were identified:

- While there has been much progress in widening participation (participation rates in the most disadvantaged geographical areas increased by 30% between 2004/05 and 2009/10) those in the most advantaged areas are still three times as likely to participate in higher education as those in the most disadvantaged areas.
- There has been no improvement in participation at the most selective universities among the least advantaged young people since the mid-1990s and the most advantaged young people are seven times more likely to attend the most selective universities than the most disadvantaged.
- The odds of a child at a state secondary school who is eligible for free school meals in Year 11 being admitted to Oxbridge by the age of 19 is almost 2,000 to 1 against. By contrast, the odds of a privately educated child being admitted to Oxbridge are 20 to 1. (Social Mobility and Poverty Commission, 2013, p.5)

In Canada, 25% of all low SES students, compared to nearly 50% of those of higher SES, attend university. This gap has remained for over twenty-five years. As Berger et al suggest, 'participation in postsecondary education in Canada is no more or less equitable in 2006 than it was in 2001' (2009, p.46). Parental income has a significant impact on participation. In fact evidence shows that low SES students are 40 times more likely to attend college than university (Berger et al, 2009). In New Zealand these trends are again replicated, with those from low SES groups being less likely to study at university. For example, those from a high decile school have a 90% chance of getting a degree qualification while those from low decile schools need to be in the top 5% of all students to progress on to a degree course (Strathdee and Engler, 2012). What we see is that the university sector in particular is still dominated by those from more advantaged backgrounds, even after a policy approach that has claimed to redress the limited opportunities and take-up of those from low SES groups.

Third, three of our case study countries have indigenous populations and these have been a major target group for widening participation. In Australia, there remain similarities between Aboriginals and Torres Strait peoples and those with low SES in that participation in post-secondary education is lower than for those from higher SES backgrounds, and this difference is well entrenched in the system (Bradley et al, 2008; James et al, 2008). Only 5% of Aboriginal and Torres Strait post-secondary students were attending university compared to 30% of young people aged 18 to 19 overall (James et al, 2008). Young Aboriginals and Torres Strait peoples were also over-represented in vocational qualifications and under-represented in postgraduate studies (Bradley et al, 2008). They are more likely to be involved in VET courses and getting lower-level qualifications (Rothman et al, 2014). When young Aboriginals and Torres Strait peoples attend university they tend to do courses in the arts and humanities, and, similar to those from low SES groups, are under-represented in the sciences and medicine (James et al, 2008). Attrition rates are also higher for Aboriginal and Torres Strait youth (James et al 2008; Gale and Parker, 2013; Rothman et al, 2014). In Canada, First Nation peoples are twice as likely to have stopped their education before completing high school. This, coupled with the fact that First Nation peoples are more likely to be in the low SES income bracket, sees their participation in post-secondary education being proportionally low. Evidence shows that, at the age of 20, only 28% of First Nation people have either completed high school or are in post-secondary education compared to 60% of non- First Peoples (Berger et al, 2009). There has been a slight increase in the number of First Nation young people attaining a university degree (from 6% to 8% between 2001 and 2006), but this growth was less than growth for the general population, suggesting that a widening gap is emerging (Richards, 2008; Gale and Parker, 2013). In New Zealand, evidence shows that while Maori students increased their participation rates in tertiary education between 1999 and 2005, much of this was in vocational training courses for certificates (Scott, 2003; Ministry of Education, 2014). This increase was a result of the development of specialist institutions (Wananga) that aimed specifically at Maori participation (Shulruf et al, 2010). Between 2005 and 2008 we start to see a leveling off and numbers actually declining (Ministry of Education 2013). Being Maori has a major impact on going to university; all the evidence shows Maori are less likely than any other ethnic group in New Zealand to access higher education and they also have the highest attrition rates (Strathdee and Engler, 2012).

Fourth, there has been a 'gender revolution' in post-secondary education, with the balance between young women and men being reversed. It is important to recognise that increased enrolment in university for young women has been happening since the 1950s (Booth and Kee, 2009). In fact as Booth and Kee (2009) show, gender parity for young women in university enrolment was achieved in Australia in 1987. Women's participation has continued to grow, to the point that 55% of the enrolled students in higher education in 2007 were young women (Booth and Kee, 2009). Between 1985 and 2007 16 out of 18 OECD countries had more women in post-secondary education than men (Lancrin, 2008). This growth is segmented, in that young women tend to be enrolled in areas such as the humanities, the arts and social sciences, and science, while engineering and mathematics still remain the preserve of young men (OECD, 2008) For example, in Australia, course enrolments of young women are clustered in traditional areas such as nursing and teaching (Carrington and Pratt, 2003), and in the UK engineering and computer science are dominated by young men (Equality Challenge Unit, 2013). While women do comprise roughly 50% of students entering the prestigious faculties of law and medicine, these areas are the least likely to have a significant enrolment from any young women from the lower SES groups. In this context, it would seem that middle-class women tend to be benefiting more from the increased access to higher education than those from low SES groups (Putman and Gill, 2011). These trends have major impacts on future career trajectories and wages (Lancrin, 2008), and can help to maintain the dual labour markets that exist between young men and women.

Similar patterns can be found in the VET aspects of post-secondary education. As we saw in Chapter Three, in the UK there has been a growth of what are called 'modern apprenticeships' that offer VET qualifications as a result of on- and off-job training. Between 2005 and 2008, the number of apprenticeships increased from 189,000 to 457,000. They are available in 150 occupations in 14 sectors (Fuller and Unwin, 203). Between 2005 and 2008 women's involvement increased substantially so that, by 2008, 59% of apprenticeships were held by young women. However, as in higher education, we see labour segregation, in that young women's participation is in the fields of health (86% female), child care (97%), hairdressing (90%) and business (81%). In comparison, young men dominate engineering (97% men), construction (98% men), and IT and telecoms (91% men). It is also the case that gender pay differentials exist in apprenticeships and training programmes in both Australia and the UK. For example, Fong and Phelps (2007) showed that while nationally the pay differential between men and women is 11% in the UK, in apprenticeships it is 21%. The highest paid sectors were also those that were dominated by young men (that is, engineering and electro-technical trades; see Fong and Phelps, 2007).

These patterns are replicated in Australia, where young women have increased their participation in apprenticeships (47% of total apprenticeships in 2007) but their involvement remains segregated in traditional areas (Miles and Bickert, 2007). In Canada, VET opportunities have always been segregated by gender (Sharpe and Gibson, 2005). In 2002, only 9% of apprenticeships in Canada were taken by young women, although variations existed between provinces with Quebec only having 2% and Saskatchewan having 16% of apprenticeships occupied by young women (Sharpe and Gibson, 2005). Apprenticeships tend to be in manufacturing and engineering and when young women are doing apprenticeships they are usually in the area of food and service (Sharpe and Gibson, 2005). In New Zealand similar trends remain entrenched (Higgins, 2002; Chan, 2011). In a study exploring the motivations for entering vocational apprenticeships, young women were seen as more likely to be working in traditional areas. For example, 99% of hairdressing apprentices were young women and similar percentages operated with young men in boatbuilding and engineering (Chan, 2011).

Even in non-traditional areas, such as information and communications technology (ICT) and engineering, gender segmentation can still take place at a range of levels within the industry. Kirkup (2011) showed, by analysing national data in the UK, how gender is operating in vocational training and apprenticeships in ICT. While young women's participation in IT is traditionally low there has been an increase of women taking ICT qualifications, not only at school but also in post-secondary education (Kirkup, 2011). However, the evidence shows a number of gendered features. First, men tend to occupy the high skills training in ICT while young women end up in 'soft skills' training which is seen as offering 'dead end' jobs. Second, young women hold few apprenticeships; it is young men who access the best and more highly skilled opportunities. In addition, a number of private providers of training that provide on the job training have a poor record of recruiting young women (Kirkup, 2011).

Conclusion

Over these two chapters on education and training we can see a number of critical patterns that are consistent across the UK, Australia, Canada and New Zealand. First, young people are clearly seeing the importance of education and training for their life course trajectories. This is reaffirmed by the fact that, even in the great recession that followed the 2007 economic crisis, participation numbers remained reasonably stable across all our case study countries. Second, post-16 education and training is increasingly being commodified by the introduction of a wide range of techniques influenced by neoliberal thinking including quasi markets, the use of NPM, the increased use of private providers in delivering services and the expansion of the 'user pays' philosophy. This has shifted the idea of universities and training from being a public good to a private good, and has brought the young closer to market mechanisms by constructing them as 'customers' who are purchasing a product (education or training). In this context they are continually expected to be active in decision making and operating as 'consumers' of education and training. Third, as was suggested in the previous chapter, this process is not experienced equally. Some groups of young people know how to work the system better than others, partly as a result of their privilege and cultural and social capital, while others struggle to understand the 'rules of the game' and the ways that they need to operate to make progress. In this new environment where choice is seen as critical, it is those who are better positioned who can get the best value out of it.

We therefore see that, even in times of massive social change, different forms of social inequality remain consistent over time. Historically, young working-class people have not had access to higher education and, while there are minor improvements, this remains the case today. But it is also the case that even when they do go to university, they do not normally get access to the best universities or to opportunities that will improve their career choices. These divisions are not just within higher education but also across sectors, in that those from low SES groups are more likely to take a trajectory through the vocational sector rather than university. This has clear impacts on future job prospects and careers. Interestingly, we do not see large numbers of middle-class young people in the VET sector, suggesting that they recognise the way to access good jobs and careers is through accessing good universities. Patterns of inequality that have been historically established also remain strong for those from indigenous backgrounds and for young women. Not only do those from indigenous populations sit in the lowest SES groups but also they are doubly disadvantaged by their indigenous status. Unsurprisingly, they are more likely to be found in the vocational sector and have low involvement in universities. For young women, even though opportunities to participate in post-16 education and training have expanded, there is still substantial occupational segregation. For example, in apprenticeships it is in traditional areas that we see young women (hairdressing, caring and so on), while in universities young women are still hugely absent from the sciences and engineering. So while expansion and restructuring of education and training have been taking place, there is still substantial continuity in experiences between different groups of young people.

FIVE

Unemployment and work: precarious futures

Introduction

In Chapters Three and Four we concentrated on education and training, highlighting how Australian New Zealand, Canadian and UK efforts to respond to the growing concerns about skills shortages in the 1990s saw governments try to improve the 'human capital' of the young. In this chapter we turn our attention to young people's relationship with paid work. Getting into paid work has always been a focal point in young people's movement into independent adulthood and citizenship (Roberts, 2003; Jones, 2009). As a field of practice, paid employment has its own rules, regulations and social practices that shape young people's transitions and trajectories (Atkinson, 2010). The ways in which these relationships are established, changed and shaped, especially for the young, have their roots in historical and contemporary processes embedded in the macro, meso and exosystems of social and economic policy and the practices of corporate business and capitalism (Mortimer, 2009, p.149).

Being 'in work' or 'out of work' puts young people into different sets of social relationships, especially around access to social resources and opportunities that can determine their future in the social structure (France et al, 2012; Shildrick et al, 2012). Moving from education into the world of work or into and through unemployment shapes both the present life worlds of individuals and their future trajectories (Atkinson, 2010; Shildrick et al, 2012). Work and paid employment are 'force fields' (Bourdieu, 1998, p.40) that can protect the young and help them to become more independent, self-reliant and socially mobile (Atkinson, 2010). They provide a critical site of social practice where habitus and cultural and social capital can play a significant part in helping young people manage their social and economic futures (Atkinson, 2010).

In the following discussion we will explore what has been happening to young people's relationships with paid work. Not only has the age entry point into work been reconfigured, but the way in which paid work is experienced by many young people has been undergoing significant changes. Following the recent economic crisis and great recession, new and deeper problems for the young have emerged, especially around unemployment and finding a career, yet as we shall see, many of these processes have been evolving for over twenty years. Our discussion will start by examining how these changes have been conceptualised, highlighting the importance of recognising the nature of these new relationships, especially in terms of insecurity and uncertainty. We will then examine what this has meant in terms of youth unemployment and young people's working environment in the UK, Australia, Canada and New Zealand. These processes are not unique to the 2007 economic crisis, although, as we shall see, they have clearly been accelerated by it: their emergence has roots in earlier political and economic processes related to the neoliberalisation of advanced economies.

'Precariousness' in late modernity

The concept of 'precariousness' has become a popular theme in discussions about paid work. It has also become a major point of discussion in youth sociology (Woodman and Wyn, 2014). Guy Standing's 2011 book, *The precariat*, has greatly influenced how changes in the labour market can be understood and his argument has gained substantial attention, especially in terms of the changing experience of the young. Standing (2011) proposes that we are now seeing the emergence of the 'precariat', or a 'class in the making', who are internally divided yet angry and bitter at the way they have been treated. As a class, he suggests, the precariat contains a diverse collection of people who are living insecure and fragmented lives, moving in and out of short-term jobs in unprotected work environments. He claims they are 'denizens' rather than citizens, a denizen being 'somebody who has a more limited range of rights and weaker entitlement to them, than the citizen' (Standing, 2012, p.590). He sees this primarily as it affects migrants but suggests that the young and those on the margins are also becoming more and more mobile and insecure, and can therefore be defined as denizens as well (Standing, 2012).

While Standing (2011, 2012) offers a new way of thinking about the new environment in workplaces around the world, he does not empirically demonstrate its existence. As a concept, the precariat has an intuitive appeal, especially in times of economic crisis, but it lacks clarity and precision, and is weak in terms of evidence (MacDonald, 2013). This is not to deny that paid work, especially for the young, may be changing and that this may be a negative experience for many.

The concept of precarious work, or work that is insecure and unstable, has a long and illustrious history (Kalleberg, 2008; Quinlan, 2012). In fact, social theorists such as Marx, Durkheim and Weber had much to say about how, for certain groups, precarious work was a normal part of their involvement in the industrial labour market (Kalleberg, 2008). Labour as a resource has always been a critical commodity for capital accumulation and, although the welfare contract after the Second World War brought protection and a partial de-commodification of labour (Polanyi, 1944), by the 1980s re-commodification had begun, especially in those states that were embracing neoliberalism (Jessop, 2002). As a result, by the late 1980s the level of precarious work increased as the welfare contract began to collapse (Bourdieu, 1998).

As outlined in Chapter Two, once neoliberalism re-established itself in the 1980s as the 'new' economic doctrine, especially in the advanced economies, new forms of working emerged as a result of changes in how the labour market was regulated (Jessop, 2002). This helped maintain and increase capital accumulation, creating opportunities for employers to develop new working arrangements. In this context we start to see, in the post-Fordist era, the increased use of 'flexible labour' and new forms of labour laws that increase insecurity and casual work (Kalleberg, 2012). This continued and expanding growth of precarious employment since the 1980s therefore correlates to the expansion of neoliberal approaches and the politics of 'market rules'. As Kalleberg (2012) suggests, this arises because of:

> macrostructural economic, political, and social forces such as the intensification of global competition, rapid technological innovation and change, deregulation of markets, increased mobility of capital and growing financialization of the economy, the decline in unions and worker power, and the continued rise of the service sector. (Kalleberg, 2012, p.429)

The creation of flexible working through the use of temporary work, casualisation and part-time work is closely related to how the labour market is regulated. This becomes a critical and essential tool in the ways nation states help businesses reduce costs and increase profitability. To what extent flexible working are global trends remains unclear (Fevre, 2007) and national governments, unsurprisingly, are reluctant to accept that the insecurity created by this practice is a permanent feature of their local and national labour markets. However, as we shall see, across the UK, Australia, Canada and New Zealand, changes in how the labour market is regulated are increasing the growth of insecurity and uncertainty in the labour market for the young.

In these changing times we need to understand and recognise that a normal experience of paid work is now non-standard for many young people. Standard work is normally defined as paid work that is full time, permanent and takes place in the daytime between the hours of 8am and 6pm. Non-standard work means 'forms of work involving limited social benefits and statutory entitlements, job security, low wages and high risks of ill-health' (MacDonald, 2009, p.168). This can include 'its contractual status (temporary or permanent) or/and length of job tenure' (MacDonald, 2009, p.168). Contemporary evidence indicates that the youth labour market, especially for those with low educational qualifications, is increasingly characterised by a high turnover of work that is temporary, interspersed with spells of unemployment and inactivity, involving part-time and casual employment or work that is outside standard working hours. Such occupations, by their nature, also have insecurity of employment contracts and low pay (MacDonald, 2013).

But of course we also need to be mindful that precariousness and non-standard work is not a new concept for the young, especially for groups such as the working class, women, migrants, and indigenous populations. Work has always had elements of precariousness for young people. For example, Goodwin and O'Connor (2005) show that even in times when the transitions from school to work seemed unproblematic, many young people had non-linear, complex and risky experiences, involving not only changes of jobs but periods of inactivity and unemployment. In the 1980s, at the height of unemployment in the UK, the types of jobs available to the young working class were limited, often being of a poor quality, insecure and without great financial reward. Experience of work was also interwoven with periods of unemployment and training that saw the young working class 'warehoused' in government training schemes (Bates et al, 1984). Also, for young women, work has always had strong elements of flexibility, casualisation and insecurity (Crompton, 1997). Therefore, if we take a longer historical perspective on work we can see that 'insecurity' in employment alongside periods of unemployment for the most marginalised and vulnerable young people has always been an issue (MacDonald, 2011; Quinlan, 2012). Those with low skills and/ or no qualifications, living in disadvantaged areas, have always had to manage insecurity and uncertainty in the youth labour market, and these issues are always exacerbated in times of crisis (Pollock, 2002; Quinlan 2012; Shildrick et al, 2012). However, what we have been seeing across Australia, New Zealand, the UK and Canada is that such work insecurities have been increasing since the early part of the 21st century, and especially since the 2007 crisis. Notions of flexible, casual, temporary and non-voluntary part-time work that is non-standard have been increasing in all sectors of the economy, and this process of precariousness is also starting to impact on other economic and social groups not traditionally used to encountering precarious work as a part of their lives.

It is also important at this point to recognise that, as this insecurity and uncertainty has grown, we have also seen the increase of workfare and national government policies that aim to 'help' the young maintain working careers and working lives. Active labour market policies have become a core area of policy across the UK, Australia, New Zealand and Canada, operating as a part of increased conditionality aiming to ensure that the young keep active in searching for, and taking work, regardless of its quality (Gazso and McDaniel, 2010; Hamilton, 2014). Attached to this we also see the greater use of sanctions, where young people who fail in their searches are punished by having their benefits removed (Wynd, 2013; O'Hara, 2014). This issue will be further expanded on in Chapter Six, but here we need to recognise the interconnection between insecurity and state policies of welfare to work and the expansion of conditionality in benefits.

Global and regional trends in unemployment

In exploring these questions, we should start our analysis by examining unemployment as a global phenomenon. When it comes to questions of crises, it is reasonable to assume that young people will suffer the highest levels of unemployment around the globe. History shows us that young people tend to lose their jobs more quickly than any other social or economic group in economic crises and they suffer most from long-term bouts of unemployment (ILO, 2013). The 2007 crisis was no exception (ILO, 2013). In Figure 5.1 we can see that between 2007 and 2009 youth unemployment increased across the Organisation for Economic Co-operation and Development (OECD) countries from 11.5% (69.9 million) to 12.7% (75.6 million). Over the following two years it declined to 12.3% (72.6 million), then gradually increased again until it reached 12.6% (73.4 million) in 2013. Projections suggest that this increase is set to continue well into 2016 (ILO, 2013). Young people are three times more likely to be unemployed than adults and they presently make up almost half of the world's total unemployed

Figure 5.1 Global youth unemployment and unemployment rate 1991–2013

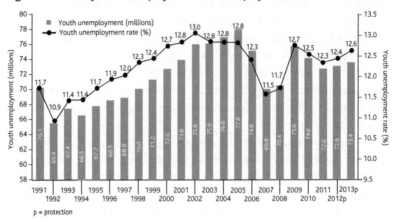

p = protection

Source: ILO: Trends Econometric Models, April 2013

(43.7%), confirming that, in times of crisis, young people are the hardest hit (ILO, 2013).

These figures suggest the recent crisis has been causing young people significant new problems but, as we can see, these levels of unemployment are not particularly new. From 1992, youth unemployment grew year on year until 2002 when it reached 13% (75.8 million). It then levelled out and dropped dramatically between 2005 and 2007 (69.9 million). Youth unemployment has been a major social problem for nation states for well over two decades, but if we look at youth unemployment more regionally we can see the diversity that exists between regions and nation states.

Table 5.1 shows youth unemployment trends across time for a number of regions. There are three main points to make. First, what we see is huge variations between OECD regions and clearly the 'world average' hides significant diversity of experience. North Africa, for example, has always had the highest levels of unemployment, ranging from 23.9% to 29.5% over the past 13 years. Unemployment is highly entrenched in certain places in the world. In comparison, some regions have consistently lower levels of youth unemployment (that is, East and South Asia). Second, when we look at the crisis of 2007, most regions saw youth unemployment increase significantly, although the biggest impact was in the developed economies and the European Union (EU; 5.8 percentage point increase), followed by the Middle East (3.3) and North Africa (4.8). The developed economies include not only the EU but also the US, the UK, Canada, Australia and New Zealand. Third, and this is a key point to note, if we go back to the

Table 5.1 Youth unemployment rates (15–24-year-olds) in OECD regions 2000–09/14

Region	2000	2007	2009	2011	2013	2014*	Change since 2007	Change since 2000
World	12.8	11.6	12.9	12.7	12.9	13.1	+2	+0.3
Developed economies and EU	13.5	12.5	17.4	17.6	18.2	18.3	+5.8	+4.8
Central Eastern European and CIS	20	17.5	20	17.9	17.7	18	+5	-2
Latin America and Caribbean	16.1	14.1	15	13.8	13.3	13.6	-5	-2.5
East Asia	9.4	8.0	9.4	9.4	9.9	10.1	+2.1	+.7
South East Asia and Pacific	13.2	14.8	13.9	12.9	12.8	13	-1	-0.2
South Asia	10.3	9.2	9.8	9.7	10	10.2	+1	-0.1
Middle East	25.5	23.9	23.7	26	26.8	27.2	+3.3	+1.7
North Africa	29.5	24.2	23.9	28.1	28.6	29.4	+4.8	-.9
Sub-Saharan and Africa	13.3	11.7	12.1	11.9	11.7	11.9	+.2	-1.4

* Projected data.

Source: This data was analysed from the OECD Factbook (http://www.oecd-ilibrary.org/economics/oecd-factbook-2013_factbook-2013-en).

year 2000, we see that the difference between that year and 2014 is actually less substantial for most regions. What we see is that over this 14–year period the biggest change has been in the developed economies and the EU. What this tells is that high youth unemployment, while not exceptional for many regions has, since the early part of the 21st century, become a major problem in the developed economies and the EU.[1] These regional figures also hide national variations. If we look

---

[1] It is important to recognise that regional trends mask the fact that these figures are a product of unemployment as defined according to ILO standards. In many countries in Asia, South America and Africa unemployment will be widespread but it will not satisfy the ILO definition and therefore the full impact of unemployment in these regions is hidden.

at the youth unemployment rates in countries such as Spain, Greece and Italy, we see figures that range from 40% to 50%. Interestingly though, we also see that in these countries youth unemployment has historically been high and, while the crisis saw a significant jump, it is important to note that the levels of youth unemployment have always been high over the last twenty years.

Table 5.2 Youth unemployment rates (15–24-year-olds) in eight OECD countries 2000–12

Country	2000	2007	2010	2013	Change since 2007	Change since 2000
Australia	12.1	9.4	11.6	12.2	+ 2.8	- 0.1
Canada	12.7	11.2	14.9	13.7	+ 2.5	+ 1.0
Japan	9.2	7.7	9.2	6.9	- 0.8	- 2.3
New Zealand	13.5	10.1	17.4	16.3	+ 6.2	+ 2.8
Norway	10.2	7.3	9.3	9.2	+ 1.9	-1.0
Poland	35.2	21.7	23.7	27.3	+ 5.6	-7.9
Spain	25.3	18.1	41.5	55.6	+37.5	+30.3
United Kingdom	11.7	14.3	19.5	21.1	+ 6.8	+ 9.4

Source: This data was analysed from the OECD Factbook (https://data.oecd.org/unemp/youth-unemployment-rate.htm). Figures rounded up to one decimal point.

In Table 5.2 we can see that a trend across most of the areas is that unemployment has continued to grow, especially since 2007. Between 2000 and 2007, youth unemployment was declining but, after the crisis, all of our case study countries saw it increase. Some interesting figures can be explained. For example, in Poland there was a substantial drop in the unemployment rate between 2000 and 2007; this is related to the readjustment being made from a communist to a post-communist state (see Chapter Seven for more details). Poland then suffered unemployment increases similar to other countries from 2010. Norway and Japan only saw a small increase throughout the recession. Again, this was related to specific local contexts that operated to lessen the impact of the crisis. Norway had a large resource in the form of its oil reserves that helped protect it from sudden jumps in unemployment and Japan had already been through its own crisis in the 1990s. As we can see, Spain has been the hardest hit, seeing unemployment jump from

25.3% in 2000 to 41.5% in 2007, and continuing to grow to 55.6%. Recent figures suggest that unemployment remains high in Spain. The main reason for this is that Spain, as we will see in Chapter Seven, has been hit the hardest by the economic crash and great recession. It is also worth recognising that, compared to Canada, New Zealand and the UK, the unemployment rate in Australia throughout the 2007 crisis and into the great recession was less pronounced. This arose because of a stronger economy as a result of its mineral trade with China. Since 2013, however, youth unemployment in Australia has continued to rise, with an increase of 1.8% over two years, and is now twice as high as the national average (ABS, 2014). This is apparently a result of the Australian economy slowing down.

Moving into 2014, evidence from our main case study areas confirms that high levels of youth unemployment remain. For example, in Australia youth unemployment remains high and the length of time a young person is unemployed has increased from 16 weeks on average in 2008 to 29 weeks in 2014, with 18% of all unemployed young people now classified as long-term unemployed (ABS, 2014). In the UK, youth unemployment jumped quite dramatically between 2007 and 2013 but has since started to decline and continued to fall until July 2014, when it had dropped to 15.9%, yet by the end of 2014 it had crept back up to 16.6% (ONS, 2014). In Canada, we see a steep increase throughout the crisis and great recession, which then levels out and starts to drop in 2014, reaching a low of 12.6% in October but rising back up to 13.3% by the end of the year (Statistics Canada, 2014b). In New Zealand, the youth unemployment rate increased to 18.9% in early 2013 then dropped to 16.3% by the middle of the year; it is now seeing a slow movement downward in 2014 (Statistics New Zealand, 2014).

If we look into the national figures for our four countries in more detail, we see that significant regional and group differences exist. Aboriginal and Torres Strait young people in Australia are three times more likely to be unemployed than other Australians (ABS, 2014). These figures can also depend on geography: Aboriginal and Torres Strait young people are 12 times more likely to live in remote areas than other Australians (ABS, 2014). Similar patterns exist in New Zealand, where youth unemployment for Maori young people is double that of those from European descent (29% compared to 14%). When issues of regional differences are taken into account, Maori unemployment in some of the more remote and rural areas can be well over 50% (Statistics New Zealand, 2014). Since the economic crisis Maori unemployment has continued to grow, even though youth

117

unemployment in New Zealand has been slowly declining in some areas (Statistics New Zealand, 2014). In Canada, First Nation youth have also been hit hard: in 2014 there was an unemployment rate of 25.9% among 15–19-year-olds, compared to a non–First Nation rate of 19.5% (Statistics Canada, 2014b). Canada also has variation by province in that unemployment among young people aged 15 to 19 ranges from 27.4% in Nova Scotia to 11.6% in Saskatchewan. The 2007 economic crisis and the great recession that followed also had variable impacts on the provinces in that Nova Scotia, New Brunswick and British Colombia had the highest increases in youth unemployment compared to the other provinces (Statistics Canada, 2014b).

Differences in our main case study areas can also exist between cities and within cities. For example, in UK cities such as Middlesbrough, Barnsley and Glasgow, youth unemployment of over 25% is normal, while Southampton and York have less than 13% (Crowley and Cominetti, 2014).Within cities with average levels of unemployment there can also be 'pockets' where unemployment is over 25%. In more disadvantaged cities these levels are even higher (Crowley and Cominetti, 2014).

This analysis suggests that:

- Youth unemployment is becoming more entrenched around the globe and is becoming normalised in some parts of the world.
- More recently, youth unemployment has been gradually increasing in the advanced economies, suggesting that it is not just a 'third world' or even 'second world' problem.
- The crisis has increased the depth of the problem – large groups of young people encounter periods of sustained unemployment.
- Its impact is not even – within nation states certain groups and geographical areas fare worse than others. This is especially relevant for those nations with indigenous populations.
- As was suggested in Chapter Four, this may well be more a problem of underemployment than unemployment: there are not now enough jobs to go around.

So what has been happening to paid work?

The changing nature of work in late modernity

As unemployment has increased, opportunities for 'decent' work have apparently also been decreasing as the very nature of work itself has been changing. These are not new developments but they have been exacerbated by the 2007 crisis. The growth of jobs for the young across OECD countries has decreased dramatically, down by 7 million from 35 million new jobs being created in 2011 to only 28 million in 2013. The types of jobs being created tend to be in the service economy in areas, such as hospitality, social care and education (ILO, 2013). These areas have seen a growth of 10% over the last decade so that 45% of all workers now work in the service sector (ILO, 2013). These are traditionally areas where the young work. However, not only are fewer jobs available but growth is mainly in part-time work, with a 9% increase in such work since 2000. We are also seeing an expansion in temporary work for the young (ILO, 2013). For example, recent evidence from Greece shows that over 41% of new employment contracts are flexible and temporary, and the proportion of full-time permanent jobs available has dropped from 79% in 2009 to 59% in 2011 (McKay et al, 2012).These trends are what have led researchers like Standing (2011) to say that we are seeing the emergence of a 'new class', the precariat, that is made up primarily of the young.

Changes to the youth labour market under neoliberalism

It is generally assumed that 'deregulation' of the labour market is closely tied to the neoliberal notion of 'freeing markets' while re-regulation is about increasing social protection in the labour market. Such distinctions are problematic in that they fail to recognise the complex and diverse ways that regulation operates, especially around freeing up labour. What we have witnessed are new forms of regulation designed to enforce market discipline on the young, rather than the overall withdrawal of regulation, as suggested by the term deregulation. The discussion that follows will focus on the different types of rules and regulations that are being used to free up labour. Such freeing up can involve not only the removal of laws but also the addition of others that operate in favour of business.[2]

Much legal activity around labour market reform suggests the removal of interventions in the labour market, especially concerning trade union membership and rights to collective bargaining. However, it also involves introducing new laws such as rights (or lack of rights) to health and safety protection, leave provisions, requirements on minimum wage laws, hours a person can work without breaks, shift length and the contractual rights a person has (Blanpain, 2010). Over the last thirty years, governments have seen regulation in the youth

---

[2] I want to thank Phil Mizen, who brought this point to my attention.

labour market as the key to economic development and tackling the youth unemployment problem (Heyes and Lewis, 2014). It has been claimed that a major problem has been over-regulation of employment law for the young, creating hindrances and blockages to the creation of new jobs and opportunities for them to get into work (Heyes and Lewis, 2014). At an international level, the drive to regulate labour markets to 'free up labour' has been led by organisations such as the OECD (1996), and the European Commission (EC; Fergusson and Yeates, 2013). More recently, the World Bank has been advocating such a position:

> some broadly based policies, especially those regulating the labor market, can hurt new entrants disproportionally. For example, minimum wages are sometimes set too high … employment protection laws provide stability to those already employed, but could inhibit employers from taking a risk in hiring promising but inexperienced workers. (World Bank, 2006, pp.51–2)

Discourses at this level have a fundamental impact on helping national governments frame neoliberal approaches to the 'problem of youth unemployment' (Fergusson and Yeates, 2013). Yet the success of such approaches remains unproven. In fact, it has been argued that, throughout the economic recession:

> EPL (Employment Policies Legislation) has had little or no influence on the labour market prospects of young European workers. The notion that weaker employment rights improve the position of vulnerable workers and encourage greater social inclusion is therefore not a compelling one. (Heyes and Lewis, 2014, p.604)

Changes in the youth labour markets in the four cases study countries discussed here have a varied and complex history. Such legislation has not been the only strategy used by governments to increase jobs, and regulation policies and practices do not follow a linear pattern. However, over the last thirty years we have seen gradual and incremental changes, at both a general level (that is, employment laws affecting all) and at a direct level that has shifted the balance so 'flexibility' and 'casualisation' have become more central in the youth labour market.

Australia

In Australia, a wide range of legislation was introduced between 1996 and 2011 that has contributed to the liberalisation of the Australian labour market (Tweedie, 2013). Changes such as the Workplace Relations Act (1996) and the Workplace Relations Amendment (Work Choices) Act (2005) were introduced by governments as a way of increasing the role of market forces over wages and conditions. This also shifted the emphasis away from collective bargaining to 'individual choice' in work contracts and reduced a number of employment rights, including the removal of full protection for unfair dismissal (Anderson and Quinlan, 2008). While the Australian Labor Party, in their Fair Work Act (2009), extended some protective rights for casual staff by creating the status of long-term casual employee, it did not radically change the situation of casual workers (Tweedie, 2013). In the youth labour market, little legislation exists at the federal level to protect young people as a special group (Stewart and van der Waarden, 2011). However, national policies have sanctioned differential payments for young people's minimum wages. This has seen different industries set different rates. For example, in hospitality the youth wage at age 15 is 50% of the adult wage, 60% at 17 and the full rate at 20. More recently, under the 2009 Fair Work Act (S27), states were allowed to retain power to pass laws on child labour (Stewart and van der Waarden, 2011). Since then, three of the Australian states have implemented new laws, but most of these laws concentrate on protecting school-aged workers and those under 16 (that is, requiring parental consent for them to work). New South Wales and Queensland did instigate new laws for 18 and under but it is unclear how much these are recognised in practice by employers in these states (Stewart and van der Waarden, 2011)

The youth labour market in Australia has been changed so that there are no special provisions to protect the young (Steward and van der Waarden, 2011). As a result, one of the major new features of the Australian labour market is its increased casualisation. Casual temporary and part-time employment has increased substantially over the past twenty years (Woodman and Wyn, 2014). In 2012, 23% of all Australian employees were working on temporary and casual contracts (ABS, 2014). This is similar to Spain (25.3%) and Poland (27%), which have the highest levels of casualisation in Europe (ILO, 2013). Some industries in Australia are more casualised than others. For example, the accommodation and food sector has over 64% of its staff on casual contracts. Other service sector occupations are also highly casualised, including agriculture and fisheries (48%). Over 20% of all casual workers in Australia are aged between 15 and 24 (Stanwick et al, 2013), although young people are concentrated in those areas of work that have high levels of casualisation (Woodman, 2012). When you take out those who are working while in education, the rate of casualisation is even higher (Stanwick et al, 2013). For example, over 65% of all young people aged between 15 and 19 (not in education) are working on casual contracts (compared to 38% of 20–24-year-olds). This is a substantial increase since 2001, when it was 45% for 15–19-year-olds and 32% for 20–24-year-olds (Stanwick et al, 2013). Part-time work is also common among the working young, with 54% of those aged 15 to 19 and 20% of those aged 20 to 24 working part time (without paid leave), compared to only 7% of 25–29-year-olds (ABS, 2014). A significant gender also gap exists, in that 72% of all young women working between the ages of 15 and 19 are working part time (without paid leave), as are 31% of 20–24-year-old women (compared to 14% of 25–29-year-olds).

The United Kingdom

In the UK, regulation has been a complex process and one that has not been linear over time (Tebbit, 2007). As a part of the neoliberalisation of the UK, Margaret Thatcher and John Major undertook a process of re-regulation throughout the 1980s and 1990s in such a way as to increase opportunities for employers to have more flexibility and increase profits (Jessop, 2002). For example, wage controls existed for a limited number of sectors and were maintained by local wages councils until they were abolished in 1992. Similarly, in the late 1990s there were major changes in employment laws, such as: a reduction in rights to protection for wrongful dismissal, to severance pay in redundancy and to join a trade union. Part-time, temporary and casual work had few restrictions in law and in fact tax incentives existed that encouraged these forms of employment (Stewart and van der Waarden, 2011). The most significant action taken by the UK government was its refusal to sign the European Social Charter, thus refusing to put into place a range of protections for UK workers. However, unlike Australia, the UK had a long history of legislation that aimed to protect young workers, with its roots in the child-saving movement of Victorian England, which made deregulation difficult. These included Factory Acts that prevented children and young people entering dangerous occupations or hazardous environments (Stewart and van der Waarden, 2011).

In 1997, with the election of New Labour, there were major changes to labour market regulation. In fact, it is suggested that this was a period of positive re-regulation (Tebbit, 2007), with over 54 major regulatory initiatives being implemented in the employment field. These included the introduction of a national minimum wage, new working time directives, increased maternity pay and the introduction of parental leave, new laws on part-time and fixed-term workers, and sex and age discrimination legislation. Among these, the minimum wage brought a modicum of financial protection to the young[3] and the age discrimination legislation aimed to ensure that young (and older) workers were not disadvantaged solely because of their age. Working time legislation (brought in in 2008) introduced the 'young worker' (aged between 16 and 17), who was to receive protection with regard to working conditions and terms of employment.[4] As in Australia, those aged over 18 had the same protections as adults.

Interestingly, in terms of the growth of flexibility in the UK labour market, these changes under New Labour seemed to make an impact (Tebbit, 2007). Labour market flexibility increased between 1992 and 1996, then levelled out throughout the first part of the 21st century, suggesting that the increased regulation imposed by New Labour slowed the growth of flexibility. Within individual sectors, however, flexibility was increased in the supply of labour (as a result of immigration) but decreased in the areas of working time, type of employment and pay (Tebbit, 2007). Such changes start to explain the situation in the UK regarding the trends in young people's employment experiences. Significant differences in labour market experiences have always existed between young people in the UK and Australia (Furlong and Kelly, 2005). Evidence from a range of sources consistently shows a low level of temporary and part-time work among the young in the UK and, while there was a gradual increase through the 1990s, by 2005 it had levelled out and declined compared to other countries (Oliveira et al, 2011). For example, between 2005 and 2008 only 10% of those aged 15 to 24 were working in temporary jobs and, while this was higher than for those aged 25 to 29 and 50 to 64, it was still one of the lowest levels in Europe (Oliveira et al, 2011). Since 2008 we have started to see some of these trends reversed, in that part-time/casual and temporary work, alongside self-employment, has dominated the new jobs being created after the financial crisis (IPPR, 2010). Between 2008 and 2010, the number of young people finding temporary work increased by 40%, while the number of part-time workers among the young increased by nearly 400,000. There was also a gender dimension

---

[3]   Although similar to the minimum wage in Australia we see it as age related.

[4]   For example, employers had to give extra breaks on the job and between shifts.

to this, in that temporary jobs increased by 53% for men and 34% for women. Involuntary part-time[5] employment increased and this was more relevant to women. Involuntary part-time work for those aged between 16 and 24 increased to more than one in four (IPPR, 2010), and young people are more than twice as likely to be employed in involuntary part-time and temporary work as other age groups (IPPR, 2010). As in Australia, the growth area for part-time and temporary work is in distribution, hotels and restaurants. Again, these are areas that are traditionally dominated by young workers (IPPR, 2010).

Since 2010, when the Conservative and Liberal coalition took office in the UK, two major developments that have increased casualisation and temporary working have been the rise of internships and zero hours contracts (Intergenerational Foundation, 2014). Interns are taken on to 'train' and work for up to six months, often with low wages or no pay. Recent research suggests that over 30% of all graduates finding employment had previously done internships for their new employer (Cabinet Office, 2012). Some industries are overpopulated with such contracts (Intergenerational Foundation, 2014). For example, 82% of new employees in journalism were working on internships (with 92% of them being unpaid). The concept of an unpaid internship is technically illegal in UK law, in that if a person works for a minimum number of hours, performs set tasks and adds value to the employer, they are entitled to be paid. This fact is generally ignored (Intergenerational Foundation, 2014). The second growth area has been the zero hours contract. These are contracts where the employer has no obligation to provide a set amount of paid hours. In other words, employees get paid only when they are needed. Employment on these contracts doubled in 2012 to 583,000 and those aged between 16 and 24 accounted for 31% of the workforce (ONS, 2014). Evidence suggests that over 47% of companies with 250 or more employees are using zero hours contracts. Traditional industries that have a history of using casual staff have increased this way of working and more recently a growing body of evidence shows increased zero hours contract usage in public services and institutions such as hospitals and universities (ONS, 2014). Other practices, such as agency working, short hours contracts and term-time contracts have also been continuing to grow as a part of the increased casualisation of the UK workforce (TUC, 2014).

---

[5]   Involuntary part-time work is a stronger indicator, in that it means young people would like to work more hours.

Canada

From the 1990s onwards, Canada's labour market policy concentrated on 'protecting and enhancing business interests through financial and other government incentives' (Tyyskä, 2014, p.153). It concentrated on developing programmes for youth that would 'create good jobs and ease the school to work transition' (Tyyskä, 2014, p.153). This included lowering the minimum wage and reducing labour costs for employers. In the 1990s, increased wage subsidies were offered to employers who were prepared to employ the young (Marquardt, 1998). Provinces gave targeted assistance to encourage employers to hire unemployed young people, and helped assist the set-up of self-employment projects while cutting social benefits (McBride, 2004). This supply-side approach to reforming opportunities for work in Canada remained a dominant feature of government intervention throughout the start of the 21st century. In terms of social protection, Canada has had a minimum wage since the 1940s, which the majority of young people of working age have received. While the federal state has responsibility for setting a national standard, provinces implement their own variations. This can provide exemptions and lower rates for some industries (Tyyskä, 2014). What had a major impact on young people's experience of paid work was the increased use by employers, supported by federal government legislation, of flexible working models and the shift from 'non-standard' work to flexible working arrangements (McBride, 2004).

Across Canada, part-time and temporary work expanded throughout the 1990s until around 2000. Major shifts took place: by the end of the 1990s a greater proportion of people were working in contract-based work, self-employment or temporary work than in full-time permanent work. Between 1989 and 1998, growth in full-time employment accounted for only 18% of all new jobs compared to 58% in the previous decade (Galabuzi, 2005). There was also a steep increase in young people working part time, rising from 10% of all those aged 15 to 24 and in work to 35% (Barlett, 2014). In terms of temporary work, Canadians aged 15 to 24 are more likely to work on a temporary contract today than at any other point since 1997 (the first point when data was collected), with 30% of all young people aged 15 to 24 working on temporary contracts by 2001 (Barlett, 2014). At this point, these trends levelled off and remained reasonably stable until the crisis in 2007, although it is interesting that this 'stability' occurred when the youth population was declining, indicating that part-time work actually grew (Barlett, 2014). Over the first two years of the great recession, the availability of full-time work dropped dramatically until around 2010, when a slow growth in part-time and temporary work became the strategy that employers and provinces used as a way of getting people back into work. Since 2010, 60% of jobs taken by young people have been part time (Barlett, 2014). Across Canada, First Nation youth continued, throughout the early part of the 21st century, to have the lowest levels of employment. In 2009, only 45.1% of First Nation youth were in employment, which was 10% lower than for non-First Nation youth. This situation continued to worsen after the economic crisis of 2007, with First nation young people twice as likely to be unemployed compared to others (Tyyskä, 2014).

New Zealand

As we saw in the discussions in Chapter Two, New Zealand not only introduced neoliberal reforms but actively embraced them as core principles governing how the country and the economy should be run. Such an approach has seen a number of major reforms of the labour market that have continued to increase flexible working and casualisation of the workforce (Anderson and Quinlan, 2008). New Zealand has always had a labour market that contained 'core and peripheral' workers (Spoonley et al, 2004): as a small nation, with fluctuations in availability of jobs, it has always been a challenge to maintain high levels of permanent employment (Campbell and Bosnan, 2005). Between 1945 and the 1980s, New Zealand was able to provide both full employment and good quality work, but after the 1970s oil crisis and the shift of the UK's trade partnerships to the European common market, New Zealand actively focused on deregulating the labour market and increasing casualisation of the workforce (Campbell and Bosnan, 2005). A wide range of legislation was introduced, such as the 1991 Employment Contract Act, which increased the ability of employers to use casual workers (Campbell and Bosnan, 2005) and individualisation of employment contracts (Humpage, 2014). Under neoliberal reform, the role of trade unions and their powers for collective bargaining were also diminished (Humpage, 2014). At one level, the 1991 Act, while increasing casualisation, also introduced a range of protections for those on casual contracts (Campbell and Bosnan, 2005), although the impact of the 1991 Act was less on existing casual workers' contracts and more on the 'core' workforce, with 'some of the rights and benefits specified in awards and agreements for permanent workers – in particular penalty rates – largely disappear[ing]',as 'the new "flexibility" opened up in connection with permanent workers, in particular the new flexibility of working-time arrangements' (Campbell and Bosnan, 2005, p.11).

In 2000, the incoming Labour government, while proposing a 'third way', remained committed to neoliberal principles and practice (Roper, 2005). For example, its first labour market legislation maintained individual agreements, although it saw the 'softening of ... restrictions on union membership' (Humpage, 2014, p.65). Labour also made improvements in workers' conditions and made nine improvements to the minimum wage (Humpage, 2014). As we reached 2008 and the economic crisis, the incoming National Party proposed a wide range of new changes that aimed to increase the pace of labour market deregulation (Humpage, 2014). By 2013 they had introduced a number of anti-union laws and deregulated contracts by introducing a 90-day probation or trial period for small businesses (1–19 employees), while also reducing starting wages for 16–19-year-old employees to 80% of the adult statutory minimum wage[6] (Rasmussen et al, 2014) and permitting a youth minimum wage for the first three months of employment.

Casualisation of the labour market in New Zealand has been increasing since the late 1990s (Spoonley et al, 2004) and 'non-standard' working has become more the norm in New Zealand. Historical data is limited although the Survey of Working Life in New Zealand (Statistics New Zealand, 2008, 2012) has a range of trends that show casual and temporary work remaining an important part of the labour market in New Zealand. In 2012 one in ten of all employees in New Zealand was working in temporary[7] work. Of these, 47% were casual, 29% were on fixed-term contracts and 14% were seasonal workers. In 2008, figures showed that over a third of all temporary workers were aged under 25 (Statistics New Zealand, 2012). In 2012, temporary workers continued to be dominated by the young in that 60% of all casual workers were aged under 35. Similar patterns existed for temporary agency workers (61.5%), fixed-term workers (47.7%) and seasonal workers (50%) (again for the under 35s). Female workers were also more likely to be temporary workers with six out of ten working in temporary work in 2012. It is also the case that temporary workers were more likely to be Maori (13%) and Pacific (10.7%). The main occupations that relied on temporary work were professional

---

[6]   Applies only to 18–19-year-olds if they have been on benefit prior to starting a job.

[7]   This includes casual, seasonal and fixed-term temporary agency work (Statistics New Zealand, 2012).

(24.7%) and labouring (23.4%). Temporary workers were much less likely to be managers, technicians or trade workers. Roughly half of all temporary employees worked part-time hours compared with only 20% of permanent employees. This is one of the most striking differences in job characteristics between temporary and permanent employees. When it comes to non-standard work,[8] evidence shows a growing pattern of New Zealanders working outside the standard work pattern. In 2008 around half of all employees (50.5%) had worked at weekends and 59.2% had done some form of non-standard work over the week, with 36% having done so more than 10 times in the previous four weeks (Statistics New Zealand, 2012).

Incentivising employers

The gradual reconfiguration of regulation in labour markets to increase the freeing of labour over the last thirty years has played a critical role in creating and expanding precarious forms of work for the young. Part of this arises as governments aim to 'free up' labour so that employers can increase job opportunities for the young, yet firms and business claim they need further changes to the youth labour market as a way of reducing costs to employ the young. What is not always recognised in these discussions is that governments, while changing the way the market is regulated, are also providing financial incentives and subsidies to the corporate sector to create work (Farnsworth, 2012). For example, the UK government recently gave the multibillion-dollar Disney Corporation over £170 million to make a film in the UK via tax breaks and other subsidies. In a similar vein, Amazon pays less in corporate tax than it receives in grants and awards from the UK government (Chakrabortty, 2014). In New Zealand the national government not only recently provided subsidies to Warner Bros. and MGM to produce the film *The Hobbit* in New Zealand but also changed employment law to reduce the legal requirement of union membership for film crew (Haworth, 2011). In a recent audit of spending by the UK government on corporate subsidies, it was identified that over £14 billion was directly allocated in 2011/12 to firms and businesses in the private sector. (Chakrabortty, 2014)[9] If you add to this other indirect payments such as tax subsidies, cheap credit and marketing campaigns by government to promote British industry, the amount jumps to

---

[8]   Standard hours are defined as between 7am and 7pm (Statistics New Zealand, 2012).

[9]   This is nearly twice as much as the Job Seekers unemployment budget in the UK.

over £85 billion a year. It is interesting that there is no public record (or awareness) of the extent and size of the investment tax payers are making in private enterprise (Chakrabortty, 2014).

When it comes to incentives in the youth labour market, governments have developed a wide range of financial processes that aim to help employers address supply-side problems. For example, the UK coalition government developed an employment allowance that allowed businesses to take on workers without paying the first £2,000 of National Insurance. Offering such incentive payments to the private sector or business is regarded as normal and legitimate, but little accountability or evaluation is built into such programmes. A large amount of money is invested, with the outcomes and impacts unknown. These practices are not new as there is a long history of such initiatives, but this approach increased during the financial crisis. For example, across all four countries massive subsidies have been given to employers to take on apprentices (£50 million in the UK in 2010; AU$100 million in Australia in 2010). Also, governments have given huge wage subsidies for employing young people. In New Zealand employers get NZ$5,000 for employing a young person in high-demand industries. In the UK, for each 18–24-year-old employed, the employer gets £2,275, while in Canada employers can claim from a budget of CA$70 million through the Career Focus programme to support an additional 5,000 paid internships for recent post-secondary graduates (Canada Budget Statement, 2013). Such programmes can also have a strong targeted approach. For example, in Canada CA$350 million per year has been provided through the Aboriginal Skills and Employment Training Strategy to First Nation organisations to provide training and employment services to these groups (Canada Budget Statement, 2013).

Not only are we seeing governments increasing their intervention in the supply-side of the market but also new firms and organisations are growing that aim to actively promote and encourage 'flexible' and temporary work. Over the last twenty years we have seen the expansion of new organisations that thrive on supplying and managing labour in flexible and casual ways. For example, in the US, there has been a reconfiguration of the employer with the emergence and growth of temporary help firms (THF) that 'assume the responsibility for hiring, allocating, paying, and firing the employees they send to their client firms' (Vallas and Prener, 2012, p.338). Such approaches are not new, as agency working has a long history, but what is new is that organisations and companies that specialise in such services are mobilising themselves to form collective pressure groups in places such as the US and Europe, while also reconstructing themselves as good employers who can make a significant contribution to the new flexible work environment that is required in late modernity (Vallas and Prener, 2012). Euroccett in Europe and the Association of Temporary Workers (ATW) in the US both operate to promote temporary work, arguing that, for many, it is a life balance choice and a way of helping them move from unemployment to full employment. The discourse they promote tends to see the employee 'redefined as a commercialiseable product' and it 'induces employees to embrace a critique of the very bureaucratic structures that had previously sheltered them from precarity' (Vallas and Prener, 2012, p.347). As a result, this discourse can then be internalised by workers to rationalise the changes that workplaces are going through as a matter of individual choice and responsibility, and something that is good for their future career directions (Vallas and Prener, 2012). Young people are significantly over-represented in agencies that promote temporary working, with 60% of agency workers in Portugal, 50% in Poland and 46% in the Netherlands being under 25 years old (Eurocciett, 2014).

Flexible work for the young – who benefits?

It is generally argued in the media and political circles that flexible working has both positives and negatives. This discourse proposes that flexible working has a number of positive aspects for employees. For example, speaking in 2014, the Conservative Minster for Employment Relations in the UK[10] argued that flexible working can be positive for business by attracting the most talented and providing opportunities for mothers and other carers to work while carrying out their domestic responsibilities. It also helps 'young people, entering the world of work for the first time, many of whom might find flexible working a useful way of combining work with further study'. Similarly, in New Zealand, Prime Minster John Key,[11] when announcing reforms on the introduction of a youth start-up wage,[12] trade union reform and changes in rights regarding constructive dismissal, argued that 'a

---

[10] Jennie Willott, speech to the Business Benefit of Flexible Working Conference, highlighting the business benefits of flexible working to employers 2014.

[11] See: https://www.national.org.nz/news/news/media-releases/detail/2011/10/27/workplace-policies-to-build-flexibility-create-jobs

[12] This was a new arrangement, where employers could employ a young person below the minimum wage for an introductory period.

flexible and fair labour market is critical for building a stronger and more competitive economy, and creating more real jobs'.

Such a discourse and narrative is a popular defence of the continuation and expansion of such work, yet, as we have seen across the four case study areas under discussion here, flexibility has increased the precariousness of youth employment. The beneficiary in such cases tends to be the employer, not the young employee. For the young we see the creation of jobs that are unstable, insecure, casual and part time, as a result of significant policy changes. Evidence suggests that such a strategy is not always necessary. For example, claims that liberalisation and re-regulation in Australia were necessary to allow the country to be competitive in the global market place have been undermined by evidence that shows a significant number of employers use the 'casual option' to avoid the costs of standard employment practices. These forms of contracts have little to do with fluctuations in work flows and the need for flexibility, as over half of all casuals are employed on a permanent casual contract for over a year, while 15% have been employed as such for over five years (Stanwick et al, 2013).

The growth of flexible working and the increased precariousness of the youth labour force have major impacts on young people. Many of these types of contracts are problematic in that they create unstable and irregular incomes which limit access to a range of financial services (for example, such workers cannot get credit or mortgages). In Australia over 25% of all casual employees experience significant fluctuations in their earnings and this is highest among those working part time (41%) (Stanwick et al, 2013). Similar problems exist for those working on zero hours contracts in the UK, in that many young people employed on such contracts have irregular incomes, making the paying of bills and meeting financial commitments difficult (Intergenerational Foundation, 2014). The increase use of non-standard work also has major impacts on young people's social life and social relationships (Woodman, 2012). Leisure becomes non-standard and being able to engage in social networks and friendship groups becomes increasingly difficult (Woodman and Wyn, 2014).

These types of employment arrangements also reduce choice for the young. Across all of our main case study areas, young people expressed a desire to have something more secure and permanent. While differences can exist, particularly for students who are working while studying, the general international trend is that many temporary, casual and part-time workers want more hours, more regular hours and more control over their working time. For example, over 40% of all temporary workers in New Zealand in 2012 expressed a wish to have a full-time and permanent job (Statistics New Zealand, 2012). Those who are best able to manage flexibility and casualisation tend to be those with the power and resources to do so. For example, internships benefit the wealthy and privileged in that it is only possible to take on such a role if you have substantial financial and cultural support from parents or have protected income from other sources (Intergenerational Foundation, 2014). In a recent UK report it was found that internships were easier to come by for those from privileged backgrounds. It was also found that these individuals were more likely to secure the most desirable internships in London. In contrast, those from more disadvantaged backgrounds did not seek London-based internships because their families could not support them. Evidence also showed that young people often had to do more than one internship (in some cases as many as 15) before getting a paid job. Again, those from privileged backgrounds are more able to do this because of family support. Evidence also showed that a gender pay gap existed for those who did get pay: young men earned £116 a week while young women earned £88 on average (Debrett Foundation, 2015).

Managing irregular incomes and financial security is easier for those with wealthy parents or substantial cultural capital. Casualisation of the youth labour market tends to have the biggest impact on the most vulnerable and insecure. Being working class, and/or being a young woman, with low attainment levels at school or post-secondary levels increases the possibility of casualisation and temporary working (Statistics New Zealand, 2012; Stanwick et al, 2013; ABS, 2014; ONS, 2014; TUC, 2014; Tyyskä, 2014). This is also highly relevant for indigenous populations in Canada, Australia and New Zealand, as they are among those most likely to be affected by unemployment and precarious work (ABS, 2014; Statistics New Zealand, 2014; Tyyskä, 2014). However, there is also a growing trend for zero hours contracts to be used in professions: a number of health professionals, university lecturers and airline pilots are now working on zero hours contracts (TUC, 2014), suggesting that such employment practices are now affecting the life trajectories of the middle classes.

One final and critical point to acknowledge is that a major impact of the casualisation of young people's employment experiences is the expansion of low pay. Most of the work that is casualised is low skilled which usually also means low pay (Keep and Mayhew, 2010; Corlett and Whittaker, 2014; TUC, 2014). Evidence from across our four countries shows that those in temporary work receive lower wages than those in permanent employment (Statistics New Zealand, 2012: Stanwick et al, 2013; ABS, 2014; ONS, 2014; TUC, 2014; Tyyskä,

2014). Permanent employees also have better terms and conditions, receiving leave entitlements, pension contributions from employers, and have more control over their working time. Temporary work continues to help keep youth wages low. In the UK over 1.5 million young workers are now on a low wage (Brinkley et al, 2013). Low pay among those aged 16 to 30 has almost doubled since the 1970s, rising from just over 20% to 39% in 2010 (Corlett and Whittaker, 2014). Since the 2007 economic crisis and the recession this number has increased at a faster pace, with a real generational gap emerging (Brinkley et al, 2013). There is also a clear gender divide in that there are three times more young women doing low-paid work than there were twenty years ago (Brinkley et al, 2013). Between 1993 and 2011, the percentage of young women aged between 16 and 24 working in low-paid occupations, such as office work and cleaning increased from 7% to 21%, while over the same period the percentage of young men working in low-paid jobs rose from 15% to 25%, or from one in seven to one in four (Corlett and Whittaker, 2014). Similar trends exist in Canada and other parts of the world (Côté, 2014). In the US, evidence shows that the real youth wage has declined: in the 1960s young men would be earning about three-quarters the income of adult males but twenty years later young males of that age group were making about half the income of older men. The proportion of the adult wage earned by young men has since declined further (Côté, 2014). A similar but more significant drop took place for young women. In the 1960s they earned almost 90% of the wages of older women, but by 2010 they earned 60% of the adult female wage (Côté, 2014). In New Zealand 56% of all young people aged 18 to 24 are working for the minimum wage, although Maori and young women are more likely to be on the minimum wage than European Pakeha and young men (Ministry of Labour, 2010).

Conclusion

We have seen dramatic changes taking place in young people's encounters with and experiences of paid work. Clearly unemployment remains a significant threat to young people. The chances of young people becoming unemployed are three times higher, on average, than for older adults. This level of risk is even higher for young people located in certain geographical areas where unemployment is more entrenched and for certain disadvantaged groups. The sustained problem of youth unemployment, especially after the 2007 crisis and through the great recession, suggests that we need to think of these trends as the introduction and embedding of underemployment, as there is now a worldwide problem with the number of jobs available for the young. However, is not merely a problem of lack of jobs: the types of jobs being created are precarious in nature and their quality is significantly problematic, especially for those with low educational skills and a lack of social and cultural capital. The growth of precarious work is not by chance but is in many cases a result of the need to maintain profits in an environment where capital accumulation is difficult. This approach, given legitimacy after the 2007 crisis and throughout the great recession, is being supported by neoliberal policies and practices that support flexible and casual working as a way of addressing the problems of labour. Alongside this, we see governments since the crisis increasingly providing incentives to business that have little to do with the creation of sustained, permanent and secure jobs but are more concerned with ensuring that work of any quality (and pay) is being made available. As a result, young people today are confronted by a labour market after the crisis that operates against them and exposes many of them to a future of insecurity, uncertainty and exploitation.

SIX

NEETs and the disengaged: the 'new' youth problem

Introduction

In the previous three chapters we concentrated on the changing trends in young people's experience of education and work. In this chapter we turn our attention to those who are seen to 'slip through the net' and end up as NEETs (those not in employment, education or training). The concept of NEETs has its origins in the UK (Furlong, 2006). Initially, work by Istance et al in 1994 used the term 'Status Zero'[1] to refer to a group of young people in Wales aged 16 to 18 who were not covered by the categories of employment, education or training. In 1999, in New Labour's social exclusion report, this term was reconfigured as the NEET category (Furlong, 2006). Since then it has become a core category in the UK and has gained substantial international currency. As we shall in the discussion that follows, other nation states have accepted it as a central way of measuring the 'youth problem'. Simultaneously, it has become a core indicator used by the Organisation for Economic Co-operation and Development (OECD), the World Bank, the European Union (EU) and the International Labour Organization (ILO) to measure national success. For example, it has now become a key statistical indicator for youth unemployment and the social situation of youth for the EU's 2020 growth strategy (Eurofound, 2012) and is also a key indicator for comparing the performance of nation states (OECD, 2014a). However, there are substantial problems with its definition (Furlong, 2006; MacDonald, 2013) and how it is used, especially in relation to targeting the 'workless'.

Connected to the emergence of NEETs is the growing use of active labour market policies (ALMPs) that have been used to tackle the problems of engagement by NEETs. ALMPs are defined as 'a wide-ranging set of measures designed to "actively" intervene in the labour market in order to improve its functioning' (Sunley et al,

---

[1]   The local careers service called those over 16 in education Status 1, those in training Status 2 and those in employment Status 3 (Istance et al, 1994)

2006, p.6). They are the opposite of passive policies, or policies such as people receiving unemployment benefits without any obligation, although the distinction between active and passive is blurred in that no benefit system has ever been entirely unconditional (Sunley et al, 2006). However, the core focus of many ALMPs in our main case study areas has been less focused on getting the young into work and more concerned with cutting welfare benefits, increasing conditionality for social benefits and pushing young people towards workfare-type programmes. In reality, as the analysis will show, many of these policies operate to regulate and control the poor, and the young in particular, and to push them into 'poor work'. This chapter begins with a review of why the NEET concept has become popular as a tool for policy makers, followed by a review of how this has sparked a range of policy strategies across the is, Australia, Canada and New Zealand that aim to re-engage the disengaged into either work or training. The second part of the chapter will then explore how governments have turned their attention to more interventionist approaches that suggest 'worklessness' is not an option for those lacking the means to support themselves, and that the state should be involved in creating ALMP welfare policies that require the young to be compliant and active in finding work. The concluding discussion will explore how these policies contact and shape the moral economy around NEETS.

NEETs as the new 'youth problem'?

It is claimed that one of the major consequences of the great recession has been a massive increase in nearly all OECD countries in the number of young people who are NEETs. The biggest and fastest increase is seen among 20–24-year-olds (OECD, 2014a). Those countries that have the highest rates of NEETs are those with the highest levels of youth unemployment (OECD, 2014a). In 2011, in countries such as Chile, Greece, Ireland, Israel, Italy, Mexico, Spain and Turkey, where the increase in youth unemployment was high, more than 20% of all 15–29-year-olds were categorised as NEETs (OECD, 2014a). Evidence from a wide range of international and national reports suggests that young people with lower levels of education are more likely to be NEETs (Eurofound, 2012; OECD, 2014a). For example, NEETs in Spain with lower levels of educational attainment comprise approximately 70% of the total NEET population (Eurofound, 2012). However, there is a suggestion that holding a tertiary degree does not guarantee not becoming a NEET, although how much being a NEET impacts on this group's future remains unknown (Eurofound, 2012).

Significant gender differences also exist, partly as a result of the inclusion in NEETs of what is called the 'inactive' category, which includes those with caring responsibilities (OECD, 2014a). For example, in Europe the NEET rate is 12.5% for young men and 13.4% for women although national variations exist, with Nordic countries having a higher male rate whereas most Mediterranean countries and Eastern European countries have a high rate for young women, partly because of the highly gendered expectations of caring (Eurofound, 2012).

The measuring of NEETs is important but there are problems. As an indicator it has started to replace the traditional measure of unemployment (Furlong, 2006; Eurofound, 2012), being seen as more inclusive in that it identifies not only those who are defined as unemployed but also those who are 'inactive'. For example, it also includes young carers, young people with family responsibilities, and people who are sick and disabled (OECD, 2014a), and is seen as offering a more positive way of capturing the heterogeneous nature of young people's relationship with work, unemployment and training (Furlong, 2006). It can also provide evidence of the diverse ways that young people are vulnerable and how policies fail to recognise why some groups are likely to be less successful (Furlong, 2006). National governments find the NEET concept a useful way of approaching the youth unemployment problem (MacDonald, 2011) in that it captures a wide range of categories beyond simply being 'unemployed' (Furlong, 2006). However, it is important to recognise that there are a number of methodological problems that make comparisons across national boundaries problematic and can create difficulties in assessing levels of change over time (Elder, 2015). Measuring NEETs as a category also aggregates a series of problems into one category, meaning that we then have to disaggregate it to understand how we might target specific policies (Furlong 2006);

> it combines those with little control over their situation with those exercising choice, thereby promoting a state of confusion about the factors associated with an apparent state of disadvantage. (Furlong, 2006, pp.554–5)

It can, in this sense, group together both the privileged and the disadvantaged, leading to a diversion of attention from the vulnerabilities of being disadvantaged and unemployed (Furlong, 2006; MacDonald, 2011). In addition, NEET constructs activity as static and as a moment in time (MacDonald, 2011). As we have seen, young people move in and out of education, employment and unemployment and the NEET categorisation does not capture this. When an approach is taken that recognises the more dynamic nature of young people's relationships with work, unemployment and education, a different picture emerges that reinforces the notion that youth transitions are complex and non-linear (Furlong, 2006). At one level, this creates significant problems with measurement, as numbers of NEETs can vary across seasons or by age group (Eurofound, 2012). More importantly, NEET fails to capture how a significant number of young people are 'churning' between work, unemployment and education, especially in the most disadvantaged and vulnerable groups. As MacDonald states, 'the fluidity, complexity and precariousness of labour market experiences [of young people] ... [meant that] churning between insecure low-paid jobs, poor quality training schemes and unemployment was the norm' (2011, p.432) thus showing that being a NEET is a dynamic process that is not adequately described by static methods of measurement.

The question remains as to why NEET has become popular as a tool for national governments and international organisations. Of course the idea of youth as a social problem has always been a dominant feature of the 'youth question' (Cohen, 1973), although it is important to recognise that the problematising of youth 'during the modern age say[s] as much about the builders as about their subjects, and the way that the concept of youth has been used clearly relates very closely to historical conditions and the social concerns of the times' (Jones, 2009a, p.4). As today's neoliberalism has expanded across the political landscape it has mobilised political groups on both the left and the right to create a new moral order or economy (Sayer, 2005). This operates not only to justify a range of economic and social policies that oil the wheels of modern market societies (Bolton and Laaser, 2013) but also creates a set of explanations of human nature, social order and the 'natural order' of how market-based societies works (Bolton and Laaser, 2013). Of course these are not uncontested (Polanyi, 1944) or without points of resistance (Thompson, 1971) but their embedded nature creates a 'moral discourse' around issues such as the role of inequality in society, how gender relationships should be organised and what are the causes of poverty. As neoliberalism has grown in influence, its moral position in relation to a market economy has been able to reshape the moral agenda. At its heart have been the question of a 'deserving' and 'undeserving' poor, with its key focus being on those not in work or those who have been defined as being part of a dependency culture. This moral discourse locates the problems of the economy as lying with the state, in that welfarism is seen as creating a generation of young people who are unwilling to work and believe in entitlement to benefits (Jones, 2009a; Tyler, 2013). Of course, this moral position is not new and has its roots in the rise of the underclass thesis prevalent in the UK under the Thatcher government (MacDonald, 1997). It later gained ground in debates raised by New Labour on questions of social exclusion. For example, Murray (1984) and the conservative governments in the 1980s and 1990s argued that dependency was a consequence of a generous welfare system that created a problem class who were workless as a result of lifestyle choices. As a result, the government started to reduce universalism in welfare benefits and introduce policies of conditionality. New Labour's 'third way' politics drew upon this discourse of the 'immoral underclass' to justify focusing on supply-side problems in the labour market and introducing further conditionality to benefits and new workfare arrangements, while also laying the blame on the poor and the unemployed for being workless (Byrne, 2005).

Political discourses in the UK then conflated the problem of NEETs with the concept of the 'underclass', which was then associated with the notion of 'anti-social behaviour' (Rodger, 2008). It has been claimed, in a number of government reports (see, for example, Department of Education and Skills, 2007), that those who are NEETS are more likely to offend, to be anti-social and to cost the state substantial sums through their need for welfare support and health care (Rodger, 2008). Hence the development of ASBOs (Anti-Social Behaviour Orders) was combined with NEETs policy to help tackle the potential risk of criminality in this particular group. The government approach to NEETs thus not only links this group with the idea of 'anti-social behaviour' but also tends to 'construe being NEET as a problem *with* young people' (MacDonald, 2011, p.431), seeing them as either making wrong decisions (Roberts, 2009) or as 'deficient in [certain] areas such as having low ambition or poor skills' (MacDonald, 2011, p. 431). Government discourses of the problems of NEETs link the concept of non-participation with certain understandings of disengagement – 'a concept directly derived from the paradigms and precepts of psychology' (Fergusson, 2013, p.21) – as 'fundamentally a negative process … [which] … is by implication a failure to act, an absence of exercise of will, or at extremes a default condition of passivity or indolence in which personal responsibility is abrogated' (Fergusson, 2013, p.21). This then reworks the problem in such a way that it is reconfigured in political discourses to be one of the individual, not the state or market, and gives governments a justification for increasing their strategies of governance (Fergusson, 2013). In this context, the role of policy is 'to begin these corrective remoralisation processes whereby reconstructed citizens take seriously their responsibilities to support themselves under whatever conditions prevail' (Fergusson, 2013, p.22). Throughout New Labour's term of office, the concept of participation, especially in paid work, dominated the discourse of entitlement, re-shaping what it meant to be a citizen:

> Rights of citizenship in the form of entitlement to welfare came to depend on 'responsible' conduct, in the form of accepting offered places in education, training or labour markets. (Fergusson, 2013, p.60)

In this context, failure or unwillingness to look for or find work requires the state to help young people 'find a route back to citizenship and the protective bosom of the state' (Tyler, 2013, p.198), although if they are not willing to help themselves then they need to be 'coerced to become included citizens' (2013, p.198). It is within this debate that the re-engagement of NEETs has become central to the 'youth problem' (Fergusson, 2013; Tomlinson, 2013; Tyler, 2013). In the UK, the coalition government of 2010 took this moral position in their approach to welfare reform. The process has been accelerated within discourses around the Work Programme in the UK (Fergusson, 2013) and discussions of the New Zealand National Party government (Strathdee, 2013), both of which conflate the term 'NEET' with the concept of being 'disengaged'. For example, David Cameron, talking in 2012 about welfare reform, suggested that the welfare system continued to promote a dependency culture in which:

> it pays not to work ... you are owed something for nothing ... [and which] gave us millions of working-age people sitting at home on benefits even before the recession hit. It created a culture of entitlement.[2]

It was these ideological and moral positioning's that reconstructed not only what the problem was (for the economy) but also how the NEET problem was to be addressed. A core strategy in tackling the problem of NEETs has been the expansion of workfare policies and practices that operate to regulate and control the poor. Before we examine them in detail, it is important to recognise that a number of policy developments have been instigated that aim to catch NEETs

---

[2]   Prime Minister David Cameron on welfare reform, at Bluewater, Kent, 25 June 2012.

early, with the intention of embedding the responsibilities of work as a core value into the young.

Strategies for tackling the NEET 'problem'

Early intervention at school

A strong focus of national policies in our main case study areas has been to increase 'early intervention and prevention' strategies, especially in schools. This approach claims to identify a wide range of 'risk factors' that increase the potential for a young person to become a NEET. As a result, policy is aimed at tackling the 'causes' of being a NEET. These risk factors are claimed to be grounded in evidence, although the predictability and interrelated nature of the risks remain unclear. For example, the source of the NEETs problem is defined in many ways, including in terms of problems of underachievement, retention and participation in school, and poor parenting and lack of support for young people (Furlong, 2006). But in a number of reports the focus is broader and linked to more individual negative behaviours or situations such as: having been in the social care system; being a substance abuser; and having family problems and conflicts. The lack of clarity about what are the main risk factors creates confusion over how to identify as it were, pre-NEETs and target resources on them (Tomlinson, 2013). For example, in a study exploring the construction of a NEET indicator, different local authorities in the UK used different ways of identifying those at risk of being a NEET, ranging from demographic data (age, gender and socioeconomic status [SES], being an asylum seeker, a refugee or from the traveller community) to individual or behavioural factors such as being identified by other professionals, being on the social services register, being registered as having special educational needs (SEN), being in care or having a medical condition (Filmer-Sankey and McCrone, 2012). In Australia the risk factors identified are similar although with some differences:

> not having an intention to complete school, coming from a non-nuclear family, being a below average academic achiever, being male, having an unfavourable attitude towards school and perceiving student– teacher relations as unsympathetic (Curtis and McMillan, 2008, p.8)

Other factors also included are low-skilled parents without successful post-secondary education (Curtis and McMillan, 2008), school size and relationships with peers (Lange and Sletten, 2002), and having links with possible future criminal behaviour. This discourse of negativity plays into the construction of this group of young people as a 'part of a "rough" underclass, separate from the rest of the working population' (Simmons, 2008, p.433), who have a series of individual 'problems' that need to be addressed if they are to be absorbed into the workforce (Mizen, 2004). As a result, we are seeing policies introduced into schools that aim to target the pupils who are seen as troublesome and problematic (Wilson et al, 2011). Concepts such as 'alternative education'[3] have then been used to develop and deliver specialised interventions. For example, in Queensland, Australia, the government created a legal requirement for young people to participate in post-secondary education (see discussion below) and, as a way of achieving this, they provided substantial resources to local schools to develop and run early intervention programmes to help maintain high levels of participation in post-16 education (Wilson et al, 2011). In total, 121 different school-based initiatives have been identified that were:

> services within state schools; annexes to state schools providing long-term education programs; flexi schools (state and non-state); community-based youth services; short and long-term education, training and employment preparation programs; Technical and Further Education (TAFE) and other training providers; and behaviour management programs. (Wilson et al, 2011, p.35)

How effective such programmes are remains unclear (Wilson et al, 2011) and concerns exist over how such programmes can actually stigmatise and problematise young people (France et al, 2012). As we have seen, risk factor targeting is not a science (France, 2008; Case and Haines, 2009): it is unpredictable and potentially can alienate young people further from the mainstream (Ellis and France, 2012; France et al, 2012). It is generally assumed that services are good for you, but it is also the case that services can be bad for you if they have unintended consequences (Ellis and France, 2012). In addition, programmes that target the most vulnerable and problematic in education tend to push them towards more vocational forms of education as a way of keeping them engaged in the education system (Tomlinson, 2013).

---

[3] Alternative education programmes are usually defined as activities that fall outside traditional school.

Making employment, education or training compulsory

While schools have been central to targeted initiatives for NEETs, a number of governments have introduced compulsory post-secondary education. For example, Ontario and New Brunswick in Canada have made post-16 education and training compulsory and Winnipeg plans to introduce this in 2016. In 2006 Ontario raised its compulsory learning age from 16 to 18 and provided a range of incentives for young people to stay in education and training. These incentives included access to the local apprenticeships scheme and tax credits for employers. The Ontario programme also had sanctions in that 16–17-year-olds who failed to comply could have their driving licences suspended, and parents could be fined for their children being absent. Employers could also be convicted for employing 16–17-year-olds during school hours (Ungerleider, 2008). While the programme was seen as a success it would seem that this success was not attributable to a single policy intervention and it was unclear whether sanctions were used and if so how effective they were.

Compulsory attendance in education, training or work has also been introduced in Australia. Queensland was the first to implement this, in 2006, followed by South Australia in 2007, Western Australia and Tasmania in 2008, and finally New South Wales and Victoria in 2010. New South Wales, for example, introduced laws in 2010 that made it compulsory for all young people to be active in employment, education or training. Parents are responsible for the participation of their children in compulsory education and training. Since 2010, in addition to parents facing legal action, young people who do not attend education can now also face legal action under certain circumstances. A wide range of subjects, with flexible timetables and targeted careers advice was made available to help students choose an appropriate career path. Schools were also required to develop and implement strategies and programmes to support the group of students who traditionally would have left school when they reached 15 years of age, often during Year 10. Under the new laws they had to stay in school until they were 17. In 2010 the federal government introduced the Compact programme. This programme established a compulsory requirement for all 16- and 17-year-olds to be in education in Australia, giving an entitlement to an education or training place to all 15–24-year-olds. Compact is intended to encourage young people to "learn or earn". It means that young people aged under 22, who are on Youth Allowance and without a Year 12 qualification or its equivalent, are required to participate in education or training in order to receive their benefit.

Questions remain regarding how successful such a strategy has been, as policing and tracking the young outside of the traditional school setting is increasingly difficult and requires the development of sophisticated (and costly) tracking systems. Such systems also require the private sector to participate in these processes, as they are seen as the only types of organisations large enough to provide adequate surveillance (Maguire, 2013).

More recently, the UK government has also set about increasing the education leaving age to 18 by 2016,[4] meaning that all young people are required, by law, to be in employment, education or training. While this measure is seen as benefiting all young people, it is targeted at reducing the numbers of NEETs in England and Northern Ireland[5] (Department for Education and Skills, 2007). How it will be implemented remains a challenge. Local authorities are charged with the responsibility to deliver the policy, but it remains unclear what constitutes 'appropriate' education and training, or how young people will be tracked (Maguire, 2013). How this will make a difference to engagement in education among 16–18-year-olds is unclear, while the highest levels of NEETs tend to be among those aged 20 to 24 and thus unaffected by this policy. The risk is that such an approach will compound and maintain the warehousing and 'churning' of 16- and 17-year-olds rather than getting them into work (Maguire, 2013).

Targeting intervention for 16–17-year-olds

Across Australia, the UK, Canada and New Zealand, a core policy has been to target 16–17-year-olds who are either 'at risk' of becoming a NEET or already are NEETs. For example, one of the major initiatives in the UK was the introduction of the Education Maintenance Allowance (EMA) in 2000. This provided a regular weekly payment (£30 a week) for those with low incomes to stay in education, subject to the condition that they attended regularly and obtained a qualification. It aimed to offer an incentive to young people and it was hoped that this would reduce the number of NEETs. In 2010, the UK coalition government removed it and replaced it with a number of other programmes. The Blair government also introduced

---

[4]   Young people aged 16 to 18 are required to be in training or education – although in effect this only applies to 16- and 17-year-olds, as they will only be required to participate until their 18th birthday.

[5]   Wales and Scotland have the option to implement this but as yet have declined.

the Connexions Programme in 1999,[6] which was a careers and advice programme that provided personal support to young people. It was intended to be a universal service but also targeted those most at risk of being NEETs (Smith, 2007). Over its life, it had major structural problems with delivery and evidence of its effectiveness in reducing NEETs was questionable (Smith, 2007). By the end of 2008, Connexions had been integrated into local schools and it no longer existed as a branded national service. Other programmes have been piloted, including Activity Agreements (Maguire, 2013). This programme provided financial incentives, individualised support and targeted assistance to those most 'at risk'. The programme had mixed success: while it increased participation of NEETs in education, employment or training, this was not always sustained. It was also the case that many of the NEETs were likely to have found jobs regardless of the intervention and so this was seen as a costly way of tackling the problem (Department for Education, 2011). In 2012 the coalition government provided £1 billion to set up the Youth Contract. This aimed to give all young people aged 18 to 24 work experience of up to 12 weeks (unpaid). It was seen as a new component of the Work Programme (Department of Work and Pensions, 2010), but it was intended to target the long-term unemployed or NEET groups as a way of getting them back into work.

In Australia the main initiative to tackle the NEET issue has been the Compact programme discussed earlier. The Compact services include individualised support, outreach work and a wide range of re-engagement activities for those under the age of 18. The main focus is on young people at risk of being NEETs in both the school setting and post-16. In total, 65 providers in 118 regions are delivering the service (Department of Employment, 2013), but how it is delivered varies across the states and territories. A recent evaluation showed that over 71,000 young people who had disengaged or were at risk of disengaging from education had been helped by Compact and that 96% of those helped were still engaged in education, employment or training six months later (Department of Employment, 2013). In 2014, the Australian Liberal government proposed abolishing the service, but at the time of writing Senate was rejecting this proposal.

New Zealand has a shorter history of NEETs, only recognising them as a formal category for data collection in 2011 (Statistics New Zealand, 2011). Prior to this, New Zealand saw formal education as the solution

---

6   Connexions did not exist in Wales, which had its own approach (National Assembly for Wales, 2000).

to future non-participation in the labour market. However, over time this strategy has been seen to have failed (Strathdee, 2013), and there has been increased targeting within the post-16 age group. For example, in 2012 the National Party government introduced the Youth Package (Office of Ministry of Social Development, 2012), which specifically targeted resources at 16–17-year-olds who were either NEETs or at risk of being NEETs. This service is called the Youth Pipeline and aims to ensure that no 18-year-old will be on a benefit. It has authority to gather information from schools and other providers to identify who is at risk of becoming a NEET so that they can be targeted (Office of Ministry of Social Development, 2014). In this programme, young people who are NEETs can get a Youth Payment, although they have to have it managed by an adviser and it is dependent on them seeking work. Providers are paid by results. The Youth Package also included the establishment of the Youth Guarantee Scheme. This provides fees-free tertiary places for eligible domestic students aged 16 to 19 years who are studying towards a qualification at levels 1, 2 or 3 on the New Zealand Qualifications Framework (NZQF) (including the National Certificate of Educational Achievement or NCEA). It aims to improve the transition process from school to work, to improve the achievement levels of Maori and Pacific students and students with special education needs, and to reduce the overall number of NEETs.

In Canada the federal government established the Youth Employment Strategy (YES) in 1997, which targeted young people aged between 15 and 30 years of age who were not engaged in employment or education. Prior to this there was no federal policy. Most targeted employment policies are based in the provinces. The YES programme provides funding for organisations in the provinces, which can apply to set up locally based interventions. Its primary objective is to enhance skills development and help young people overcome barriers to finding work. In 2003, it established three streams of funding: Skills Link, Career Focus and Canada Summer Jobs. Skills link applies to: young single parents; people of First Nation descent; people with disabilities; recent immigrants; youth who live in rural or remote areas; and youth who have dropped out of school. The Career Focus stream gives attention to those with post-secondary qualifications and the Summer Jobs stream is aimed at helping students get work. At its conception the federal government allocated CA$315 million and in 2013 it added a further CA$50 million to be spent over two years. Management consultants undertook an evaluation in 2009 and highlighted its successes, although they also raised concerns over the lack of transparency on how money was allocated and on gender disparities, in that young men who accessed the Skills Link programmes tended to end up earning more than young women who entered the programme (Human Resources and Skills Development, 2009).

Welfare-to-workfare programmes

What we see in the discussion so far is a range of policies that aim to target and re-engage NEETS by changing the landscape of education and training for those aged 14 to 18. Many of these initiatives are seen as offering a preventative and supportive focus, yet as we have seen, some can bring policies of conditionality (that is, EMA in the UK and the Pipeline programme in Australia) or have potential risks of increasing surveillance and monitoring, especially of the poor (tracking systems for compulsory post-16 education). But governments in our four case study areas discussed here have gone further and have tried to develop a wide range of active labour market strategies to tackle the 'problem' of NEETs. Such strategies target unemployed, but underpinning them is a desire to make active the inactive and to stop young people becoming dependent on welfare. They therefore tend to be targeted more towards highly disadvantaged groups, the young and those who are seen as being more at risk of becoming NEETs (Kluve, 2014). How these strategies have developed in each country varies, although the use of such approaches has grown in all our case study countries, especially over the last fifteen years.

United Kingdom

The birth of individual activation policies and especially the welfare-to-work programmes in the UK can be attributed to the Thatcher government in the 1980s. Not only did she reduce the value of benefit payments to the young she also strengthened conditionality in the system by requiring individuals to be available for work, to actively seek work and to accept any work available. Even though there were strong calls for such programmes (Murray, 1984), the conservative governments did not implement some of the harsher programmes such as working for benefits. Previous experience of managing mass work experience programmes had involved huge costs and bureaucracy and it was recognised that getting employers involved in such programmes was problematic and risked 'distorting the market' (Mizen, 2004). As a result, US-style welfare-to-work type programmes were not implemented. The early UK programmes were maintained and expanded by the Major government. For example, unemployment benefit was replaced by a Jobseeker's Allowance for 18–24-year-olds, which again reduced benefits while increasing the obligations to seek work. In 1997, with the election of Tony Blair and the introduction of 'third way' policies, the New Deal programme was introduced. Funded by a large tax on the profits of privatised utilities it introduced a range of programmes aimed at young people aged 18–24 and required them to participate in order to receive benefits. Sold in the election manifesto as a new deal or settlement between the individual and the state, it introduced the first-ever compulsory scheme in the UK. In 2007 it was expanded to include the New Deals for disabled people and for lone parents. In 2010, with the election of the Conservative and Liberal coalition, the New Deal programme was replaced by the Work Programme and attempts to restructure benefits towards a 'universal credit' system, merging out-of-work benefits with in-work benefits in an attempt to smooth the transition between work and the benefit system.[7]

The Work Programme increased the welfare-to-work approach initiated by the previous Labour government by requiring those receiving a Jobseeker's Allowance to be part of the programme. It has a strong focus on 18–24-year-olds and NEETs aged 16 and 17. Following recommendations from the Freud Report (Freud, 2007), provision of services to the unemployed was to be contracted out using a 'payment by results' approach. Non-compliance by young people at various stages of the Work Programme brings a wide range of sanctions including the loss of benefits. In 2014 the government increased restrictions on young people getting access to Jobseeker's Allowance and introduced the 'Help to Work' programme for those who have been out of work for over two years. Before they get any benefits they have to attend the Job Centre every day and either work for free or undertake training.

Australia

In Australia there have been similar developments; young people's entitlements to social benefits have been restricted and a new social contract with penalties has been developed (Hamilton, 2014). The move towards this model started in the 1980s, after the Hawke government commissioned a review of social security. It recommended active job searching and labour market preparedness, including a work test. This aimed to increase contractual reciprocity and placed obligations on the claimants. This saw the introduction of the 'New

---

[7] This has still not been achieved.

Start' programme that included intensive interviewing. This approach was further extended by the Keating government, which, as part of its 'Working Nation' programme, introduced the 'Job Compact'. This guaranteed a job to the long-term unemployed but, in return, claimants had to accept any 'reasonable' offer of work. It also introduced harsher penalties for non-compliance.

In 1996, under the Howard coalition government, the concept of 'obligations' was expanded, alongside the expansion of regulations and harsher penalties for non-compliance. It was at this stage that the government introduced the 'Work for Dole' (WfD) programme. Under this scheme all unemployed 18–24-year-olds who had been on a benefit for six months were forced to participate in a range of job preparedness programmes as a condition of receiving benefits. Conditionality was also continually strengthened. The Howard government also introduced 'income management' for Aboriginal and Torres Strait communities that aimed to ring fence part of their payment for priority needs.[8] With the arrival of the Labor Party in power these trends continued. The concepts of 'social contract' and mutual obligations littered the policy arena of welfarism. Being on the political left did not mean Labor disagreed with such approaches; in fact, it argued for increased responsibility and attacked the corrosive effects of welfare dependency (Hamilton, 2014). Labor introduced the 'Compact with Young Australians' programme (discussed earlier), which provided government-subsidised training places for young people aged 15 to 24, but entitlement to benefits was conditional upon participation in and completion of education and training. It also expanded income management schemes to vulnerable families in other geographical areas. Julia Gillard, who was prime minister from 2010 to 2013, continued this approach, increasing conditionality for families with children while also creating harsher punishments for non-compliance (Australian Labor Party, 2010). Sanctions on benefit claimants have also been increasing. In 1997 a new penalty regime was introduced which gave providers of employment services power to penalise those on benefits for a breach (OECD, 2013b) and which saw a substantial increase in instances of benefits being removed from claimants. It was claimed that such a process was unfair and harsh, and that it was deeply flawed, punitive and lacking safeguards for the vulnerable (Jobs Australia, 2011). While governments explored ways of reducing its negative impacts, in 2011 it was extended by the Labor

---

[8]   Such a programme has since been rolled out in New Zealand (see the New Zealand section later in this chapter).

government, which gave substantial new powers to providers to suspend payment to jobseekers for failure to attend interviews or go on the WfD programme. This move saw the use of sanctions increase once again, with eight-week suspensions of benefit increasing substantially (OECD, 2012).

In his first budget in 2013, the newly elected Tony Abbott revealed that job seekers applying for a New Start or Youth Allowance, who had not been previously employed, would face a six-month waiting period before they were eligible for payments. They would also need to undertake 25 hours a week in the WfD programme. Once they had spent six months on the programme, they would lose income support altogether for another six months unless they undertook further training or study after completion.[9] People under the age of 25 would not be eligible for the dole and instead would have to apply for the Youth Allowance, which is approximately AU$100 less per fortnight. More recently, the Australian Liberal government has been attempting to reform welfare further. In a recent report from a commission on welfare in Australia (Commonwealth of Australia, 2015) it is proposed that young people under the age of 22 must be engaged in some form of education or employment before they receive any form of income. At present, young people under the age of 22 who are studying, doing an apprenticeship or looking for work may still be eligible for some Youth Allowance benefit, depending on their parents' income. Under the new proposals, unless a young person under 22 is deemed fully independent, any income support will go to their parents. The report proposes the Age of Independence as 22 years, on the grounds that young people are living at home longer.

Canada

Major welfare reform that brought in welfare-to-work policies in Canada took place in the 1990s. As discussed in Chapter Two, the end of the Canada Assistance Plan (CAP) and the introduction of the Canada Health and Social Transfer (CHST) had a major impact on the finances of provinces and their ability to use federal money to implement welfare-to-work programmes. How the provinces responded varied and was greatly influenced by local culture and histories and financial situations (Little and Marks, 2006). Significant attention is usually given to the changes that took place in Ontario,

---

[9]   At the time of writing these plans are still be discussed by Senate (Commonwealth of Australia, 2015).

but other provinces also implemented variations of the welfare-to-work models that restructured young people's relationships with the local state.

In 1996, Ontario, under the leadership of the Conservative Mike Harris, created a new contract between the local state and its inhabitants with the introduction of 'Ontario Works' (OW). Harris argued that welfare should be 'a hand up not hand out', arguing that 'there is a philosophy, that is about creating a cycle of dependency, paying people more money to stay at home and do nothing, versus give people an opportunity, give them training, give them work experience, give them a job' (Ontario Legislative Assembly, 1995, pp.1430). From this point on Ontario embraced policies and practices of welfare-to-work (Little and Marks, 2006; Maki, 2011). OW has three components: Employment Support, Employment Placement and Community Participation. Similar to other schemes in the UK and Australia, OW includes requirements for participants to undertake job searches and basic skills training alongside other job-ready activities. It has a requirement that, in return for welfare payments, participants must also do up to 70 hours of community service a month. Recipients have to take a placement and if they do not stay or are thought not to be making enough effort they receive a warning. After two warnings their cheque can be suspended for up to six months. Re-entry into the programme is complex and slow (Little and Marks, 2006).

Other provinces did not implement a programme of this size and cost, although most made changes that altered the relationship recipients had with benefits. One factor that seemed fundamental was cost: it became evident that introducing a model similar to OW had substantial costs and required significant investment (Little and Marks, 2006), and this led to other provinces looking for alternative ways of reducing the welfare budget while increasing the responsibilities of the young. However, in states including Alberta, British Columba and Saskatchewan, new enforcement practices were introduced. For example, in British Columbia participation in the Youth Works programme was mandatory for young adults aged 19 to 24 who were on social assistance. In Alberta and Saskatchewan, the learning of employment skills was imposed on claimants by forcing them to attend obligatory sessions and to set employment plans. These 'case plans' (set in consultation with a professional), usually require them to outline their strategies for getting into work (Gazso and McDaniel, 2010).

A number of provinces have also changed benefit eligibility rules. For example, in British Columbia (BC) the focus was on restricting eligibility and reducing benefits: the benefit for a single person was cut by up to 21% (Little and Marks, 2006). The BC government also created a new application procedure. Built into it was a requirement for claimants to prove they had searched for work: if what they had done was deemed inadequate, then the application could be refused. Even if successful, claimants would still have to wait six weeks for payment. BC also included a 'prior work history' criterion. To be eligible, claimants must have either earned at least $7,000 a year or worked at least 840 hours for two consecutive years. Those over 19 years of age also had to have been independent for at least two years before they could access benefits (Gazso and McDaniel, 2010). These reforms, it is claimed, were made to 'promote self-reliance and employment and discourage patterns of dependence on income assistance' (British Columbia Ministry of Human Resources, 2002, p.26). Such programmes have significant impact on the ability of young people to access assistance, as they do not always have a strong employment record or the ability to live independently without some form of financial support from others (Little and Marks, 2006). Welfare claimants, once receiving benefits, also have to develop an 'employment plan' outlining the conditions they have to meet to continue to receive it. If they do not follow this they are at risk of having their welfare cheque removed or reduced (British Columbia Ministry of Human Resources, 2002). More recently the federal government has provided CA$241 million over five years that will go to job training for First Nation youth who are receiving income assistance. Approximately half the money will go to setting up the programmes on reserves while the other half will go to pay for personalised job training, which will only be accessible if welfare recipients agree to participate in the programme.

New Zealand

As we saw in Chapter Two, New Zealand faced significant economic challenges in the 1980s that had major impacts on social welfare policy. The government created a welfare system that is residual and only for the poor. While 'reform' has been on the agenda a number of times over the last thirty years, the system remains fundamentally unchanged other than seeing increased measures that reflect neoliberal principles and practices (St John and Rankin, 2009; Humpage, 2014). In the 1990s the National Party government raised the question of welfare dependency and advocated a number of critical reforms that saw the introduction of reduced benefit rates, increased conditionality and sanctions for claimants who left work voluntarily. It also saw the introduction of the 'Community Wage' (St John and Rankin, 1997), which aimed to get the unemployed to undertake unpaid work in the community while out of work. Strong resistance emerged in New Zealand that eventually saw the government back down on the Community Wage and soften some of the harsh rules on compliance (Humpage, 20014). The newly elected Labour government in 2000 introduced the 'work first' approach:

> In the 'Third Way' rhetoric, employment was promoted as the best way, even the only way, out of family poverty; the state's role was reduced to 'enabling', with selective work incentives and childcare subsidies. (St John and Rankin, 2009, p.8)

At the same time, the Labour government softened many of the workfare approaches introduced by the National Party government, although over time they set up a new jobseeker's agreement, increased case management systems, introduced work testing and created a new pre-benefit requirement (Humpage, 2014).

By 2007, welfare-to-work and ALMPs were well established in the New Zealand welfare system. The arrival of the new National Party government in 2008 saw a renewed focus on welfare reform. This included a tightening up on the rules that apply to getting benefits and the introduction of new measures that increased workfare-type approaches to benefit claims (Humpage, 2014). For example, the unemployed are now required to actively look for work, accept any suitable job offered and undergo work experience. Sanctions have been increased and, for the first breach of the work obligations contract, the main benefit of claimants will be reduced by 50%. For a second breach, all benefits will be suspended and for a third, the claimant's benefit will be cancelled. Other initiatives have seen the introduction of policies that act to 'quarantine' behaviour. For example, government has introduced the Youth Payment for 16–17-year-olds, but they can only claim it if they have exceptional circumstances or come from a low-income family: payments will only be distributed through redirections (for accommodation and utility costs), a payment card (for food and groceries) and an in-hand allowance. Beneficiaries must be in full-time education, training or work-based learning, and they must undertake an approved budgeting programme. But the National Party government elected in 2008 has also increased the powers of the state to introduce sanctions (Wynd, 2013). Evidence shows that, since 2010, there has been a massive increase use of sanctions and penalties for those who are seen not to comply (Wynd, 2013). By 2011, over

58,000 beneficiaries had been sanctioned and lost benefit. How many of these were under 24 remains unknown. Much remains unclear about who is being sanctioned and why, and about the impact of these processes on people as the National Party government in New Zealand does not have a transparent system in place for evaluating its actions programmes (Wynd, 2013).

What we therefore start to see as we examine these four countries is three main developments. First, there has been the introduction of welfare-to-work programmes: while variations exist in how they have been implemented, they have been universally introduced and increased as a way of dealing with youth unemployment. The policy of activism as opposed to passive welfarism is now the norm when it comes to young people having access to social benefits when they are unemployed or inactive in the labour market. Second, across all the case study countries, conditionality is at the heart of the active programmes. Those who are unwilling or unable to follow the requirements are facing stiffer sanctions and penalties. It is suggested that 'receiving financial support from the state when unemployed or unable to work is harder now than at any time in the last 60 years' (Wright, 2011, p.5). Third, while the central claim as to why these programmes are being used is that it is to get people back to work, there remains a strong focus in the policy narrative on reducing the social welfare bill. The programmes are seen as having a dual focus: getting the young into any type of work and reducing the welfare bill by getting people off benefits. What we are seeing across all four countries is the establishment and roll out of a form of citizenship that shifts the emphasis from entitlements to responsibilities, where individuals are expected not only to take more responsibility for their own lives but also to stand on their own two feet financially, without support from the state.

The 'big business' of unemployment: quasi markets and private sector providers

Before we explore the impact of the expansion of these welfare-to-work programmes it is worth recognising the growing role of the private sector in delivering these types of services. It is clearly big business for the private sector. As we have seen in the previous three chapters on education and employment, quasi markets and the involvement of the private sector in the provision of services to the young has been on the increase as a part of the neoliberalisation of society. This process is clearly evident within the welfare system that the young encounter. The creation of the new architecture of capitalism and the reconfiguration of the relationship between public and private has been a central aspect of how young people now experience the welfare services that they must deal with when unemployed or in need of help. Having private sector involvement is not new, yet what we are seeing is an increased use of such approaches to deliver local services. For example, in the UK when the New Deal programme was at its height, 60% of the total service was provided by 900 private or third sector providers (Finn, 2009). In Canada, new partnerships between the private sector and/or non-profit organisations were established between 1993 and 2004. This policy brought with it new private sector practices such as the introduction of performance-based contracting with 'payment by results' (Gazso and McDaniel, 2010). In Australia, public sector employment services were abolished in the mid 1990s and replaced with a system of private and non-profit providers. Currently there are over 100 providers competing for contracts at over 2,300 sites across Australia (Martin, 2014). Contracts are offered on a 'pay-for-performance' basis and ineffective providers are driven out of the system. The OECD (2014a) claims it is a very efficient and effective system, although little evaluation has been done and in fact evidence suggests it has had limited impact on getting young people into work (Fowkes, 2011).

In the UK, the use of private sector providers for welfare-to-work programmes has increased substantially, with 16 of the 18 major contractors now responsible for the delivery of new services under the Work Programme being from the private sector. One major development in the UK is not only payment for results but also what is called the 'black box delivery model', whereby providers can deliver whatever service they think is best for the client (Martin, 2014). As a way of avoiding providers working only with those who are quick to turn around, the government introduced differential pricing, ensuring higher rewards for getting the hard-to-engage into work. Evidence from a recent UK evaluation suggests that the payment by results model has major problems in that it is not seen as suitable for clients with 'multiple barriers'. Providers are focusing on those who are 'job ready', as they are seen as cheap and easy to turn into successes. 'Differential pricing' is not working as the cost of providing support and help for those in most need has been too high (Department of Work and Pensions, 2014). Concerns have also been raised about the way that the market may marginalise the third sector and not-for-profit organisations, with recent research reports suggesting that the new contracting model disadvantages the socially based organisations (Hudson et al., 2010). For example, the financial risk in bidding is seen as prohibitive for many of these organisations, and the private sector is seen as squeezing out voluntary sector involvement (Rees et al, 2013). Evidence also suggests that the private sector companies 'park' the most difficult young participants with the third sector companies, indicating that a substantial amount of 'gaming' goes on in the system, ensuring higher rates of profit for the private sector (Rees et al, 2013). Similar evidence of 'parking' and avoidance of high-need and high-cost groups was also evident in the Australian WfD programme, along with standardisation and minimum standards set as the target, ensuring costs were kept low for the private sector (Fowkes, 2011)

Does welfare-to-work work?

The question remains: do welfare-to-work programmes work? In a recent study reviewing OECD evidence on the effectiveness of ALMPs, it was claimed that there was evidence, at the macro level of analysis that they can impact upon levels of unemployment (Martin, 2014). Evidence suggests that, even when labour demand is depressed, some form of labour market activation can make some difference. However, what policies (or combination of policies) work is not clear, and evidence also suggests that any impact is best achieved with those unemployed people who are relatively 'job ready' or who are in need of child care support (Martin, 2014). Where these programmes are less successful is in areas of high and entrenched unemployment, and with those who are sick, disabled or have a mental illness. Activation policies may increase employment, but the work often tends to be temporary, casual, insecure and low paid (Martin, 2014).

Other research supports this claim (MacDonald and Marsh, 2005; Simmons et al, 2014), showing how policies that try to re-engage the disengaged tend to reinforce positions of marginalisation and exclusion rather than increase employment. In those communities and geographical areas where limited work exists, and where families with long histories of unemployment live, activation policies result in churning the poor in such a way that little change takes place (MacDonald and Marsh, 2005).

Looking at the types of programmes that come directly under the welfare-to-work rubric, evidence of their effectiveness also remains unclear (Sunley et al, 2006; Lane et al, 2013; Martin, 2014). For example, when discussing their evaluation of the UK New Deal welfare-to-work programme, Sunley et al (2006) found significant geographical differences in impact. Those areas with depressed labour markets in effect churned young people through the system while doing little for their work opportunities:

> What is clear is that the dysfunctional and damaging outcomes of these differences have included higher rates of recycling through the programme and higher rates of movement onto non-means tested benefits in depressed local markets. (Sunley et al, 2006 p125)

Major problems also emerged from the recent evaluation of the UK coalition's Work Programme (Meager, et al, 2014). Evidence showed that the drop-out rate from the programme was high, with only 55% who were referred actually starting the programme. For those who did start the programme, the impact was essentially non-existent. Overall, the maximum impact was a 5 percentage point reduction in benefit receipt, and only 13 weeks after starting the programme the impact had disappeared completely.[10] On average, someone referred to a mandatory work programme spent just four fewer days on a benefit as a result. In fact, unsurprisingly, the biggest impact on benefit reduction was via those who were sanctioned (as they actually lost their benefits). Looking at long-term results, evidence showed that those referred were 3 percentage points more likely than other people who had not been on the programme, to be on a benefit after 13 weeks. Results also showed that getting young people into work was not successful. Major issues were also raised about the purpose of the programme, in that it seemed to be more about getting the young off benefits than getting them into work. Throughout the programme, sanctions for non-compliance have been increasing. Interestingly, while ALMPs are seen as providing a broad range of options in the UK, the focus has fundamentally been on workfare and tackling welfare dependency (O'Hara, 2014). For example, in 2012 the coalition's Universal JobMatch programme was introduced. This was designed to monitor jobseekers' job search activity, to ensure they were complying with the requirement to search for jobs. To comply, individuals have to do three job searches a week. If they fail to do this they are automatically sanctioned and lose benefits. Evidence suggests that the loss of benefit comes first, before an individual can explain why they may not have met targets. They then have to go through an appeal system to get put back

---

[10] Impact was being measured in-house by the Department of Work and Pensions using a multivariate analysis of participants, exploring their time on the programme and their outcomes.

onto benefits (O'Hara, 2014). In 2013, a damning submission made to the House of Commons Work and Pensions Committee showed a massive increase in sanctions and the disallowing of benefits for minor failings, such as missing appointments, not completing forms on time or being unable to attend a meeting due to illness (O'Hara, 2014). In this sense, the programme was more about getting people off benefits than about getting them into work.

Similarly, a recent UK report based on a five-year evaluation of the effectiveness of sanctions reached the following conclusions:

- Those under 25 are hit hardest by the sanctions imposed through conditionality.
- International evidence shows that benefit sanctions substantially increase the number of people coming off benefits, and also increases short-term job entry – but there are negative longer term effects in terms of earnings, job quality and keeping a job.
- Vulnerable people and those with multiple and complex needs, such as lone parents, disabled people or homeless people, have been disproportionately affected by the recent expansion of welfare conditionality.
- Sanctions also have a number of unintended consequences that include distancing people from social support; creating hardship; and displacing rather than solving issues such as long-term worklessness and substance misuse (Watts et al, 2014).

Results of the OW programme in Canada were different; the evaluation showed that welfare case-loads dropped by 54% over the duration of the programme, although it was unable to attribute this to the programme. At the time of the evaluation Canada was in a period of high economic growth and low unemployment, suggesting this might have been a major factor. What happened to those who left the programme is unclear: a local survey of 800 OW participants found that 56% left for jobs, although much of the work they found was insecure and poorly paid (with 30% getting temporary jobs and a further 30% getting part-time work). Of those entering work, over a third were paid less than $10 an hour (Crisp and Fletcher, 2008). The report concluded that the programme has:

> limited focus on skills development in social assistance [which], along with the precariousness of the labour market, mean[s] that recipients who exit social assistance do not escape poverty and are forced to cycle through periods of

receiving and not receiving social assistance. (Crisp and Fletcher, 2008, p.14)

The Australian WfD programme was also seen as unsuccessful in its aims. Research found that WfD was 'ineffective in helping participants to find sustainable employment with only one-quarter in work three months after leaving the programme and 14 per cent employed in full-time jobs' (Crisp and Fletcher, 2008, p.16). What is interesting about all of these reports and reviews of the welfare-to-work programmes is that, even though the programmes have been shown to have little positive effect on getting people into work, policy makers still see this policy as the primary way of tackling the 'problem' of NEETs. Why?

The rise of the 'workfare state'

To answer this it is necessary to consider what other role welfare-to-work programmes might play. Peck (2001) sees them as having a distinctive role to play in terms of regulating the poor and most vulnerable:

> Workfare is a creature of these political-economic circumstances, mobilizing and socializing workers for jobs at the bottom of the new economy. Under conditions of wage stagflation, growing underemployment, and job casualization, workfarism maximizes (and effectively mandates) participation in contingent, low paid work by churning workers back into the bottom of the labour market. (Peck, 2001, p.80)

As the previous evidence from the evaluations suggests, Peck's argument that workfarism operates to churn the most vulnerable and poor into poor work is correct. It operates not only to socialise but also to shift poverty from 'out-of-work poverty' to 'in-work poverty', while reducing the welfare budget of national economies. Such a strategy aims to bring the unemployed closer to the labour market but in reality it creates a 'reserve army' of labour that can be drawn in and out of the labour market as and when required (Peck, 2001). As we have seen, welfare-to-work programmes have emerged unevenly and in different shapes and sizes across time (and place), although internationally 'workfare has become the institutional codification of work-oriented welfare reform – and as such it must be understood as *both* a reactive, reform strategy *and a* would-be successor to the welfare state' (Peck,

2001, p.81). In this context, it is fit for purpose for the new political and economic context driven by neoliberalist ideals and principles (Wacquant, 2011). But such regimes also have a strong connection to the moral economy of neoliberalism that shifts the responsibility (and blame) from the state to the individual in very clear ways. For example, as we saw in the discussions over NEETs, across the policy discourse on welfare reform there has been a shift from one of 'entitlement' to one that emphasises the new social contract of personal responsibility (Hamilton, 2014). Such discourses are moralising and powerful in shaping public opinion and perspectives of what is right and wrong in the welfare system (Humpage, 2014).

Welfare-to-work programmes can also then operate to police and monitor the poor. As we have seen, such programmes are usually embedded with forms of surveillance that can dehumanise or ignore human rights, especially of the powerless (Maki, 2011). For example, there are a number of examples of intrusive practices by professionals in the OW programme, with up to eight surveillance practices being introduced (Maki, 2011). These include unannounced home visits being used to ensure compliance, enforced drugs testing, and increased surveillance and monitoring of leisure and home life. The programme also introduced welfare fraud hotlines that passed information onto Eligibility Review Officers, who have powers to investigate suspicions and have direct legal access to both homes and private communications (Maki, 2011). Similar issues can be found in the UK Work Programme, where surveillance is a central part of monitoring conditionality and participation (O'Hara, 2014). The development of such approaches reasserts the notion that the poor are untrustworthy, feckless and immoral and need to be continually under surveillance (Gazso and McDaniel, 2010). Regulation and policing of the poor, and of young people in particular, are central to the ways these programmes are organised (Wacquant, 2009).

What we also have to recognise in this discussion is the gendered nature of some of these processes. Welfare-to-work is perceived traditionally as targeting those young men who are seen as 'dangerous' and a risk to the security of the majority. Yet inherent to and embedded in these programmes is a set of values and beliefs about the role of women that take a particular moralising position (McDowell, 2004). For example, at the heart of the Blair reforms in the UK, parents (and mothers in particular) were seen to be central in that they should 'ensure their children do not truant, do not stay out late at night, do not hang about on the street corners nor indulge in various behaviours that might upset the neighbours' (McDowell, 2004, p.154). If they did not fulfil this moral duty, they were penalised by being fined for their children not going to school and/or forced to undertake parenting classes to learn how to be a 'good' parent. At the centre of this discourse is a belief that these mothers are part of an underclass and a cause of their children's problems. But it is not all women: it is usually mothers who are poor who are seen as the problem to be tackled. For example, in recent debates in the UK, the Conservatives' approach to mending 'Broken Britain' proposes that a fundamental cause of this state of affairs is the breakdown of the family and poor parenting on the part of mothers in some of the disadvantaged areas (Lister and Bennett, 2010). In this context welfare-to-work policies have targeted young solo-parent mothers. In much of this rhetoric, young women from poor areas are seen as having children as a means of accessing housing and benefits and avoiding work, suggesting they are part of the dependency class and that welfare-to-work policies are needed to get them into work. For example, in New Zealand a whole range of policies have been activated targeting young solo mothers, requiring them to be actively seeking work once their child reaches a certain age. Similar policies are being implemented in Australia and the UK. There remains a strong ethic and belief that work pays, even for solo mothers and that it is an individual's responsibility to earn for their family (MacLeavy, 2011).

But it is not just in terms of parenting that gender becomes an issue. Much of the debate on dependency and the role of welfare-to-work reforms has assumed that the 'real' problem of unemployment is young men. The New Deal programme in the UK was only sensitive to gender questions to the extent it was thought there was a crisis in masculinity in post-industrial times (McDowell, 2003) and women's issues were 'given a short shrift because the feminized labour market with its flexible work patterns, low pay and low status employment was perceived to be readily accessible (and acceptable) to women' (MacLeavy, 2011, p.13). Similar issues arise over the use of wage subsidies and access to training and apprenticeships, as discussed in the previous chapter. These were targeted originally at sectors with high male unemployment, such as the manufacturing and construction industries. Such a perspective suggests that unemployment and work is a male issue and fails to recognise the socioeconomic structural processes that impact not only young women's choices but their actions. It fails to recognise the low rewards for much of the work young women have access to, or the balancing act that young women have to manage between caring and work (MacLeavy, 2011). Neither does it recognise the different starting points and lack of training and opportunities for many disadvantaged young women, which in effect ensures getting a job is a reinforcement of 'poor work' (MacLeavy, 2007). Since the 2007 crisis, there has been increasing pressure on the welfare-to-work system to respond to the problems of young women and unemployment, especially as female unemployment grows. For example, in the UK national statistics, young women claiming Jobseeker's Allowance reached a 15-year high in 2011 (Fawcett Society, 2009). Clearly, gender equality is unlikely to be advanced by policies that fail to recognise the underlying structural causes and barriers for young women in both accessing work and being able to use activation policies that would aid their career development (Lister and Bennett, 2010).

Conclusion

What needs to be recognised is that being defined as a NEET or being on welfare is now seen as a moral 'disease' of the poor that is seen to be eroding the living standards of the middle class, the wealthy and the privileged. While uncertainty remains over who NEETs are and how we should define them, policy is continually connecting them to the category of 'undeserving', making them the new social problem of our time. This has increasingly become the case since the 2007 crisis and throughout the great recession. Symbolically, they are used politically as a way of highlighting the reasons why the state needs to intervene in a particular way. Of course, as was outlined, NEETs are not only constructed as a problem because they are viewed as not accepting their responsibilities, they are also seen as the group most in need of welfare-to-work programmes that are building on the ethos of both breaking the dependency culture of the workless and the 'something for nothing' culture associated with NEETs. These programmes have expanded substantially since the 2007 crisis and throughout the recession, and this is not a coincidence. They are surrounded and underpinned by a range of political arguments that operate symbolically to reinforce the moral economy of neoliberalism. This operates at a broader political level to give legitimacy to a set of powerful ideas about the young ('feckless', 'lazy' and 'dangerous') as in need of increased control. NEETs are the 'new' social problem after the crisis; they are the 'welfare scroungers' and the 'anti-social', who are taking and not giving, living their lives as part of the 'underclasses'. In this context they are the 'undeserving class' identified by Charles Murray (1984) in the 1980s. This then justifies governments, especially since the crisis, in expanding and extending the ALMP programmes that extend surveillance, disciplining and sanctioning practices as a way to control and regulate their behaviour.

It should also not go unrecognised that, as recession hit in 2009 and beyond, governments used such programmes and practices as a way of reducing the 'welfare bill', while handing out large sums of state resources to the private sector through subcontracting these services.

SEVEN

Divergence and difference: contrasting cross-national experiences of being young

Introduction

In this chapter we begin by outlining how Norway, Japan, Poland and Spain have been encountering and engaging with neoliberalism. We will also explore what impact the 2007 crisis and the great recession that followed has had on these countries, and how it has influenced their relationship with neoliberal approaches to policy and practice. As in Chapter Two, the analysis will show how each of these states has evolved and how they have interacted with neoliberalism historically. It will also outline the impact of the crisis and how, at a macro level, public policy has responded. The chapter will then explore the implications of what it means to be young in these four countries, highlighting the way social citizenship has been constructed in each of the nation states. In this process we will see that what it means to be young in Norway, Japan, Poland and Spain not only varies between the different countries but also in comparison to the other four case study areas discussed previously. Ideas of citizenship and 'being young' are shaped by the different contexts in which they are constructed.

In Chapter Two we identified four key trends that were evident across the UK, Australia, Canada and New Zealand. These were:

- The growing and expanding role of neoliberalism and neoliberal ideology in shaping the policy agenda of the nation state. While the historical trends were not always linear or unresisted, it was evident that neoliberalism has been having a significant impact in the UK, Australia, Canada and New Zealand.
- This drive towards neoliberalisation was not just driven by the political right – in fact the 'third way' politics of the left was fundamentally built around the principles of neoliberalism. When the political left were in office they did not reject or repeal neoliberal policies but tended to 'tinker' with them to soften the social impact.

- Throughout the 2000s there was a strong emphasis on 'rolling out' and embedding market principles into public services. Quasi markets and public–private partnerships for delivery became the norm.
- Neoliberalism is not just an economic project; it has embedded within it a strong moralising agenda, one that aims to shift responsibilities (and costs) towards the individual.

So how far can we see these trends operating in our other four case study areas discussed previously? The following section will give a brief history and explanation of the relationship each country has had with neoliberalism.

Norway and the social democratic state

Norway has a strong tradition as a country that operates according to the Nordic model of social democratic principles and practices. These are usually seen as:

> a comprehensiveness of social security systems, institutionalized universal social rights, a high level of public support, and a high level of equality, which grew out of a combination of public commitment to the principle of universalism and equality of income distribution, which, in turn, is partly attributable to the strength of trade unions. (Sejersted, 2014, p.6)

Esping-Andersen suggests the Nordic model of the welfare state is a fusion of welfare and work that is committed to guaranteeing the incomes of its citizens over their life course and in whatever circumstances they encounter. It is 'a right to work and a right to income protection' (Esping-Andersen, 1990, p.27). While there are clear differences across nation states in the Nordic region in terms of how the model operates (Berglund, 2010; Olofsson and Wadensjö, 2012), it is underpinned by core commitments to principles of collaborative interaction between representatives of the state, trade unions and the business sector (Gooderham et al, 2014) and, while there are country differences in how the model operates, the welfare state is traditionally seen as socially democratic. This has historically provided strong welfare support that is universally available, alongside high taxes, giving lifelong support and ensuring security even in times of hardship (Sejersted, 2014).

As a result, Norway has been a moderate and reluctant adopter of neoliberalism, although as we shall see, there are variations in how neoliberalism has penetrated different sectors of Norwegian society. Historically, Norway has maintained a strong state presence in economic and social planning, although the social democratic model is built within a corporative model that has always included partnership between the state, business and the trade unions. Over the last twenty years one major development has been an increase in privatisation, with a number of significant public companies such as Telenor and Statoil being sold off and partially privatised in 2000 (OECD, 2003). Since this period there have also been major changes in how the state operates and in the role of the private sector. This has seen not only increased sales of previously owned state assets but also the introduction of market logic in areas such as aviation, the running of hospitals and labour market organisation (OECD, 2003). This approach saw the state shift towards a regulatory state (rather than a provider), where competition and privatisation had a role to play in service provision (OECD, 2003). For example, Norway has seen the liberalisation and commercialisation of its Public Employment Services (PES) in that the private sector has now a larger role to play in providing training, helping jobseekers to get work and running other active labour market policy (ALMP) programmes (OECD, 2003). However, many of the reforms have been largely concerned with 'structural devolution' and have been driven by pragmatism rather than ideology. They seem more concerned with increasing efficiency than with dismantling public services or the state (Mydske et al, 2007). Norway's pathway to a neoliberal destination has been incremental, with, to date, no political parties displaying a particularly voracious appetite for major neoliberal reform (Mydske et al, 2007). While public attitudes towards neoliberal ideology became more supportive from the 1970s onward, leading to the election of a conservative government in 1981, this support had waned considerably by the new millennium. An analysis in 2007 by Rose and Heidar concluded that neoliberal values had made only a moderate impact on Norwegian society, which remains a strongly social democratic political culture.

Like other Nordic countries, Norway experienced a severe banking crisis in the 1990s, the effects of which were still in the minds of bankers and regulators in the lead-up to the current crisis, creating a more prudent approach and an understanding of the necessity of maintaining adequate capital requirements. Of course, Norway has been much aided in this with its natural wealth, which has been well stewarded by the state. The discovery of oil in the North Sea in late 1969 transformed the country's economy, and Norwegians have been happy for the state to manage their resources and look after their communities. They have, however, had to adjust to the new global capitalism. Incremental change towards a combination of state control and global competition has taken place, although Norway has been able to cling on to more of its social democratic habits than its neighbours (Sejersted, 2014). The oil boom helped to maintain public spending throughout the global recession after the 2007 crisis, and the public sector today still accounts for 52% of Norway's gross domestic product (GDP). This makes it a rich country and, thanks to oil and continued marine resources, it did not suffer significantly from the GFC (great financial crisis) or the European debt crisis. It was not entirely immune, however. Social and wage inequality is growing, and neoliberal policies are creeping in, championed by the previous Labour government (Brandal et al, 2013). Neoliberal values and ideals, influenced by think tank Civita (financed by employers' organisations) and the Organisation for Economic Co-operation and Development (OECD), have done their best to suggest that the Nordic welfare state model is no longer viable and that Norway needs to adapt to a more neoliberal approach. With the election of a right-of-centre coalition in 2013, will we see an increasing adherence to neoliberal policies? Erna Solberg, leader of the Conservative Party and now prime minister of Norway, sees competitiveness as one of the key issues in Norwegian politics, suggesting her party is concerned about the relaxed approach to public expenditure and reforms, and that neoliberal approaches may be central to the future direction of policy.

Japan and the 'developmental state'

Japan is a major economy in East Asia and its relationship with neoliberalism has to be understood by recognising how developmentalism has shaped the region (Beeson, 2007; Child Hill et al, 2012; Shibata, 2008; Tsukamoto, 2012). The neoliberal movement is firmly entrenched in countries such as the US, the UK, Australia, Canada and New Zealand, but Japan and others in this region can be seen as 'late developers'. Industrial nations in East Asia have been strongly influenced by what has been called the 'developmental state' and while 'the spread of developmentalism among nations in the Asian Pacific has been uneven, contested and shaped by the local context and selective appropriation' (Child Hill et al, 2012, p.8) it has had a major impact, not only on how nation states have constructed economic and social policies but also how they have engaged with neoliberal ideology and practice (Beeson, 2007; Child Hill et al, 2012; Shibata, 2008).

Developmentalism in East Asia is:

> an ideology holding that economic progress is best achieved when the state leads the nation in promoting economic change. Public ownership, planning and goal setting are institutional means to achieving national economic development. Public and private sectors cooperate under the overall guidance of a pilot planning agency. The state further encourages co-operation among businesses and between businesses and labor to speed the adoption of new technology, reduce production costs and expand the nation's share of global markets. (Child Hill et al, 2012, p.6)

Policy making is dominated by a political-bureaucratic elite who see industrialisation as the primary goal. This is not a model that rejects market forces and the private sector, in that it tries to combine industrial policies with increasing competition among private sector firms. In this approach, intervention by the political-bureaucratic elite is central, and aims to protect domestic industries and adjust economic policy so as to benefit the internal workings of the national private sector. But developmentalism also rejects the ideological rationale of classical liberalism, seeing it as a form of Western imperialism (Child Hill et al., 2012). Japan is recognised as the first nation in the region to have embraced developmentalism as a policy. It created a distinctive approach that was a reaction to threats of economic domination and military conquest by the West. As a result, Japan created a strong nation state that emphasised capitalist development that was to be managed. It also drew on the Japanese identity and culture of religion and 'one people' to create 'a state-crafted ideology, rooted in economic and cultural nationalism and Confucian philosophy [that] played a crucial role in Japanese developmentalism' (Child Hill et al, 2012, p.9). In terms of social welfare, unlike other nation states, social policy is secondary to the 'growth first' strategy in developmentalism in Japan. Universalism and comprehensive rights of citizenship are marginal to national policy (Shibata, 2008; Child Hill et al, 2012). Responsibility for social security is located more in the family, the neighbourhood and, most importantly, the 'firm'. In Japan the firm is an ideology that operates to create an 'enterprise family' and community. It takes on a wide range of responsibilities, including those traditionally performed by the market (for example, helping with job mobility, employee housing), the state (training and pensions) and the community (leisure, health and fitness, and social events). As a result the interrelationship between the firm and security for individuals ensures that company (economic) growth becomes critical to all members (Child Hill et al., 2012). Developmentalism in Japan was hugely successful, especially after the Second World War. It transformed not only the economy but also social benefits and welfare. It increased living standards and made Japan a leading economy in the world (Beeson, 2007).

While tensions and clashes remain between the key principles and practices of developmentalism and neoliberalism in Japan, especially over the role of the state, it has been recognised that they are not completely antagonistic or exclusive (Beeson, 2007: Child Hill et al, 2012). For example, both approaches prioritise economic performance and capital accumulation, and both value methods of state intervention that are focused on market incentives (Child Hill et al, 2012). However, it is claimed that the approach taken by Japan has basically ensured that 'neoliberalism and its underlying market-rational individualism have never had real purchase as an ideological basis of government reform in Japan' (Tsukamoto, 2012, p.74). Others suggest that, while neoliberalism has not been a driving force in Japan, the political-elites have borrowed the tool of neoliberalism when they felt they might help them create a hybridisation of 'developmental neoliberalism' (Child Hill et al, 2012, p.15). For example, Tsukamoto (2012) shows how neoliberal ideology infiltrated a range of developments in Tokyo during the 1990s and 2000s, which changed the governance structures and approaches being used. What is clear is that, over the last two decades, Japan has come under increasing pressure to move away from developmentalism as an economic strategy. For example, after the end of the Cold War the US was highly critical of the Japanese model and, with support for the US opinion from the International Monetary Fund (IMF) and the World Bank, Japan and other East Asian states were put under pressure to adopt neoliberal practices. This pressure was implemented by attaching structural adjustment requirements to any financial assistance programmes such countries received (Child Hill et al, 2012). The 'turning point', where neoliberalism took hold, came in the 1990s, when Japan and its 'bubble economy' fell into decline after forty years of sustained growth. The problems were further exacerbated in 1997 after the East Asian financial crisis took hold, leading to over twenty years of stagflation in Japan (Beeson, 2007: Child Hill et al, 2012). This then led to increased liberalisation of the financial sector, and the reconfiguration of the Japanese firm. International pressure and the need for overseas finance saw many Japanese firms relocate production offshore, leading to an erosion of their commitment to the Japanese nation/people (Pempel, 1999). What we start to see over this period is increased use of neoliberal tools in economic and social policy (Beeson, 2007).

Unlike the US and other European states, the crisis did not hit Japan through the banking sector. Like Australia and New Zealand, it was hit hardest by the contraction of global trade (Tiberghien, 2012). Banks in Japan had not fully recovered from the 1990 crisis and had not bought into the subprime markets. However, the GFC's impact on the Japanese economy was significant, with a drop of over 20% in export trade and a drop of 3.3% in GDP in one quarter, leading to a decline of 6.3% over the year (IMF, 2011). Japan, like other nations, implemented a number of fiscal packages as a means to stimulate growth which, alongside increased exports, saw the economy make a good recovery by 2010. The great recession also coincided with a regime change in Japan. In 2009 the Democratic Party of Japan (DPJ) defeated the conservative Liberal Democratic Party (LDP). This saw a new party in power for the first time since 1995.[1] It had social democratic ideals and aimed to reverse neoliberal tendencies (Tiberghien, 2012). For example, it promised child support allowances, generous unemployment benefits, greater regulation of temporary work and a reduction in inequality. It was attempting to return to a coordinated market economy model (CME), but with a stronger emphasis on social welfare as a state responsibility. But by 2012 Japan's economy was moving towards stagflation and the DPJ was in disarray. Not only had it failed to implement its radical reforms, it had also lost the support of the Japanese public (Bix, 2013). In 2012, the election of Shinzo Abe from the LDP led to the introduction of a strategic plan that has since been named 'Abenomics'. It introduces the idea of the 'third way' (or 'third arrow') that integrates neoliberal philosophy with traditional Japanese state management, proposing using a fiscal stimulus through public spending, (Bix, 2013). For example, it aims to spend ¥5.3 trillion in public works with another ¥25 trillion promised over five years to help address the problems of the 2011 quake and tsunami (Boesler, 2013). Abe is also looking at providing more child care resources so that women can return to work. A range of neoliberal reforms to the economy are planned, including an increase in monetary stimulus through central bank policy, making corporate tax cuts, and making structural reforms to the Japanese economy in areas such as deregulating the labour market by giving greater powers

---

[1]   Apart from a 10-month period in 1993/ 4.

to employers to terminate employment and increasing flexible working and privatisation (Bix, 2013). This is the 'third arrow' of Abenomics and reflects neoliberal ideology.

Poland and the emerging post-communist state

Poland's relationship with neoliberalism arose in 1989 with the collapse of the Berlin Wall and the removal of the rule of Soviet communism. After the Second World War, Poland came under the control of the Soviet Union and was a communist state that introduced a managed and planned economy. Throughout the decades that followed, and through the Cold War, Poland, like other states that came under Soviet control, struggled to deliver minimum living standards for its people. As a result there were a number of rebellions and periods of unrest that challenged the system. The Polish elite and political class attempted to introduce reforms such as market socialism, although they continued to fail to provide resources for Polish citizens. In 1989, led by the Solidarity movement, Poland broke away from the Soviet bloc and made a leap towards market liberalism, embracing the core principles of neoliberalism (Hardy, 2009). It 'jump started the market ... using a so-called "shock therapy"' (Hardy, 2009, p.1) approach that was implemented overnight. It introduced immediate policies of monetary contraction and policies controlling supply of money, austerity measures and public sector cuts, removing price controls, liberalising foreign trade, ending state control over incomes and introduced a plan for the privatisation of major industries (Belka and Krajweski, 1995). Its primary architect, Leszek Balcerowicz, intended to rapidly restructure the Polish economy from a centrally planned economy to a market-based economy. Its immediate effect was lowering of wages, increased unemployment, closure of major factories and economic crisis. As Hardy suggests 'it was a lot more shock than therapy,' (2009, p.1) throwing the country into chaos.

The radical reconfiguration of the Polish economy in a short period of time initially created substantial stress and pressure. One of the major consequences was a sharp fall in GDP, with a drop of over 11% in the first two years. Across all sectors and all economic indicators, output and investment levels dropped dramatically. Inflation reached 584% in the first year, although it declined to 43% by 1992 (Poznanski, 1996). Unemployment increased significantly, with a leap to a rate of 11% and, within the first five years, over 2.8 million jobs were lost. By the middle of the 1990s, unemployment had dropped Poland then entered the 21st century with a youth unemployment rate almost double the

European Union (EU) average. In the first quarter of 2000 it was almost 38% for young people aged 15 to 24, and between 2002 and 2003 it almost reached 44%. From 2004, the unemployment level then continuously dropped until the end of 2008, when it was at 17% (Polakowski, 2012).

The rebuilding and construction of the Polish economy into a neoliberal state was further expanded in the following years. Representatives of the Polish state and the trade union movement embraced neoliberal economic development ideas, which were strongly supported by external organisations and international partners. First, countries such as the USA and UK, along with the IMF, supported the increased liberalisation of Poland by providing loans and aid that required neoliberalisation of the economy. For example, USAID gave billions of US dollars in aid and, between 1990 and 2001, USAID was involved in 400 activities in which millions of dollars were injected to ensure neoliberal principles were introduced (Hardy, 2009). The US also created over 1,500 organisations within Poland that aimed to increase a range of activities, such as private and financial sector development, and local government reform that aimed to instal a free market model of capitalism into public services (Hardy, 2009). Second, although the initial development was chaotic, moves towards joining the EU helped stabilise Poland and restructure the way the country did business. Again, in this process European funding and incentives helped to consolidate neoliberal reforms (Hardy, 2009).

While the 'shock treatment' approach brought initial chaos and economic crisis, Poland has since been seen as one of the most successful post-communist countries. Over the following twenty years its economy stabilised, GDP improved and unemployment declined. In the process a shift took place in the types of jobs that emerged. For example, between 1993 and 1996 there was a shift in employment from the public to the private sector (Puhani, 1999). It is claimed that by the start of the 21st century Poland was 50% wealthier than when it was under Soviet rule (Sachs, 2005). However, this process has been uneven; inequality within Poland has grown throughout this period (Hardy, 2009; Brzeziński and Kostro, 2010). For example, significant differences in wealth distribution exist between rural and urban areas in Poland, with those living in the cities more likely to have benefited from the restructuring that took place in 1989 (Brzeziński and Kostro, 2010; Polakowski, 2012). Similarly, women have lost out in terms of labour market restructuring in that they 'have often been the first to lose jobs and have found it more difficult to find work, experiencing longer periods of unemployment' (Hardy, 2009, p.121). It is also the case that there has been a polarisation of wages, creating 'in-work poverty', especially for those working in low-status jobs (Hardy, 2009). At the same time, similar to other post-communist countries, groups of high-earning professionals working in finance have emerged in urban areas, increasing the levels of luxury consumption (Smith et al, 2008), Levels of inequality across Poland have continued to grow at a faster rate than in other advanced economies. A recent report on the levels of inequality in Poland noted that evidence showed, 'Overall, it seems that Poland is more unequal with respect to wealth than most of Western Europe' (Brzeziński et al, 2011, p.1). In reviewing Poland's policies since 1989, the report claimed that one of the major causes of inequality was a lack of attention or concern among political elites, suggesting that the dominance of neoliberalism in Poland:

> offers little place for caring about economic inequality, [so] it is not surprising that it is hard to find any evidence for socio-economic policies in Poland being shaped by concerns about inequality. In fact, even the post-Communist party expressed a conviction that economic growth-promoting policies are the best method of poverty eradication. (Brzeziński et al, 2011, p.98)

One final point to note about Poland is that since 2004, when it joined the EU, the number of Polish people living abroad has almost doubled. At the peak of this trend, it was estimated that almost 2.3 million Polish citizens lived abroad, with the biggest pulling factor being work (Szafraniec, 2011). This is a point we shall return to in Chapter Eight.

Unlike the rest of Europe, Poland managed to avoid the worst impacts of the 2008 financial crisis that hit the EU. It has been the only EU member state not to have undergone a recession since the outbreak of the financial crisis. It maintained high levels of public spending between 2008 and 2012, which helped maintain growth. Paying for this was achieved by a range of means, such as using funds from the EU and privatising state-owned enterprises. For example, between 2008 and 2011 Poland sold 562 companies to the private sector, bringing in an income of around €10.3 billion. It is in the process of selling a further 300 with the aim of bringing in another €3.5 billion (Rae, 2012). It also set about a programme of reallocation of funding that saw increased commercialisation and privatisation of the health care system. Similar plans are being developed for education (Rae, 2012). There have also been labour market reforms and increased deregulation. In 2012 Poland re-elected its centre right coalition, ensuring that the neoliberalisation of Poland continued. Not only did it continue its privatisation programme and increase its deregulation of the labour market, but there has also been an increased focus on austerity that is aimed at 'reducing deficits' and introducing more public sector cuts (Skóvra, 2013).

Spain and the Southern European model

Since Esping-Andersen (1990) introduced his typology of three welfare regimes, there has been substantial debate about the existence of a fourth; the Southern European welfare model that operates in the Mediterranean region of Europe. It is claimed to be different from the conservative, the social democratic and the liberal models Esping-Andersen constructed (Minas et al, 2014). Traditionally, he located countries from this region in the conservative regime, but it has since been suggested that countries such as Portugal, Italy, Greece and Spain (collectively known as PIGS) have distinctive features that separate them from Esping-Andersen's three original regimes (Castles and Ferrera, 1996; Bonoli, 1997; Minas et al, 2014). While this debate continues, there is a growing body of evidence that suggests a Southern European and Mediterranean model should be included. Minas et al (2014) show through detailed analysis of European data that these countries 'are similar enough to one another, and different enough from the conservative countries, to constitute a grouping separate from the conservative countries' (2014, pp.145–6). What makes them significantly different is the role of the family, especially in the provision of welfare and the way that the state is constituted. This is not just the Western 'nuclear family': it includes the important role of the extended family (Allen, 2006). The family is seen as being a major provider of support and welfare in these Southern European countries, while the state has a limited role in providing public welfare services. For example, Spain historically spent low amounts on welfare services (only 22% of GDP) and only one out of ten adults worked in the welfare state, compared with one in six on average in the rest of Europe (Navarro, 2013). However, this commitment to family-based welfare is not simply a top-down process or a cost-cutting exercise: a moral ethos exists in these countries that has been historically and culturally formed. This ethos means that families themselves assume these obligations as natural and right (Holdsworth, 2004). This has had significant impact on family forms and transitions into adulthood:

> South Europeans have tended to follow distinctive practices during their life-cycle, such as late emancipation from the parental home, frequent co-residence with parents after marriage, or spatial proximity between the homes of the elderly and their offspring. (Moreno and Marí-Klose, 2013, p.494)

A strong social contract exists between generations in countries like Spain, where parents will provide substantial and extended support to their children throughout the process of leaving home and setting up a family (Allen, 2006). Parents will make huge investments, even at times of economic downturn, to help protect their children. In return it is expected that the children will, in later life, look after their parents, including having them live with them in the family home (Moreno and Marí-Klose, 2013). Such an approach has significant gendered impacts, in that social care within the family is predominantly the responsibility of women (Holdsworth, 2004; Moreno and Marí-Klose, 2013). This is not only because it is seen as culturally appropriate but also because 'patronage reinforces patriarchal power relations within families because access [to welfare] is mediated through the male heads of extended families' (Allen, 2006, p.268). However, Spain has been changing, with more women entering the labour market, families becoming smaller and distribution of household tasks being shared more equally, especially among the young. Attitudes have also been changing in that Spanish people now see cohabitation and divorce as more acceptable, and welfare services are increasing their levels of support, especially since the early part of 2000. This has led to some claiming that Spain is taking a 'Nordic path' to future development (Moreno, 2013).

The organisation of the state in Spain went through radical transformation in the 1970s, with the collapse of the fascist dictatorship led by Franco. In the post-Franco era, the state reconstituted itself, aiming to increase the democratization and liberalisation of the economy (Engel, 2007). However, even though the fascist regime in Spain had a strong national protectionist policy, early signs of liberalisation of trade and markets emerged in the 1970s and 1980s (Engel, 2007; Ban, 2011). Once freed from the fascist ideology, Spain underwent constitutional reforms that saw the creation of a 'State of Autonomies' that formally recognised 17 autonomous communities as partners in the sovereign state. This was a radical restructuring that shifted the government away from being a centralised strong controlling state to one that aimed to be democratic and inclusive. While it seemed a Socialist government of 14 years would offer an alternative to the growing interest in neoliberalism, many of the practices of neoliberalism were used in shaping how the economy should run (Ban, 2011). For example, major re-regulation of the labour market occurred, making hiring and firing easier. Free market economic principles were also used in determining how to manage public services and develop the economy (Ban, 2011). This is not to say that Spain is a neoliberal state, as what we see is a combination of drivers at both local and national levels, some pushing the country towards neoliberalism and others towards a more Keynesian and welfarist approach (Engel, 2007).

As a strategy for growth and expansion, Spain elected to embrace the European ideal, seeing it as a point of arrival to aim for. The European system was seen as a 'master symbol' of modernisation and a way of increasing good practice (Moreno, 2013, p.219). Spanish politicians saw it as critical to Spanish development and, as a result, Spain incorporated European objectives, indicators and procedures and practices into its own policy-making process, creating a way of legitimising (or de-legitimising) certain political and economic strategies. This included the creation of a 'fully fledged European welfare state' (Moreno, 2013, p.218) alongside increased forms of market liberalisation. However, the forms of economic order created were fluid and 'incorporated market, non-market and mixed forms of economic co-ordination' (Moreno, 2013, p.220). This, combined with economic aid provided by the EU to help build Spain's infrastructure and strong growth in its tourist industry, saw the Spanish economy grow in strength throughout the 2000s. But its active courting of Europe brought it closer to neoliberal strategies. For example, it accepted the Maastricht Treaty reforms, which included reductions in public spending, inflation targeting, and deregulation of labour markets (López and Rodríguez, 2014). By 2010 it was ranked 12th in the world in GDP and was included in meetings of the G20 group. Its per capita GDP rate was comparable to that of other European states (Moreno, 2013).

Under the Franco regime the welfare state had been established using the 'Bismarckian principle', which aimed to protect workers and their dependents rather than provide universal social protection (Guillén and Luque, 2014). In this context:

> The social order revolved around conservative principles: men should sustain families and women should stay at home taking care of children, the sick, the elderly and the disabled. (Guillén and Luque, 2014, p.265)

Following the move towards European integration, the Spanish welfare state moved towards a pattern of generalisation and universalisation of entitlements, moving it away from the Bismarckian approach of income maintenance (Rodríguez Cabrero, 2011). How successful this was remains unclear, in that the language of universalism was never incorporated into law and welfare systems still have a strong emphasis on availability being conditional on being a worker. It remained 'de facto' not 'de jure' universalism (Guillén and Luque, 2014, p.269) and became an incomplete universal system 'of an institutionally mixed nature, relatively fragmented in several levels of social protection' (Moreno, 2013, p.221), although over the last twenty years the Spanish state has increased its spending on public services and welfare to the point that it is now at the EU average. One of the major developments in this Europeanisation has been the increased usage of ALMP and reforms around employment practice. Here we see Spain introducing key principles of neoliberal ideas on causes of unemployment that locate the problem in the individual and supply. As the EU embraced new employment reforms, Spain adopted and created new legislation in 2003 that increased the use of activation policies for the unemployed, extended entrepreneurialism as a core self-insurance, and required greater responsibility and flexibilisation of young workers (Moreno, 2013).

While Spain's government increased its spending between 2000 and 2007, it only carried a small deficit, with the economy growing, on average, by 4% per year. Employment also grew, with over 7 million jobs created in this period. One of the major growth areas was home ownership, with 7 million new homes being added to the housing stock and house prices increasing 220% between 1995 and 2007 (López and Rodríguez, 2011). This massive growth in property ownership saw the nominal wealth of households increase threefold. As a result, borrowing also tripled, from €260 billion to €900 billion between 2000 and 2008. This in effect added €1 trillion to the Spanish banks' balance sheets, creating debts equal to 290% of GDP by 2008 (Wolf, 2014).

When the crisis came, Spain was badly hit, with GDP dropping to −3.6% and seven successive quarters in recession alongside a deflation that lasted eight months. This created major problems for the people of Spain. Over 1 million properties remain unsold and houses prices devalued by almost 30%. The government's public finances also spiralled into a deficit of −11.5% in 2009, the highest in the eurozone. The number of personal bankruptcies increased over fivefold, going from an average of 900 a year to 5,000 between 2007 and 2013 (Wolf, 2014). One of the biggest casualties was employment, with the national unemployment rate rising dramatically between 2008 and 2013. By 2010 it had reached 20%, peaking at over 25% in 2013. This figure was even higher for the young: among young people aged between 15 and 24, unemployment rose from 17% to 20% in one year (2007–8) and by 2010 this figure had doubled to 40%. This increase continued until it peaked in 2013 at 55%. Major regional differences also existed; in some parts of Spain unemployment was as high as 70% for the young (ILO, 2013).

In responding to the crisis the Spanish government followed others from around the globe in drawing on Keynesian strategies of demand management, but by 2010 it was recognised by the Socialist government that it needed to implement austerity measures that included cuts in public services, a 5% reduction in wages, a salary freeze for all public employees, pension reform (increasing the retirement age) and a removal of child allowances. After these measures were proposed the Socialist government lost the election and was replaced by a right-leaning government that not only continued these reforms but also introduced further changes drawing on a wide range of neoliberal tools (Banyuls and Recio, 2013). For example, the number of people employed by the state continued to fall dramatically between 2010 and 2013. As a part of this process there has been increased privatisation of public services with large-scale private operators running core services. While this process was first introduced in the early reforms advocated by the EU, under the new government this process has been accelerated. Spain has also seen fees for university places increased by almost 100%, along with a reduction in student scholarships. The incoming government made major changes in the labour market, including 'the creation of a new type of contract that makes possible free dismissal during the first year, the liberalisation of collective redundancies … the conferring of rights … on companies with regard to internal flexibility and collective bargaining' (Banyuls and Recio, 2013, p.52). This internal flexibility allows companies the right to change working conditions without agreement from the employee. The government is also introducing major changes to benefit systems, limiting access to health care and social benefits for under-26-year-olds, based on how much people have paid into the social security system (Banyuls and Recio, 2013). Spain therefore, as a part of its austerity programme, has clearly made a substantial 'neoliberal turn', introducing a wide range of reforms that not only reduce public spending but also reform the education and labour market infrastructure of post-16 education (Banyuls and Recio, 2013).

The state, youth and citizenship

In the previous four chapters we have seen what it means to be a citizen in the UK, Australia, Canada and New Zealand, and that this has been changing significantly for young people since the 1990s. These trends have been expanded and accelerated as a result of the 2007 crisis and the great recession that followed. In the next chapter we will explore the differences that exist across Norway, Japan, Poland and Spain, and their differences from our four other case study countries. What we have seen in the previous four chapters is that since the late 1990s there has been:

- a reconstitution of pathways in the field of post-16 education, training and work; the school-to-work transition has been reconfigured to one that sees young people having to navigate this stage of the life course by moving in and through different components at different stages (being in work, a student, unemployed, in training, or a mix of any of these);
- an emphasis on development of human capital and qualifications as a critical driver of young people's behaviour after the age of 16;
- an increasing trend for paid work to become harder to find, more precarious and insecure, and for work not to form a major part of young people's personal identities until later in life;
- a growing requirement for young people to be responsible, to make choices and to accept that any failure is theirs, not the system's;
- an increasing tendency for social welfare policy and education policy to be built around the notion that the young have to 'pay their way' and that financial responsibility must be taken by them (or their parents);
- an increasing use of ALMP to force through the use of sanctions and punishments as a way of ensuring the young are 'active' and 'responsible' citizens.

Of course, given the different contexts highlighted in this chapter, it is to be expected that what it means to be a citizen in Norway, Japan, Poland and Spain will be significantly different for young people. The process of 'being and becoming' is shaped and constituted in different ways. For example, the welfare state and its institutions will frame the types of experiences the young will have during their transitions (Walther, 2006). It is therefore important to recognise that not only is the state operating in diverse ways in these four countries, but also notions of what it means to young people to 'become a citizen' are significantly different from our other case study countries. What we have seen in the UK, Australia, Canada and New Zealand is the establishment of neoliberalism as a political project, not just an economic one. This has clear implications for what it means to be a citizen (Kelly, 2000). Poland, since its break from the communist regime, has clearly embraced a market-driven form of citizenship. Under communism, social rights were universal, and employment and minimum incomes were guaranteed, while most public services, such as education and health care were free (Heinen and Portet, 2002). While such a system was seen not to work efficiently, it had a strong welfarist model of citizenship at its core (Hardy, 2009). After the transition and 'shock therapy', it shifted from a universal to a residualist model where rights and benefits, as in most liberal economies, were conditional (Heinen and Portet, 2002). Major changes have taken place that have shifted the responsibility from the state to the individual. This model took time to establish and created major disruption yet, by the early part of 2000s, it was well established. As we shall see in the discussion that follows in the next chapter, Poland's youth policy and practice is strongly influenced by neoliberal ideas of responsibility and obligations.

In Norway things are clearly different. While neoliberalism has started to impact on policy, Norway has remained resistant and has retained a strong focus on maintaining the consensual relationship between the state, the market and the individual in particular localised ways. For example, citizenship in Norway is built on a social contract between the individual, the state and private enterprise, and is embedded in a wide range of universal rights. It is socially democratic and the state takes a major responsibility for protecting its citizens and for encouraging inclusion (Thun, 2012). As we shall see in the discussion that follows, this means there is strong support for young people's movement towards adulthood. For example, Norway is one of the highest spenders per head on education in the OECD (OECD, 2014a) and it allocates more resources to social welfare than any other country in Europe (Olofsson and Wadensjö, 2012). Education is also free and a large number of social benefits remain universal. This does not come without personal responsibilities but there is a strong emphasis on the responsibility of the state to its citizens (Thun, 2012). As Lister argues, the Nordic model (which includes Norway) is seen as an exemplar of social citizenship in that 'equality, solidarity, and universalism are values that explicitly underpin the Nordic model's commitment to the principle of inclusionary and equal citizenship' (2009, p.246). In this context, it is suggested that this is an 'advance autonomy model of independence between generations' (Moreno, 2012, p.26) in which the young can move out of the family home with ease.

In Japan, becoming a citizen is again a different experience, not only to Norway and Poland but also to our other case study areas. Being Japanese brings with it a strong responsibility to the nation state. Obligation and duty are embedded as key principles of social and economic life. 'Japanese society exhibits the characteristics of an ethnic national community bound together by a subtle and complex web of obligations, etiquette and custom ...' It is assumed to be a 'birth right (*kokuseki*) which translates as "duty to the country"' (Gifford et al, 2014, p.85). Yet when it comes to social rights and benefits, the state in Japan is less forthcoming (Inui, 2003): responsibilities for welfare and protection are located in the family and the firm. Social policy, for example, is weak; very few benefits exist and when they do there are very tough eligibility criteria (Inui, 2003). In this context, the family has always been seen as central, providing financial support for children well into their twenties, although the state provided a 'seniority wage system'. This aimed to help cover the increased costs of child care for families, but it was limited in that only large firms provided it and its focus was on male breadwinners only, meaning it had limited impact (Inui, 2003). One of the main sources of social benefits was the firm. As outlined above the firm has had a major role in post-war development in Japan. For the young, the 'firm' was critical to their transition into adulthood. It was not only the main source of employment (and income) but also provided a wide range of social benefits, offering child care, accommodation, and personal guidance and advice. For example, in the 1970s most large firms had dormitories located close to the factory which were used as a way for young people to leave home (Inui, 2003). In this sense, the firm had a critical role in terms of training the young as citizens (Gifford et al, 2014). After the collapse of the 'bubble economy' in the 1990s major changes took place, which created significant tensions and problems for Japan in training and socialising the young as citizens (Inui, 2003; Gifford et al, 2014).

Finally, in Spain, citizenship for the young is again very different from our other case study areas. First, while Spain has been increasing its welfare provisions since the 1990s, welfare rights and policies for the young, unlike in Norway, remain weak. In his comparative study of welfare regimes that support young people in Europe, Moreno (2012) found that social expenditure on youth is low in countries such as Spain and Italy compared to those in Northern Europe. In fact, evidence shows that the distribution of spending between generations is unequal in Spain and young people cannot rely on the state to provide them with the resources to gain independence (Moreno, 2012). It is argued that, for the young in Spain, the model of emancipation is not from the family, but a form of emancipation within the family (Sgritta, 2001). The concept of a 'familistic' model of support suggests that the relationship with the family is central to young people's experience of emancipation, and autonomy and citizenship (Moreno, 2012) in that 'the lack of [an] institutional framework of social support policies for youth has created a link of solidarity between the young and parents' (Moreno, 2012, p.26). Young people remain longer in the family home than most other Europeans, with 64% of all 15–29-year-olds in Spain still living at home in 2005 (Holdsworth and Morgan, 2005). Parents also continue to support their children (both financially and emotionally) until they have established their own home (Moreno, 2012). But, as we saw, citizenship for the Spanish is highly gendered in that the 'Bismarckian principle' of social benefits being linked to employment, alongside the cultural values of Spain towards women's and men's roles, means that the experiences of being and becoming a citizen are structured around well-defined traditional gender roles. While there are changes taking place, being a young woman in Spain has a different set of obligations and duties attached to it (Holdsworth, 2004).

Conclusion

So how far are these four countries similar to the UK, Australia, Canada and New Zealand? It is clear that each country has a very different history and political culture, not only with regard to the other four case study countries but also to each other. Each country has had a very different developmental history, which has established particular principles that underpin social and public policy.<bullet list>

- Norway has its social democratic 'Nordic way' built on partnership and welfarism.
- Japan is characterised by its state-crafted ideology, rooted in economic and cultural nationalism and Confucian philosophy, and underpinned by a strong developmentalist model of planning.
- Poland, as the newest of the case study states, was created in resistance to state socialism, leading to a political objection to state-led planning coupled with a desire to be a market-based society.

- Spain, as a Southern European state, emerged from the Franco fascist period and embraced the European ideal. It also has a strong emphasis and commitment to welfare that is reliant on the family.

As a result, there have been diverse reactions and responses to neoliberalism in these four countries. In Norway and Japan we see a history of resistance towards neoliberalism with Norway wanting to continue its social democratic way, seeing neoliberal ideology as a threat, and Japan seeing neoliberalism as a form of Western imperialism. Of course, as neoliberalism has gained strength around the world and international organisations such as the World Bank, IMF and OECD have encouraged its beliefs and practices, resistance has become harder to maintain. For example, as the Japanese economy weakened and it began to rely more on external markets, its political-bureaucratic elite began experimenting and drawing upon neoliberal tools. However, in Norway the lack of a national political movement that supports neoliberalism (coupled with the availability of oil resources) aids resistance, ensuring that its use is not ideologically driven.

Of course, while local context is of critical importance in resisting neoliberal ideology, even in Norway and Japan policies have still drawn upon neoliberal ideas and applied them more regularly. For example, over the last two decades, Norway has used markets in delivering welfare services and Japan has moved towards a hybrid state that is more attuned to neoliberal modes of operation. Of course in Poland and Spain things have been different. In Poland, the embracing of 'markets' was at the heart of its resistance to the previous communist regime; this meant that neoliberal policies underpinned the expansion and development of the new economy. The West, and the US in particular, strongly supported the idea that bringing Poland into the liberal economic model was an advantage for other Western nations, as it created new markets in which to sell their goods. Spain, too, has never objected to using neoliberal ideas and practices in its attempt to catch up. Spain's Socialist government, while embracing the European model, is willing to accept the neoliberal requirements of membership, although it does not 'fully' buy into the approach (seeing the growth of the welfare state as fundamental). However, it has adopted key neoliberal economic mechanisms, especially around labour market regulation. It is also worth acknowledging that even Norway was not immune in this period, in that market philosophy gained more ground, even with a social democratic government, as it was seen as a natural way of bringing about more efficiency in public services while also selling off national assets.

Finally, it is important to recognise that the impact of the economic crisis and its aftermath was not universally experienced. However, as in the UK, Australia, Canada and New Zealand during this period, neoliberal principles and policies have been established or introduced to varying degrees. The extent of their impact has in many cases been determined by the political will or ideology that dominates. For example, Poland established neoliberal practices as a way of moving away from the Soviet regime and as a result they have become normalised as a way of running the economy. It is unsurprising, therefore, that Poland's response to the broader crisis has been to extend neoliberal practices in its policy making. On the other hand, Norway was least affected by the crisis and had substantial resources to maintain its social democratic approach. It did not see neoliberalism as the 'solution' and therefore its adoption of neoliberal practices has been essentially for pragmatic reasons. Spain and Japan have found themselves in a position where choices about how to respond have become more limited and they have either been forced (for example, through conditions for loans), or simply had to adapt to new economic climates (having to open their borders to external competition in the case of Japan). Therefore, while it is safe to say that neoliberal ideas have become more widespread and influential as a result of the crisis and the great recession, the extent of their influence has been mediated by the ability and willingness of states to take on their practical application.

EIGHT

Education, work and welfare in diverse settings

Introduction

The discussion in this chapter will look at how neoliberalism in Norway, Japan, Poland and Spain has influenced and shaped youth policy over the past twenty years. We will begin the analysis by focusing on the question of education and training, followed by an examination of the strategies that each country has developed for dealing with unemployment, work and welfare. The review will also show how the different states have been developing their post-16 education policies, highlighting the importance of the local context in how they are responding to the neoliberal agenda, especially since the 2007 crisis. We will also examine the significant differences in strategy not only between these four states but also in terms of how they vary with regard to the UK, Australia, Canada and New Zealand that were discussed in detail in the first part of the book.

Post-16 education and training

As we saw in Chapter Three, both the levels of participation and the number of qualifications that a young person gets have increased over the last fifteen to twenty years in all eight countries. Since the 2007 crisis, and throughout the recession, participation has continued to expand. However, differences continue to exist not only in the level of participation but also in how education and training is provided. In Norway and Spain, education is funded substantially from public funds, while in Japan education is run and managed fundamentally by the private sector. Poland, in its adjustment to a new European state, has created a partnership between public and private providers. One key feature in all eight countries is that young people's level of engagement in post-16 education is strongly influenced by what is happening to employment opportunities, although local factors also make a difference. This is clearly evident when considering Norway, Spain, Poland and Japan, and there are some interesting trends. In Norway, when the young were able to access good quality jobs (between 2000 and 2007), their level of involvement in education declined, but this changed in 2008 (OECD, 2014a). In Spain, the relationship between unemployment, work and local factors is more complex. The proportion of young people involved in post-16 education after the Franco period (in the 1970s) until 2007 was one of the lowest in Europe and the Organisation for Economic Co-operation and Development (OECD) countries. Part of the reason for this was that a house-building boom in the early part of the 2000s saw young people entering the building industry and therefore spending less time training (OECD, 2014a). Spanish workers have not always seen post-16 education as central. Past generations have had low levels of educational attainment and involvement. While the share of the population who have obtained the certificate of obligatory (lower) secondary education has increased from 71% in 2007 to about 74% in 2010, this is still very low in international comparisons. It is also the case that the number of graduates from tertiary education has also always been low in comparison to others (OECD, 2014a) and, while this had started to change, numbers entering and graduating from post-16 education and training still remained low. In fact Spain is one of only five OECD countries where less than 60% of 25–64-year-olds have attained upper secondary or tertiary qualifications (the OECD average being 75%). However, the number of young people aged 25 to 34 who now hold an upper secondary education qualification is almost double that of the older generation (OECD, 2012). Clearly a major driver has been the economic crisis and the great recession, as young people started to see education as a route to a future job.

In Poland there has been a similar growth spurt but for different reasons. In the early part of the post-communist era, Poland adopted a system that made participation in post-16 education compulsory up to the age of 18. As a result it has one of the highest participation rates in the OECD[1] (OECD, 2014a). Prior to the changes, only 10% of adults had higher education qualifications, but by 2009 this had doubled to 20%, although this is still two and half times lower than the average in OECD countries (OECD, 2014a). The main increases are among the young; by 2011, on average 32% of all 25–34-year-olds had a university degree. This is three times higher than in the oldest sector of the population and almost on par with the OECD average, making it one of the most dynamic increases across all OECD countries (OECD, 2014a). After the fall of communism there was a major drive to get

---

[1]   The participation rate in Poland was 92% compared to the OECD average of 81% (OECD, 2013a).

an education, which was seen by Polish young people as the route to prosperity and social mobility (Kwiek, 2013). Unlike our other case study countries, the drive was less about increasing high-level skills for a new knowledge economy, or reducing unemployment, and more about getting a university degree in its own right. This massification of higher education was a key driver. After leaving communist Europe, the Polish people had growing aspirations to have access to university qualifications:

> Poland became a country of people intensely pursuing education, and the education sector was the first to experience the population surge. Since the beginning of the 1990s the enrolment rates at the top of the educational ladder have increased nearly four times. (Szafraniec, 2011, p.92)

In the initial stages, little concern or attention was focused on the quality of these qualifications, as 'Higher education credentials from any academic field, any institutional type and any mode of studies were viewed by the newcomers as a ticket to the good life and rewarding jobs' (Kwiek, 2013, p.240). In addition, limited attention was given to questions of equity or social justice; those from rural areas and low socioeconomic status (SES) groups failed to gain as much from the process as the middle classes or those living in urban areas (Szafraniec, 2011)

In Japan, the post-16 education and training sector is significantly different again, although it has historically always had a central role in nation-building. It consists of a university sector that specialises in academic subjects and graduate training, junior colleges that provide two-year sub-degrees and routes into university, while also providing a wide range of vocational opportunities (normally aimed at 16–18-year-olds), and colleges of technology that undertake high levels of vocational training (Newby et al, 2009). The post-16 sector in Japan has a number of important features that make it unique and different from all our other case study areas. Japan created an education and training system that is seen not simply as a mass education system but a universal one (Trow, 1974) without it being made legally compulsory (Ikuo, 2014). For example, throughout the 1970s and 1980s, participation in post-16 education held steady at 36–37%, but by 1995 it had reached 42%, increasing again to 51.5% in 2005 and 55% in 2013. If special training and other vocational providers are included, the rate increases; 78% of young people in Japan are involved in education and training after leaving school. This is one of the highest participation rates across all OECD countries (Ikuo, 2014).

The issue of the role of vocational training in these case study countries is also an interesting one. Japan has always had a small but popular vocational sector. After the 1990s crash, Japan devoted substantial resources to developing its vocational sector (Goodman et al, 2009). Numbers going to non-university vocational schools (*senmon gakkō*) doubled between 1992 and 2004 from 10% to 20% of school leavers (Goodman, 2012). But it was not just school leavers who swelled the numbers; many students who entered vocational training had completed university or junior college degrees – in fact over 25,000 students enrolled after dropping out of university. Some students even combined study, attending university and a *senmon gakkō* simultaneously (Goodman, 2012). Traditionally, *senmon gakkō* were dominated by young women (80%), but by 2012 the sex ratio had attained parity (50:50). Part of the reason for this was the collapse of graduate employment; opportunities to get work after university dropped from 80% to 60%, while in *senmon gakkō*, 80% of young people graduating got a job (Goodman, 2012). However, it is important to recognise that the vocational sector in Japan is small in comparison to most OECD countries, and most young people still go to university and junior college (Newby et al, 2009).

In Norway, vocational education and training (VET) evolved under the social democratic principles of cooperation between state, business and the unions, although it was separated from the mainstream until the early 2000s. It is now well established and students can do over four years' training with state support. In fact in 2007, 46% of young people who left school went into some form of VET programme (OECD, 2008). It was seen by the state as a major way in which to aid its economic growth (OECD, 2008). Spain, while not always having a strong VET sector, has also seen growth, especially since the 2007 crisis. Historically, involvement in VET had been low, with only 8% of the population having a vocational qualification in the late 2000s[2] (OECD, 2014a), but by 2011 the numbers in VET had dramatically increased to 28%. This was higher than the OECD (16% in the early 2000s and 19% in 2011) and the eurozone (11% in the early 2000s and 15% in 2011) averages (OECD, 2014a). But this growth is not consistent across our case study countries. Traditionally, the Polish post-16 system had a strong reliance on vocational education, but after the fall of communism there was a major decline in young people taking this route. In fact,

---

[2]   The OECD average was 34% (OECD, 2014a).

between 1995 and 2010 young people's participation in vocational training declined from 70% of all 15–19-year-olds to 40% (Szafraniec, 2011). Young people clearly wanted to get a university qualification.

Neoliberalism in post-16 education

How have neoliberal ideas and principles been operating in Norway, Poland, Japan and Spain over this period? In Norway, education is seen as a 'public good' and attracts substantial investment from the national government. Norway is the third highest spender on education among OECD countries, with 1.5% of gross domestic product (GDP) being spent on post-16 education. While other Nordic countries spend more, this is still one of the highest percentages in Europe (Nielsen and Andreasen, 2015). Unlike in other developed economies, over 96% of the total spend on post-16 education still comes from public finance (OECD, 2014a). More recently, higher education has gone through significant changes. In 2003 a new bill on higher education quality reform was introduced, which aimed at changing a higher education system built on the Germanic Humboldt system to one akin to the Anglo-Saxon model (Arthur, 2006). Alongside this came reforms bringing increased competition between universities, the introduction of a new public management (NPM) practice, and elements of state funding being linked to results. For example, the new system consists of three main components: a basic grant (60% of the allocation) and two components based on performance, with 25% based on educational output and 15% based on research output. However, the university sector is still strongly driven by the state and is seen as a 'reluctant reformer' in this area, rejecting moving to the quasi-market models being used in other parts of the world (Arthur, 2006). Given that the state still has a strong role in the governance of universities and still provides most of their funding, it clearly remains influenced by the social democratic Nordic model that has had such an impact on Norway.

In Japan, market principles have been central to the post-16 education system since just after the Second World War. The Japanese model is fundamentally run by the private sector although the state remained to have a regulatory role. Historically, the state never took a major role in developing this sector and, from the 1960s onward, its expansion was taken forward by the private sector. For example, in 1960, two-thirds of all students found places in in private universities (Kariya, 2012). In 2006, out of 4,167 institutions that provided education and training in this sector, 3,709 were in the private sector. Out of 716 universities, 566 are private and 384 of 413 junior colleges are run by private organisations. The only exception to this is in the colleges of technology, where only 3 of 63 institutions are privately run (Newby et al, 2009). However, a number of vocationally oriented professional training colleges (*senmon gakkō*) exist almost exclusively within the private sector and are focused on delivering employability skills. They remain separate, however, from the university/junior college sector and, as such, are relatively free of regulation by government (Newby et al, 2009).

This infrastructure means that over 75% of all students using post-16 education and training are being taught in the private sector (Newby et al, 2009). This is exceptional; even in countries such as the US, which is renowned for using the private sector to deliver education, the proportion is usually the reverse (Ikuo, 2014). This continued and expanding reliance on private education and training, especially in higher education, accelerated in the 1990s, when it was thought that the best way of preparing for the knowledge economy was to draw on neoliberal practices. The perception was that it 'was not through bureaucratic but market solutions that the diversification of higher education could be realised' (Kariya, 2012, p.74). As a result, as the higher education sector grew concepts such as deregulation, diversification and liberation were critical terms used by the state to increase and maintain the high level of privatisation embedded in the system. This massive privatisation of the post-16 education and training sector is reflected in the state expenditure of only approximately 0.5% of GDP on this sector, compared to the average of 1.1% in OECD countries. Such expenditure is, alongside that of South Korea, the lowest in the OECD countries (Goodman et al, 2009).

While Poland is different, similarities do exist. Poland's post-communist approach to the market means that its post-16 system has been strongly influenced by neoliberal ideas and practice since the 1990s. After separation from the Soviet Union, demand for post-16 education from young people in Poland increased. Most young people wanted some form of university qualification, which was where growth was highest. The university sector in Poland was one of the oldest in Europe and, while under Soviet control, it had been delivered by a highly controlled state sector and a number of elite universities. As Poland moved into being an independent state, it achieved the expansion of higher education by creating a 'complicated inter-sectional public–private dynamic', which has led to 'one of the highest degrees of marketisation of the system in Europe' (Kwiek, 2013, p.234). Between the 1990s and 2008, 350 private universities were created, teaching over 630,000 students a year. In fact, over 32% of all students were enrolled at private universities – the highest proportion in Europe (Siwinska, 2011). Since the recession, Poland has seen a decline in the private sector, although this is less to do with the economic crisis and more a result of demographic and population changes. As a result, a number of private universities have closed (Siwinska, 2011).

Spain, on the other hand, had historically seen its post-16 education mainly funded by the national government and the 17 regions. In total, 85% of all funding for education in Spain comes from public funds, and the public sector remains a key funder and provider of services. After Franco, successive socialist governments continued to be the main funders, although expenditure remained low and below average compared to other OECD countries. Spain only spends 5.6% of its GDP on education (compared to an average of 6.3% in OECD countries and 5.9% in the eurozone). However, over the last twenty years, there has been a growth in Spain of private institutions operating in the post-16 educational sector (OECD, 2014a). For example, 14% of all tertiary students are now taught in private universities that do not receive public funding (compared to the 28% OECD average). In the VET sector the delivery of training is again mainly by the public sector, although 21% of students are taught by private sector providers. Compared to other OECD countries this is a relatively low percentage (the OECD average is 41%).

A public good or private responsibility?

The growth of education for the knowledge society has been an important focus of recent policy in all the countries discussed here, although the movement towards private responsibility varies. Norwegians, for example, have easy access to postgraduate studies and an increased take-up of Master's-level education (Næss, 2011). This is encouraged by the fact that all post-16 education is free. In higher education there are no tuition fees and in fact it is free to all Norwegian residents, regardless of citizenship status. A loan and grant system exists to help with living costs, but the young person (over 18) is treated as an adult in their own right. Loans and grants are available to all, although generally students get a grant level that reflects their personal situation (that is, living away from home or at home). One of its key objectives is to ensure equality of opportunity to all (Hovdhaugen, 2013). In the vocational sector students are guaranteed a place. This built on previous attempts by national government to provide a Youth Guarantee, in which all young people would have either work or training (Hummeluhr, 1997). In 1994 the government introduced new legislation that established a statutory right for all young people to have access to a minimum of three years' upper secondary education, which aimed to lead to either university entrance or a craft certificate. It also introduced a 2+2 model for VET, with two years of school-based education followed by two years of enterprise-based training. Those not gaining an apprenticeship place could take a one-year advanced school-based education and training. Again, this was free and, in terms of apprenticeships, young people would receive a wage throughout. In fact, while post-16 education is not compulsory, over 99% of 16-year-olds begin either education or training (Hovdhaugen, 2013).

In Spain, similar to Norway, post-16 education and training systems remain fundamentally a 'public good', although over the last thirty years there has been a process of catch up. Under Franco, investment in education was low (Martinez-Lucio and Stuart, 2003). As we saw in the previous chapter, Spain's strategy of rebuilding was to decentralise many of its resources and policies to the regions while also embracing Europeanisation (Engel, 2007). This offered ways of resisting neoliberalism while also embracing it. Regions were less willing to draw upon neoliberal policies, while policies and procedures from the European Union (EU) increased pressures on the national government to draw upon and use neoliberal tools (Engels, 2007). As a result, post-16 education was a core responsibility of the regions and much funding for education was protected and determined by local areas. However, pressures from the central state for reform saw an increase in private universities (OECD, 2014a) and private providers in VET (Souto-Otero and Bjorn Ure, 2012), although the regions still have a major role in the delivery of education. Student fees are some of the lowest in the OECD and most Spanish domestic students receive grants. Presently, students do not have to directly pay tuition fees (these tend to be covered in their grants) and in 2007 the national government provided interest-free loans to graduates so that they could continue their education beyond first degree level.

Japan and Poland are very different. One of the implications of the privatisation of the post-16 sector in Japan is that the 'user pays' philosophy has dominated since after the second world war Tuition fees are the fifth highest in the OECD, and this is creating substantial problems in terms of student and family debt (Kariya, 2012). Japan has a student loan system but only about a third of students can access it. For example, only 37% received loans in 2011 (Kariya, 2012). Similarly, a small number of students receive scholarships (3% in total in 2011). In reality, what happens is that the key player in funding young people's post-16 education in Japan is the family. With education being provided mainly by the private sector this has increased since the 1980s, so that by 2002, 60% of the costs of post-16 education and training were being met by the household (Kariya, 2012). When students do take out loans, they have major problems repaying them. Japan does not have an income-contingent repayment scheme, which means that students have to pay them back once they have graduated whether they have a job or not. In the recession this is causing significant problems; with over 1.3 million borrowers, over 330,000 of them are unable to pay, thus generating ¥474 billion (US$5 billion) in unpaid loans (Billones, 2013). Poland is similar, in that with the growth of privatisation, the 'user pays' philosophy has been shaping the delivery of post-16 education and training since the 1990s. Traditionally, full-time study was free in the elite universities, while part-time study involved the payment of fees. As the private sector took a more central role, it increased provision while also increasing fees for both full- and part-time study. However, 'who pays' varies; as massification of the system took place, the new middle class maintained their position in the elite public sector universities that were non-fee paying, while those new to the system and with lower incomes increased their participation in the private sector where fees were required (Kwiek, 2013). This growth did not mean better services or even different services – it meant more higher education services becoming available that had to be paid for (Enders and Jongbloed, 2007).

Who participates and who benefits?

In terms of widening participation, Norway does not have a policy that explicitly targets certain groups. Proposals in the Higher Education Quality Reform Act (2003) aimed to increase access for all and provide a universal system but this was in reality the continuation of a practice that has always been central to the Nordic model. However, there is evidence of groups that are under-represented. For example, students from the most educated families were almost nine times as likely to enter higher education as students from the least educated families, although between 1999 and 2011 this was reduced to just four times as likely (Hovdhaugen, 2013). There are still major differences, in that only 14% of students from the least educated families attend higher education compared to 58% of students from the most educated families. Similar trends exist in retention rates, with higher numbers of lower SES students not completing their education. Under-representation exists among ethnic groups and migrants. One-third of Sami peoples aged

19 to 24 are students, while 16% of first generation and 39% of second generation immigrants attend university (Hovdhaugen, 2013).

In Japan, it is important to recognise that the universal model of post-16 education and training is perceived to be open and fluid. In fact, as the private sector has expanded its provision, the availability of places has outstripped demand. This has led to a number of institutions not being able to recruit to capacity and has led to a drop in the entry requirements, raising concerns that Japan is lowering its standards and creating an open-access system that does not address core skill requirements (Newby et al, 2009). A second point to note is that while Japan has a universal system, there remains an imbalance between genders. In contrast to the global trend, the balance is reversed, with young women being under-represented in post-16 education and training. For example, in 2005, 51.3% of males and 36.8% of females enrolled in university Bachelor's degree programmes, and 15.1% of recent male college graduates proceeded to graduate programmes, compared to 7.7% of females (Newby et al, 2009). As we shall see, this gender question also remains critical to discussions over employment. Apart from the gender question, Japan has given little attention to accessing educational impact on different SES groups. It assumes that it has a relatively open system that creates opportunity for all. However, evidence shows increased inequality in Japan, and a breakdown in the belief that Japan is one large middle-class society raises concerns that the system benefits the wealthy and privileged (Goodman, 2012; Kariya, 2012). As Newby et al suggest in reviewing the higher education system in Japan:

> This growing income inequality – when coupled with the growing role of private high schools, populated by children of wealthy parents; sizable payments required for tutors in preparing students for university entrance examinations; and relatively high and rising tuition fee levels in universities – all point to the likelihood that growing numbers of youngsters from low-income families will be unable to gain admission and pay for university education. We simply cannot imagine any other situation obtaining, given what we understand about the financing of higher education and the process of admission. (2009, p.57)

A similar situation exists in Poland. Its focus on massification has seen little concern about or attention to who participates. (Kwiek, 2013, p.240). In fact it would seem that this process has had little impact on social mobility and inequality. While the expansion of higher education did increase access, there remains little evidence to suggest that it brought about changes in the levels of inequality between groups, especially with regard to those living in the rural areas of Poland and the poor (Szafraniec, 2011; Kwiek, 2013). However, one key feature of growth in Poland was the increased levels of participation by young women. Similar to our other case study areas discussed earlier, parity between the genders was achieved in the mid-1990s, and by 2011 60% of university students were young women and 40% were young men.

In Spain, the expansion of post-16 education and training, while still not matching the European or OECD average, has seen three particular trends. First, similar to Poland and other countries, Spain has seen a growth spurt, driven by young women entering education and training. This trend started in the late 1980s and parity with young men was reached in 1995. This continued and accelerated throughout the recent great recession (OECD, 2012). Again, as in other countries, disciplinary segregation remains, in that young women are more likely to go into the humanities, teaching and arts, while young men enter the sciences and engineering (Vincent-Lancrin, 2008). Significant intergenerational differences also exist, suggesting that parental education now has less of an impact on young people's participation in post-16 education (Ferrer-i-Carbonell et al, 2013). Evidence shows that the link is not as strong in Spain as in other parts of the world. However, a third issue relates to the impact of social class; when it comes to selecting a career trajectory, young people from working-class backgrounds are more likely to choose the vocational rather than the academic path. Class remains a significant influence on the pathways chosen by young people in Spain (Bemardi and Reguena, 2010).

Graduate employment

Apart from in Norway, the underemployment of graduates is a significant theme. Recent research in Norway suggests that the problems other graduates around the world are facing are not such a problem there (Næss, 2011). According to the OECD, Norway has among the highest numbers of graduates per head of population (OECD, 2014a), yet most graduates are finding highly skilled work; in fact it is suggested there are still not enough graduates to fill all available vacancies. The major shift is that the growth in graduate jobs tends to be in the private sector. Previously, over 50% of all graduates entered the public sector, but this has now changed (Næss, 2011). Graduates are also being paid higher wages than twenty years ago, although there is not a marked differential between those with university degrees and those without (Næss, 2011).

Major problems exist in Japan. Prior to the 1990s, Japan had a school-to-work transition system that helped maintain low unemployment. It was 'highly centralised and designed to produce what the workplace needed in order to drive the Japanese economy' (Goodman, 2012, p.16). It produced male workers who would embrace the ideology of the firm, while socialising young women into caring roles (Goodman, 2012). Lifelong employment was guaranteed to the best graduates leaving university, and schools worked closely with large firms to create smooth transition routes into the company for school leavers (Brinton, 2011). This created secure, lifetime work for the young:

> Schools were charged with the responsibility of helping students move into full-time positions in companies. Growing numbers of young male workers ... experienced the benefits of strong attachment to a particular firm or workplace. (Brinton, 2011, p.11)

Such an approach operated successfully to create secure employment and strong social attachment to particular workplaces, especially for young men, until the 1990s. After the crisis and 'bursting of the economic bubble', major changes took place in the labour market that reconstructed the school-to-work transition (Toivonen, 2013). With the collapse of the economy and of employment, firms and large corporations reduced the number of recruits they took from school leavers and university graduates (Genda, 2005). Rather than lay off middle-aged graduates, firms reduced their uptake of new young recruits. The number of jobs available for new graduates almost halved (Kariya, 2012) and firms increased non-standard work for those aged 15 to 24. In effect, this meant that 50% of jobs created in firms for young women and 42% for young men were non-standard, which was an increase of over 30% (Kariya, 2012). In this context, the lifelong employment tradition was broken (Brinton, 2011; Kariya, 2012; Toivonen, 2013).

Similarly, Spain also has a problem of underemployment, especially of its new graduate population (Peiro et al, 2012). Graduate jobs have been slow to grow and a mismatch exists between demand and supply. There is a growing body of evidence that suggests graduates who find work are overqualified (Minguez, 2013). Spain has the highest proportion of young graduates working in jobs that do not utilise their skills and knowledge. Over 35% of young graduates who are in employment are overqualified. Compared to the EU27 average (21%) this is exceptionally high (Minguez, 2013). There also remains a major concern that a number of those not in employment, education or training (NEETs), especially in the 20 to 29 age group, are graduates who, once qualified and unemployed, find their ability to participate in further training or education restricted because of lack of finances (OECD, 2014a).

In Poland, the massification of the higher education system, alongside growing unemployment among the young in the late 1990s and early part of 2000s, created a significant problem for new graduates. They had trained for highly skilled employment but competition within Poland was fierce. Two major trends resulted. First, even though a number of graduates had been trained in the regions, Poland saw a large movement of the young to urban centres where the highly skilled jobs were located. Second, partly as a result of the opening up of the EU to Polish citizens, there was massive migration of young graduates to find jobs elsewhere. Estimates show that, in 2004, only 24,000 Polish nationals were staying in the UK for longer than two months, but by the end of 2007 the number was estimated to be 690,000 (Trevena, 2011). However, benefits for these graduates are not guaranteed, in that Polish graduates who migrate are more likely to be in low-paid, insecure jobs in cities such as London (Trevena, 2011). We will return to this point in the next chapter.

Unemployment and the NEET question

So far our focus has been on education and underemployment, but what has been happening to work and policies that aim to increase young people's participation in employment? As we saw in Chapter Five, youth unemployment in these four countries varies, partly as a result of local circumstances. Norway and Japan avoided high youth unemployment throughout the economic crisis and great recession, and in fact Norway saw increases in youth unemployment only from 2007 until 2009, which then declined and levelled off by 2012, although the percentage has slowly crept back up and stands at 9.3% in 2015. Compared to the OECD and European youth unemployment figures, this is well below average (Djernaes, 2013). It is also lower than all the other Nordic countries[3] (Djernaes, 2013). Japan followed a similar path,

---

[3]   The way countries in the Nordic region measure youth unemployment can vary. For example, Finland includes full-time students in its figures while Demark and Norway do not.

although its rate of youth unemployment has continued to decline. In 2008 it had a youth unemployment rate of 7.2%, which increased to 8.8% in 2009, then dropped to 8.2% in 2012. Unlike in Norway (and other advanced economies), the rate has continued to drop, and by 2015 it was 5%, which is one of the lowest levels in the world, though this may be a consequence of the strong growth of temporary contracts. Poland and Spain have fared worse. Poland entered the 21st century with a youth unemployment rate almost double the EU average. In the first quarter of 2000 it was almost 38% for young people aged 15 to 24, and between 2002 and 2003 it reached almost 44%. From 2004, the youth unemployment level continuously dropped until the end of 2008, when it was at 17% (Polakowski, 2012). However, this figure was still one of the highest in the EU (Szafraniec, 2011). As Poland entered the economic crisis, the youth unemployment rate dropped to 19.5%, but then rose to 25.8% in 2012. This rate has remained reasonably static and in 2014 the rate of youth unemployment was 27.4%. Since then it has started to drop and in August 2015 was at 19.3%.[4] Of the four countries discussed here, Spain has been hit the worst. Youth unemployment has always been high in Spain, but between 2000 and 2007 it dropped from 26% to 17.9%. This was partly because of the growth of jobs in construction and the expanding role of the tourist industry in Spain's economy. But when the crash came, it impacted on the young immediately, with unemployment rising from 17.9% to 37% in 2009 and then to 52.4% in 2012. It finally peaked in July 2013 at 55.8%, but was still at 49.9% in March 2015[5].

Of course these figures mask the unequal impacts within countries. These are especially marked in Poland and Spain. In these two countries, unemployment had a substantially greater impact in rural areas. In Poland, the growth of new jobs in services tended to be in urban areas, while agriculture and forestry (the main employers in rural areas) were in decline (Szafraniec, 2011). In Spain, a number of regions top the overall EU unemployment league table, and seven are in the top ten. In these regions youth unemployment is the highest in Europe, with Ceuta having 72.7% of its 15–24-year-olds unemployed, while Andalusia has 66% and the Canary Islands 65%.[6] Similarly, male unemployment is the highest in Europe, with six regions filling the top of the league table. Women too are badly hit, with Ceuta coming

---

[4]   https://ycharts.com/indicators/poland_youth_unemployment_rate_lfs
[5]   See https://ycharts.com/indicators/spain_youth_unemployment_rate_lfs
[6]   See http://ec.europa.eu/eurostat/statistics-explained/index.php/Unemployment_statistics_at_regional_level

top for female unemployment (44%). A major reason for the wide differences is the types of industries that exist in different parts of Spain. 'Regions which before the crisis had higher levels of specialisation in activities such as construction and related industries, and services with lower added value, have been particularly badly affected' (Sánchez, 2012, p.9).

But it was not only differences in regional impact that affected Poland; there were also substantial gender differences. Young women aged 15 to 24 were far more likely to be unemployed than young men, although this was reversed for older groups (those aged 25 to 29). These differences continued throughout the recession, in that 30% of young women aged 15 to 24 were unemployed, compared to 25% of young men.[7] Major differences also existed between the types of educational attainment young people had managed to achieve. Across most advanced economies, the level of attainment achieved in education and training impacted on the risk of unemployment (OECD, 2013a). This was especially stark in Poland, in that those with the lowest levels of qualifications, such as vocational qualifications and/or university diplomas, were more likely to be unemployed or inactive. While massification of education in Poland had seen an increase in qualifications, it was those with graduate or postgraduate degrees who fared better in the crisis (Szafraniec, 2011; Polakowski, 2012).

One final point to highlight relates to the NEET question. Unlike the other four case study countries discussed earlier, the question of NEETs varies quite substantially between these four states. Numbers of NEETs in Norway are exceptionally low compared to other regions and countries in Europe. For example, in 2012 Norway had only 8% of young people aged between 15 and 29 years old classified as NEETs compared to the OECD average of 16%, although, like other countries, Norway did see a 2% increase between 2008 and 2011 (OECD, 2013a). In Poland, the NEET level is not exceptional (similar to the UK rate): since 2005 it has remained stable at approximately 12% of the 15 to 24 age group. In fact, in Norway and Poland there seems to be little political interest in NEETs. Spain and Japan, on the other hand, are different. In Spain they are known as 'ni-nis' (*ni estudian ni trabajan*), that is, neither working, nor studying, and have been described as a 'lost generation', who have failed to find opportunities because of Spain's economic crisis. The level of NEETs was already high in comparison to other OECD countries prior to the economic crisis, but from 2007 to 2011 it nearly doubled, to 20% of 15–24-year-olds.

---

[7]   See: https://www.quandl.com/collections/poland/poland-unemployment

When broken down by age, the older young people were more likely to be NEETs, with 19% of 15–19-year-olds and 25% of 20–24-year-olds being NEETs (Sanchez, 2012). Unlike many OECD countries, Spain's NEETs were more likely to be unemployed than inactive. This can be explained by the high levels of young people moving in and out of short-term contracts, interspersed with spells of unemployment (Sánchez, 2012). It is worth noting at this point that across these three nations the moralising that normally focuses on the NEET question is absent. Much attention is given to causes that tend to be structural (that is, problems with the labour market) or to do with low educational attainment.

In Japan the situation is different again and, unlike in Poland, Norway and Spain, there is a strong moralising component. Early on, governments' attention in discussions on the growth of unemployment was on groups who were seen as making moral or lifestyle choices that worked against them getting back into the labour market. Initially, concern was raised about 'freeters', that is, 'freelancing youth who avoided company drudgery to pursue their dream' (Toivonen, 2013, p.2). It was claimed that this group would rather be in part-time or temporary work than find full-time employment in a firm. Similarly, anxiety existed over 'parasite singles', that is, affluent females who worked as a hobby but lived at home and consumed luxury goods. Both these groups were seen as making lifestyle choices that were changing the traditional work model and threatening to create greater social problems in the future (Toivonen, 2013). Concerns were also being raised over '*hikikomori*'. These were unemployed youth who were socially withdrawn and isolated, and were seen as both immature and having mental health problems (Horiguchi, 2012). Again, this located the problem in the individual, seeing their unwillingness to be involved in work as a form of mental illness (Horiguchi, 2012). What is evident is that significant claims were being made about the extent of the problem, yet evidence about the extent to which these groups, and the type of social problem being attributed to them, existed remained unclear. In a historical review of Japanese youth policy, it is suggested that it was not uncommon for claims to be made in that:

> perceived youth problems do not correspond in any straightforward way with socio-economic conditions, even if they partly reflect the economic, educational and demographics of the day. They are rather driven by 'industries' of interested actors, commercial enterprises,

> private or semi-private youth support groups, the media
> and the government. (Toivonen, 2013, p.33)

By the mid-2000s explanations of the 'problem' focused on NEETs. How this group was defined differed, in that it included 'young people' between the ages of 15 and 35, as well as a wide range of other groups that seemed to expand the extent of the problem (Toivonen, 2013). In fact the size of this group ranged from 400,000 to 2.5 million, depending on how researchers and politicians approached age and gender (Toivonen, 2013). More importantly, as concerns about this category of non-worker grew, they also took on a negative set of meanings that saw them as lacking in key social skills of communication and confidence, and being lazy 'adult children' who rejected established work norms (Genda and Maganuma, 2004). This then created an 'industry' that attempted to define the 'causes' of the problem and which sensationalised the negative by constructing them as 'workshy,' 'lazy' and 'undeserving' of public support (Toivonen, 2013). By the time of the economic crisis in 2007, NEETs were the key problem that government had to address.

Precarious work

Across the UK, Australia, Canada and New Zealand we have seen, quite clearly, that precarious work has been increasing, driven by both economic requirements and national policy changes that operate to re-regulate the youth labour market in particular ways. But how have our other four countries fared? In Poland, job creation, especially since the economic crisis, has seen a slow growth of new jobs that are fundamentally temporary in their nature (Polakowski, 2012). Poland has the highest number of workers in any EU country that are employed on temporary contracts. This form of work has grown at an alarming rate in Poland over the past decade, increasing from just 5.8% of all employees working temporarily in 2000 to almost 27% in 2011.[8] It is young people who have been hit the hardest by this growth of temporary work. Since 2004 and through the economic crisis, the average percentage of young people aged 15 to 24 working in Europe on temporary contracts has increased 6.6% to 42.5%, and in Poland the proportion increased from 60.6% to 66% (Polakowski, 2012). This is the second highest number of young people in Europe working in temporary employment (with Slovenia being over 70%). As we saw in

---

[8]   The EU average is 14.1% (Eurofound, 2013).

Chapter Seven, Poland has been re-regulating its labour market over the last fifteen years (Szafraniec, 2011; Polakowski, 2012). This has seen the loosening of terms and conditions and a reduction in basic rights. For example, temporary workers only have a right to one week's termination notice, and they have no right to social security or the minimum wage (Polakowski, 2012). Much of the work is contracted through agencies that offer few benefits but take a substantial fee from the employee for finding them work. Over the last ten years these private agencies have grown, with over 3,000 operating in Poland in 2010 (Trappmann, 2011). Young people, who are more likely to be on temporary contracts or working through agencies, are also likely to be the most unskilled and those with the lowest levels of qualifications. In a study undertaken in 2012, 48% of all temporary workers were shown to have only primary or lower secondary education levels (Polakowski, 2012).

Spain has been going through a similar set of processes to Poland. It too has seen job growth after the recession being in temporary jobs. Since the early part of the 2000s, short-term contracts have become a far more normal part of the job market for young people aged 15 to 24. In 2004, 64.8% of young people were working in temporary jobs in Spain compared to 37.6% in the rest of Europe (Eurofound, 2013). When the economic crisis of 2007 came, the number of temporary jobs available in Spain declined quite dramatically. This happened as a result of the massive unemployment that saw those already working in temporary jobs being hit the hardest. By 2012 the numbers had crept back up to 64.7% of all new jobs being created for the young being temporary positions (Eurofound, 2013). Again, part of the reason for this was changes that had been made to the labour market. Since the early 1980s, a number of reforms have been introduced that directly impact on the young. In 1984, the Spanish government introduced laws that created new forms of temporary training and practice contracts and new employment promotion programmes of fixed-term contracts. These reforms were specifically targeted at new and peripheral workers (or 'outsiders') who were either unemployed or new entrants to the labour market. These changes effectively protected permanent workers and pushed the young into temporary forms of employment (Golsch, 2003). Other reforms, especially around dismissal and temporary work, were introduced throughout the 1990s and 2000s, and as a result young people's involvement and opportunities in the labour force were marginalised (Banyuls and Recio, 2012). As a result of these changes, Spain has created a precarious youth labour market that creates a particular structured experience:

> the most influential factor with regard to the vulnerability of young people to the crisis in Spain is the high level of precarious work, which is such a key structural characteristic of the labour market for this group of the population that it could almost be said to be endemic. (Sánchez, 2012, p.11)

In fact evidence shows that while education may be a variable that partly explains stability of employment, it is only relevant for the over-25s. This 'indicates that the temporary work contract represents the way into the labour market for Spain's youth, irrespective of their level of education' (García, 2011, p.10). Yet, in discourses over causes, the problem is never constructed as one of structural problems of labour market failure. It is either defined as one of limited and low skills and education of the young, or a rigid labour market that needs to be further deregulated to increase flexibility (OECD, 2013a). As we saw in Chapter Six, there remains limited evidence that such practices increase the number of jobs available. Nevertheless, the 'blame' for the high level of youth unemployment in Spain is seen either in terms of individual deficiency or unionisation (Sánchez, 2012). These types of reforms have continued since the 2007 crisis. In 2012 the national government introduced sweeping labour market reforms that continued to aim to regulate the labour market that directly impacts on the young. These include legislation such as Law 3/2012 that:

- increases employer's rights to act unilaterally to reduce compensation for dismissal – and to change wage rates without arbitration;
- creates greater flexibility in apprenticeships and training, allowing employers to extend contracts to three years and keep young people on training wage rates;
- increases the power of employers to act unilaterally over terms and conditions and to modify these without consultation with individuals or unions, along with a reduction of union powers especially around collective bargaining;
- creates new temporary contracts that establish a compulsory probationary period of one year, during which time a worker can be made redundant for any reason whatever, without any compensation.

In Japan, with the collapse of the firm as the traditional route into work for the young, major problems were caused by a labour market dualism that saw, as in Spain, permanent full-time employees protected from the high level of unemployment that followed the bursting of the economic bubble. This dualism saw a growth in non-regular work[9] especially for the young, with over 31% of young workers aged 15 to 24 working in non-regular jobs in 2007 (OECD, 2010).[10] This type of work tended to be insecure and low paid. Evidence also showed that movement from non-regular to regular work was very limited, meaning that large numbers of the young had declining opportunities to access lifelong employment. This dual labour market created 'a wedge between regular and non-regular contracts' (OECD, 2010, p.10), leading the OECD to call for increased legislation to increase flexibility for older workers and create more opportunities for the young. One of the major implications of dualism in the labour market was increased levels of inequality, especially in terms of gender. Evidence shows that women make up over 70% of the non-regular labour force (Aoyagi et al, 2015). The creation of the dual labour market came about as a result of the social contract made by the unions, government and business in the 1960s, which established protection of the 'male breadwinner' in terms and conditions that were fundamental to the operation of the firm, and which fed into the re-regulation of the labour market in the post-1990s crisis, increasing protection for some while limiting it for others:

> a combination of deregulation and re-regulation codified part-time and temporary work as distinct statuses with few of the benefits or social protections associated with the corporate-centred, male-breadwinner reproductive bargain. (Gottfried, 2014, p.465)

As a result, part-time and temporary work became defined as non-regular work which received less protection.

Norway is the only one of our four case study areas discussed here that has managed to protect its young, although, as we shall see, even here there are worrying trends. While over the last twenty years there has been an expansion of temporary and part-time work, its impact has been minimal in comparison to other European states (Berglund, 2010; Brinkley, 2015). In fact, since the early part of the 2000s, Norway has seen a decline in temporary work. The number of young people working in temporary work was 31.2% in 2004 (6.4% below the

---

[9] In Japan they measure 'non-regular' work to include both temporary and part-time work unlike the Eurostat which only includes temporary work in its measure

[10] This does not include students working part time. When they are added, the figure increases to 46% of young people aged between 15 and 24.

European average); this dropped to 27% in 2007, 25% in 2009 and 24.4% in 2012. However, Norway does have a higher number of part-time workers and this does tend to be gendered, with 69.5% of young women and 40.7% of young men working part time in 2009. Some of this could be attributed to young people working while in education, but it has been a growing trend over the last ten years. Similarly, temporary work in Norway is seen as a 'specific youth phenomenon' (Berglund, 2010, p.113), with most new jobs now being created for young people being temporary in their nature. Young women and immigrants tend to be more likely to have temporary jobs than others. Norway also has some of the highest levels of young people working part-time and in temporary positions in the Nordic region, yet it also gives the best opportunities across the Nordic region for young people to move into permanent work; the odds on a temporary worker becoming inactive or unemployed are low. However, those who are inactive or unemployed are more likely to get a permanent job than other such young people across the region (Berglund, 2010). Norwegian workers also have stable working hours, with over 80% of workers having stable and regular hours regardless of their employment status (permanent, temporary or part time).

There are two reasons for these trends. The first is the high level of security built into the labour market, compared to other nations. Historically, the tripartite model of cooperation and the use of collective agreements has created contracts that help protect employees from the worst aspects of free market enterprise. Trade unions have been active partners in building up protections and, although Norway has some of the lowest levels of union membership in the Nordic region (Olofsson and Wadensjö, 2012), membership is still high compared to other parts of the world. This has helped create an employment environment that is highly regulated. For example, there are strict rules on how, when and who can be employed on temporary contracts. More recently, attempts have been made to relax these, but the law, while passed, was not enacted.[11] Similarly, part-time work has the same forms of protection as full-time work (Berglund, 2010). A range of equality laws are also in place. For example, in 2008, Norway introduced an affirmative action responsibility for employers to undertake non-discrimination in recruitment, working conditions and promotion, alongside protection against harassment. It also introduced affirmative action in the employment of applicants with a minority background,

---

[11] A new law was passed in 2005 but the incoming Labour government did not enact it.

even if the applicant was ranked behind the most qualified candidate. In 2012, this changed so that public employers have had to choose the applicant with a non–Western background if the person has approximately the same qualifications (Halvorsen and Hvinden, 2014). In a recent report comparing labour market regulation across the OECD (Brinkley, 2015), it was shown that Norway comes out high on a range of key factors. It has one of the highest levels of permanent employment (85%) and lowest levels of involuntary part-time work (8%). It also ranked third in job quality (76%) and second lowest in poor quality jobs (8%), with job security being high. Norway was also identified as the OECD nation where it was easiest to find a job of similar wage (Brinkley, 2015), suggesting that its level of precariousness is low compared to other developed economies.

The second reason for the trends discussed is that in trying to address the need for flexible working Norway has adopted the Nordic idea of 'flexicurity'. As a policy objective this aims to increase opportunities for flexible working (for workers and employers) while also maintaining security and incomes (Madsen et al, 2013). It emerged in Demark prior to the economic crisis and, over the last few years, it has been adopted in most Nordic countries. The European Commission and the Organization of Petroleum Exporting Countries (OPEC) have also been advocating developing it as a way of addressing growing concerns about precariousness in the youth labour market. However, while there remains political interest, the concept of 'security' across the globe is complex and needs to be considered in relation to job security (for example, protection from dismissal), employment security (ease of getting a job if made unemployed), income security (protection of income across changing circumstances) and combination security (balance in work and family life). These types of policies can have economic consequences and ideologically run counter to neoliberal strategies (Berglund, 2010).

Finally, in terms of labour market reforms in our countries, it is important to recognise the recent growth in Europe (and Spain in particular) of policy that has seen the expansion of self-employment as a strategy for tackling the unemployment problem. The European Commission has been encouraging this as a strategy to dealing with high youth unemployment (European Commission, 2013) and evidence suggests that those countries with the highest numbers of NEETs are seeing an increase of young entrepreneurs. In fact during the recession countries in Southern and Eastern Europe have seen an increase in the number of young people who take on this form of working (Eurofound, 2015). Of course, such activity is increasingly precarious and not without high risks. In many cases this is not 'real' employment, in that it operates to move financial risks from the employer, giving the self-employed person few social or legal forms of protection:

> In a number of countries and sectors, bogus self-employment (when an independent worker is contracted to provide services to a single client or work provider in much the same way as if they were an employee) is widespread. This practice is used by employers as a means of reducing the costs of employment by lowering the social contributions payable and avoiding the costs imposed by employment protection legislation. (Eurofound, 2013, p.1)

While measuring this is difficult, it is a growing trend with between 4% and 15% of young people, depending on the country, working on these types of contracts. These figures increase in certain industries, such as construction, where over a third of employees could be on these types of contracts (Eurofound, 2015). In Spain this approach is being supported by youth policy; in the 2012 reforms, the government introduced new 'entrepreneur contracts' that create open-ended contracts for young entrepreneurs with no or limited employment protection. Similarly, in Poland self-employment has become a growth area, with a fifth of all new jobs being created this way (Gebel, 2008). One of the reasons for this has been the introduction of the 'civil contract' (Polakowski, 2012). These are contracts where employees are contracted to carry out a set of tasks. These contracts are not subject to the Polish labour code and give very few rights to the individual. For example, they do not provide sickness and maternity leave, or health insurance cover. They are also not subject to regulations on the minimum wage, working time directives, holidays or overtime payments. Again, evidence shows that it is the young, especially young women, who are more likely to be on these types of contracts. (Polakowski, 2012). The growth of such contracts has occurred because an increasing number of firms and sectors are attempting to 'flexibilise' employment relationships (Eurofound, 2015).

Active labour market policies and welfare-to-work

As we saw in Chapter Six, active labour market policies (ALMPs) have become a central feature of work and welfare policies in the UK, Australia, Canada and New Zealand. While there has been some variation, national governments have reconstituted social policy towards the young by creating policies that aim to create active rather than passive welfare recipients. Part of the strategy used by governments is to introduce various conditionality requirements and/or penalties that act to ensure participation. There is also a strong focus on cutting the cost of the welfare bill while increasing the idea that financial (and social) responsibility is a central requirement for those receiving benefits. It was clear from the analysis of our other four main case study areas that there also remained a strong moral position taken by neoliberal influenced governments that constructed and promoted the behaviour of the poor as immoral and an affront to decent citizens. Its strong moral undertones clearly operate to justify the actions of the state, and to set out the new social contract of personal responsibility.

So how have our four countries discussed here engaged with this debate? What strategies have they adopted and how have they connected to debates on morality? First, it is important to recognise that while the roots of welfare-to-work type programmes emerged from the US the concept of ALMPs was first credited to Sweden in the 1980s. The language of 'workfare' or 'welfare-to-work' was replaced with the concept of ALMPs as a way of avoiding the negativity attributed to schemes that seemed to target and problematise the poor (Kildal, 2001). From these early beginnings, ALMPs and workfare-type programmes became popular in the Nordic region. Countries such as Sweden, Denmark and Norway used them, although the rationales for this varied between nations. Four key areas of policy have been identified under this broader banner of ALMPs: job search assistance; labour market training and/or the increase of human capital; private sector incentives for employing the unemployed; and, finally, public sector employment (Kluve, 2014). Others have wanted to segment ALMPs by distinguishing between those aspects that are about improving human capital and those that use negative incentives to move people into work (Bonoli, 2010). Each of our countries has, as we shall see, taken a different approach to these issues.

Norway expanded its ALMPs in four key areas; labour market training; temporary public employment; wage subsidies; and work practices and experience. The latter was targeted more at 16–20-year-olds and the largest investment was in wage subsidies and labour market training. These approaches were expanded in the great recession, alongside an increase in public funding to counter the impact of the economic decline of external demand. Norway has the largest number of ALMPs in Europe and invests over 50% of its annual spending on labour markets in these programmes (Rønsen and Skarõhamar, 2009).

Poland, on the other hand, started developing its ALMPs in 2004 and by 2007 it was spending the OECD average, although the impact of this was limited (OECD, 2009). The largest part of its investment has been in training and apprenticeships, although recent cuts as a result of austerity measures have limited the level of investment. For example, in 2012 Poland launched the 'Young People in the Labour Market' initiative, which provided young people with vouchers to purchase training and education, but it was underfunded and targeted graduates only. While there is some justification for targeting training, the major problem in Poland is the lack of jobs. It is not directly a supply problem (Polakowski, 2012). Poland has also increased the use of the private sector in delivering ALMP initiatives. As funding in this area has grown, so has the role of the private sector, with over 83% of all training services now being provided by private trainers. However, the type of training provided and the quality delivered remains questionable, in that it only provides low level 'soft' skills and requires only limited investment (Polakowski, 2012). Other developments in Poland have opened unemployment services to the private sector through a partnership for employment. The government has also brought non-governmental organisations (NGOs), not-for-profit organisations and the private sector into the administration of unemployment (Sztandar-Sztanderska, 2009, p.629).

Spain has increased its ALMP activity and spending as well. Between 2005 and 2009, 30% of all those under 25 years of age were involved in some form of ALM programme. While Spain's spending on ALMPs relative to GDP has been higher than the average in the EU15, the amount spent per individual has been 12% lower than the EU15 and three and four times lower than countries such as the Netherlands and Denmark. Almost half of all the resources spent on ALMPs have actually gone to the hiring and retaining of personnel (usually by subsidising companies' social security contributions for hiring someone); again, in comparison to other EU15 countries, this is exceptionally high[12]. In fact, only 25% of Spain's ALMP budget in this period (2005–9) was spent on training, which was 15% lower than the EU15 average. The training being provided is also imbalanced, with a bias towards those in work. Evidence showed that only 7% of those who received training were unemployed, with the rest already being in some form of employment contract. When unemployed people did undertake training, it was usually found to be at the lower end of specialisation and through short courses (García, 2011). Finally, the focus on subsidising

---

[12]   The average in the EU15 is 25% of spending (OECD, 2014a).

employers tended to generate policies that created 'deadweight' and 'substitution' effects. The former refers to new jobs being generated that would have been created regardless of subsidies and the latter refers to new employees getting jobs that would have been occupied by others who did not participate in the programme. The evidence suggests that both effects are sizeable and that they have accounted for 90% of the jobs generated by such measures (Garcia, 2011).

In Japan, until 2002 only 0.2% of GDP was being spent on ALMPs, which is approximately a third of the OECD average (OECD, 2010). Underpinning these types of initiatives was a strong emphasis on blame directed at the young, which limits their willingness to be involved (OECD, 2010). Many of the programmes also lack clarity about who they are targeting, as terms such as 'freeters' and NEETs remain ill-defined and too general (OECD, 2010). In 2004, the Japanese government produced the Youth Independence and Challenge Action Plan, setting out a number of initiatives that aimed to tackle the problem. These included the Job Café,[13] the Japanese Dual System[14] and the Independence Camp, yet the amount of resources aimed at helping get the young back into work is seen as small in comparison with the problems they face (OECD, 2010). For example, the Independence Camp, which was targeted at NEETs and provided residential experiences for young people who suffered from joblessness, only had national resources for involving 700 young people. Given that the target group was claimed to be well over 1 million it was therefore unlikely to make much difference (Honda, 2005).

In terms of policies that require the young to be active, it is reasonable to say that while they have increased in these four countries, the active aspects of interventions in this area are focused more on job search activity than on traditional welfare-to-work type programmes that make young people work for their benefits. However, reducing benefits, especially for non-compliance, has been a central feature in a number of cases. Japan is the exception in the way ALMPs have been activated, since issues of conditionality could not be included in activation policies because 'Japanese policy-makers did not have at their disposal the notion of incentivising "inactive" youth by manipulating the benefits system' (Toivonen, 2012, p.12). Japan had no pre-existing

---

[13] This was a one-stop-shop model, where a range of services that would help young people get information and support for getting back to work were provided in one location.

[14] This is a system for integrated occupational training in which young people study at vocational schools while training as apprentices in firms.

youth unemployment system to manipulate. As a result, they tended to turn more to providing independence support that included careers guidance, and supply-side initiatives that developed policies involving some form of punishment for non-compliance (Toivonen, 2012).

Poland is probably the state that operates in ways closest to those in the UK, Australia, Canada and New Zealand in that ALMPs have clearly been used to cut benefits. ALMP policies are believed to have started in earnest after Poland joined the EU. Prior to this, the focus was on passive measures that aimed to 'soften the negative effects of unemployment ... primarily in the form of a safety net' (Sztandar-Sztanderska, 2009, p.626). It soon became clear that budgetary restrictions existed, especially following the massive increase of unemployment in the early 1990s. Joining the EU created opportunities for new resources to be made available from structural funds and created policy messages and directives that encouraged active measures (Rashid et al, 2005). ALMP was defined as the 'individualisation of services and conditionality of access to social protection based upon the "job readiness" of its recipients' (Sztandar-Sztanderska, 2009, p.624). This 'activation turn' in social policy was extensive in Poland. For example, the main funding of ALMPs was to be achieved by resources from the Labour Fund. This was not only used to fund unemployment benefit but also activities that would help get the unemployed back to work. Between 1993 and 2008 a huge shift of resources took place. In 1993, 84% of all funding from the Labour Fund was for passive policies while 11% was for active policies. By 2008 this had changed substantially, with 58% of all spending going on active policies and only 33% on passive policies (Sztandar-Sztanderska, 2009). There has been a significant decline in the level of the unemployment benefit and the number of unemployed people who can access it. In 1996, 52% of those registered unemployed had access to an unemployment benefit but by 2008 this had been reduced to 18%. For young people, the eligibility criteria[15] mean that only 12% have access (Polakowski, 2012).

---

[15] An unemployed individual has to register at a local labour office and meet several criteria in order to be eligible for unemployment benefits: a) having worked on the basis of a work contract or another contract for at least 365 days during the last 18 months, earning at least a minimum salary (which excludes part-time workers in low paid sectors); b) during this work period, the unemployed person and his/her employer need to have paid all mandatory contributions due from at least a minimum salary. (Sztandar-Sztanderska, 2012, p.626)

Eligibility is increasingly hard for the young to achieve as most jobs are now temporary or civil contracts. The rate available also dropped from 31% to 19% of the average salary between 1996 and 2008 (Sztandar-Sztanderska, 2009). This has since been reduced further because the rate now drops after three months of unemployment (Polakowski, 2012)

Norway, in line with its commitment to maintaining full employment, introduced a Youth Guarantee scheme for all young people under the age of 20 in the late 1980s. In the 1994 welfare reforms this was extended to include those aged 20 to 24. This had two main components. First, those who were unemployed for more than four months would be required to design an action plan and, second, this would list a set of key activities that they would undertake in the process of searching for work, such as undertaking unpaid work placements, participating in job clubs, or undertaking further education or training. Non-compliance would bring sanctions and the possibility of losing benefits. Over time, a shift has taken place that has seen the focus of these programmes being more on work experience than training (Olofsson and Wadensjö, 2012). How effective this approach has been is unclear, although Norway does have the lowest proportion of long-term unemployed of all the Nordic countries (Olofsson and Wadensjö, 2012).

Finally, Spain has been slow to adopt ALMPs into their practice. The first signs of conditionality were seen in 2002 legislation, but little change took place until 2011 when the newly elected conservative government introduced a key requirement for all unemployed to develop 'Job Action Plans' that set out their strategies for getting work. Attached to this are issues of conditionality, in that they have to sign up to this programme to receive benefits. It is proposed that sanctions will be used for non-compliance (OECD, 2012), although it remains unclear how these will work. These reforms were further strengthened in 2013 when conditionality and the obligation to take up suitable work were increased, especially for those who had run out of benefit. The unemployment benefit is cut in the seventh month by 50%. Enforcement and sanctions were therefore also increased (OECD, 2012a).

Conclusion

In this and the previous chapter, we have explored how the key trends and developments identified previously have operated in Norway, Japan, Spain and Poland. What is clear is that, as a result of their different histories, political ideologies, national cultures and local circumstances, the influence and impact of neoliberalism has been more variable. We can see in Norway the strong belief in social democratic practice that has helped protect the young from being exposed to the worst practices of neoliberalism. Strong management by the state, supported by business and the trade union movement, in a wide range of areas has helped in this process. That said, with the 2007 crisis has come reform and the infiltration of neoliberal thinking and, in some places, practice. While the level of influence remains small, it is clearly making some inroads. At the other end of the scale, Poland, which has embraced a number of key neoliberal ideas in its political ideology and practice, has reshaped the institutional experiences and forms of protection available to the young. As a result it is fair to say that Polish youth find themselves continually having to manage their lives in a strongly market-based economy, with less and less social protection from the state. This has had major consequences for young people since the 2007 crisis and throughout the great recession that followed. Spain is different again, in that while there were a number of developments that indicated the state had been drawing on neoliberal practice prior to the crisis, it was not until 2007 that the pace of change increased. This arose partly as a result of demands by external bodies who offered loans to make changes, but with conditions attached (the EU and International Monetary Fund [IMF]). For the young, this is creating changes in how they are protected from high unemployment by the state. While families have always been an important source of support, the changes and lack of state support are clearly putting families under stress. Finally, Japan has been able to avoid some of the worst effects of the economic crisis, although its own 1990s crisis set in motion a range of neoliberal-type changes that continue to impact on young people's lives. As we shall see in the chapter that follows and the conclusion, these changes create other consequences for what it means to be young.

NINE

Youth and mobility: inequality, leaving home and the question of youth migration

Introduction

In this chapter we examine some of the broader consequences of the changes identified previously. Our focus in this discussion is on the idea of 'mobility'. Its usage here is broad and our aim is to examine the underlying practices and processes that underpin the ability of the young to be mobile in different contexts (Holdsworth, 2009). We begin with the notion of social mobility or the 'categorical movement up or down the scale of socioeconomic classes' (Sheller, 2011, p.1), in which we examine the nature of inequality; in particular, the impact recent changes resulting from the crisis and recession are having on social mobility. The discussion will also re-examine how inequality *between social groups* in all of our case study areas has been playing out, showing that one of the major consequences has been that social mobility for the young remains limited, and this tendency is entrenched and shaped by the continued impact of class, gender and indigenous inequality. The second part of the chapter will explore the issue of mobility through young people's relationships with leaving home and gaining independence. Moving into independent living is seen as a critical stage in the process of growing up (Jones, 2009a); how the recession has impacted on this is therefore important for our understanding of young people's lives. Finally, we will turn our attention to geographical mobility and in particular to international migration, where young people 'move from one country, state or nation to another, to reside elsewhere at least on a temporary basis, often more permanently, the purpose being more than a visit or tourism' (O'Reilly, 2012, p.1). Mobility research of this nature is concerned with a wide range of groups and processes (Sheller and Urry, 2006; Urry, 2007), but our focus here is specifically on the shifts that have been taking place among high- and low-skilled young migrants, and on the movement of international students. The young are more likely than any other group to be migrants and, again, the crisis and recession has seen major changes in this experience for young people.

Mobility: social mobility, inequality and the crisis

Thomas Picketty (2013), in his book *Capital in the twenty-first century*, gives us an interesting perspective on inequality. In his discussion he highlights its history, showing how it has played a key role in capitalist development. Through a detailed empirical analysis he shows that what is important is not just income inequality but also the concentration of wealth ownership among a few. This, he suggests, helps maintain privilege and position, especially for the top 1%. While inequality was reduced by the Great Depression, two world wars and post-Second World War social policies, since the 1970s it has started to spiral upwards again, reaching levels not far short of the early industrial era. Picketty shows that 60% of the national income increase in the US between 1977 and 2007 went to the top 1% of earners. The only section that did better is the top one-tenth of that 1%, while the top 0.01% has done best of all (Picketty, 2013). This, he argues, arises because of the tendency for free market economics to benefit the rich and wealthy. However, while giving us an historical analysis of how income and wealth ownership are central to our understanding of inequality, Picketty fails to explain how they relate to the notion of crisis (Harvey, 2014). While most economists reject the importance of the political (Perugini et al, 2016), Galbraith (2012) reminds us that the bad distribution of income and wealth is predominantly a political, not an economic, decision. Others also highlight the importance of political responses as a cause of inequality, suggesting that the architecture of capitalism has been shaped by the ways in which governments have tackled problems of demand or responded to political pressure to operate in certain ways. This is not unreasonable as an explanation, in that the conditions for crisis were driven and shaped by political actors, especially in the deregulation of the financial sector (Konzelmann, 2014). The interconnectedness of such policies and practices, especially in countries like the US and the UK, increased not only the risk of crisis but also continued to increase levels of inequality and wealth ownership.

So what has been happening to the trends in the income inequality gap?[1] When we look at the global trends it is clear that certain groups have not only been maintaining their position but improving it,

---

[1]   This is measured by the Gini coefficient that scores 0 when everybody has the identical income and 1 when all the income goes to one person.

while others have been losing out. Figure 9.1 shows that since 1985, income inequality has been growing across almost all Organisation for Economic Co-operation and Development (OECD) countries, with a widening of the income gap for over three decades prior to the 2007 financial crisis (OECD, 2015).

Figure 9.1 Inequality in OECD countries between 1985 and 2013

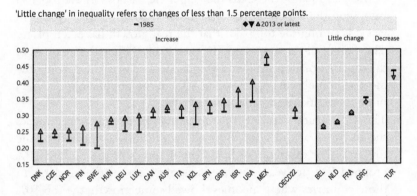

'Little change' in inequality refers to changes of less than 1.5 percentage points.

Data year for 2013 (or latest year).
Source: OECD Income Distribution Database (IDD) www.oecd.org/social/income-distribution-database.htm.

In this period average real disposable household income rose by 1.6%, but in three-quarters of all countries the household incomes of the top 10% grew faster than those of the poorest 10%, which led to a widening of income inequality. For example, in 1980 the top 10% earned seven times more than the poorest 10%; by 2015 they earned almost ten times more (OECD, 2015). Figure 9.1 shows that the Gini coefficient stood at 0.29 on average in the mid-1980s, but by 2013 it had increased 10% to 0.32, rising in 17 of the 22 OECD countries. We can see that the growth of income inequality was faster in some countries than others. For example, we see substantial raises in Nordic countries and New Zealand alongside the USA and Israel.

As a result of the crisis the income inequality gap increased across most OECD countries at a faster pace (OECD, 2014b). Over the period 2008–11 it increased more than during the previous 12 years (OECD, 2015). Income inequality is greatly reduced through redistribution, especially through taxes and cash transfers such as unemployment benefits, but neoliberal approaches to social welfare and protection in the decade prior to the crisis mean that income inequality has not been held back. The weakening of distribution policies resulting from the growing cuts and reconfiguration of welfare services worldwide has reduced important forms of social protection (OECD, 2015). As we moved into crisis and recession, the lack of protection accelerated. As a result of the crisis and the lack of protection a number of key trends have emerged that are important to note:

- In the period after the crisis the 'super rich' (those in the top 1%) have seen their incomes increase faster than any other group. In fact it is among the top 0.1% that the real growth has taken place.
- The pain of the crisis was not shared equally. While the incomes of the top 10% made a small and gradual decline over the period, low income households, representing 40% of the population, declined more substantially and at a faster rate.
- The decline hit the lowest 10% the hardest. In a number of countries the incomes of the poor dropped significantly compared to the top 10%. For example, in Spain the incomes of the poorest 10% dropped 13% per year compared to only 1.5% for the top 10%. In those countries where incomes showed some growth, the top 10% always did better than the bottom 10%.
- Overall real average disposable incomes[2] stagnated or fell in most OECD countries. In Greece they fell by 8%, and in Spain, Ireland and Iceland falls exceeded 3.5%.
- Over the first three years of the crisis 'anchored poverty'[3] increased. Between 2007 and 2011 this rate increased by just over 1% to 9.4%, yet in countries such as Greece (27%) and Spain (18%) it almost doubled over this period.

By 2010, austerity approaches started to have an impact; there was a shift in focus from fiscal intervention to consolidation, which saw cutbacks in social benefits and public services. How these policies will contribute to inequality post-2013 remains to be seen, but if the trends identified here are anything to go by, increases in income inequality are likely to continue.

---

[2] The amount of money a person has after they have paid all their bills.
[3] Anchoring the real low-income benchmark to pre-crisis levels gives a stronger sense of absolute changes in the living standards of the poor than the notion of 'relative' poverty (OECD, 2015).

Wealth inequality

As Picketty (2013) reminds us, it is important to recognise that wealth ownership is also unequally distributed and has in fact become more concentrated among the top 10%. Wealth ownership follows similar patterns to income inequality, although wealth inequality tends to be higher on average by at least 20% (Shorrocks et al 2014). If we look at Table 9.1, we can see the majority of our case study areas are located in the medium inequality category; the three exceptions are Norway and Poland (high inequality) and Japan (low inequality). Norway is interesting in that it has low income inequality yet has one of the highest levels of wealth inequality. The reasons for this are unclear, although it is thought that two key issues make a difference. First, while taxation is

Table 9.1 Current wealth inequality in developed countries and emerging markets 2014

	Developed economies	Emerging markets
Very high inequality top decile share >70%	Hong Kong, Switzerland, United States	Argentina Peru Brazil Philippines Egypt Russia India South Africa Indonesia Thailand Malaysia Turkey
High inequality top decile share >60%	Austria Israel Demark **Norway** Germany Sweden	Chile Mexico China **Poland** Colombia Saudi Arabia Czech Republic Taiwan Korea
Medium inequality top decile share >50%	**Australia** Netherlands **Canada** **New Zealand** Finland Portugal France Singapore Greece **Spain** Ireland **United Kingdom** Italy	United Arab Emirates
Low inequality top decile share <59	Belgium **Japan**	

Note: The names in bold are the Eight case study countries.
Source: Credit Suisse (2014: 30).

high in Norway, wealth such as property and inheritance is not taxed, and, second, the redistributive policies in Norway that provide strong social protection also discourage savings and wealth creation among the middle classes, as they do not have to build up resources for protection (Van Bavel and Frankema, 2013). In Japan, on the other hand, it is thought that the low level of wealth inequality has an historical basis, in that the nation was built on core principles of equity; while there has been a slow and gradual increase in the gap between rich and poor, the growth of this gap was held back by the crisis of the 1990s, which impacted on the savings and wealth accumulation of the rich (Ohtake et al, 2013). In terms of Japan's stronger income inequality, it is thought that the country's protectionist policies favour the secure, while those on non-standard contracts find their incomes decreasing (Ohtake et al, 2013).

The distribution of wealth among the top 10% across the globe shows some interesting trends, especially since the crisis. Until 1989 the gap between the top 10% and the other 90% remained reasonably static, but between 1989 and 2007 the level of wealth owned by the top 10% increased from 67% to 72% and continued to increase. In 2010 it reached 74.5% and by 2013 it was 75.3% (Shorrocks et al, 2014). Second, between 2000 and 2007 only 12 countries saw a rise in inequality, while 34 recorded a reduction, but between 2007 and 2014 this was reversed. Inequality rose in 35 countries and fell in only 11 (Shorrocks et al, 2014). Third, this growth in wealth inequality tended not to be in the advanced economies:

> it appears that wealth inequality did not increase in some of the major countries closest to the center of the global financial crisis; this result may be explained in part by the fact that the crisis saw the wealthy lose proportionally more than those at lower levels of the pyramid. (Shorrocks et al, 2014, p.33)

At the same time, we have to recognise that debt is not equally distributed. Approximately 10% of households in 18 OECD countries are over-indebted.[4] The largest share of indebted households is found in the middle-income bracket (outside the top and bottom 10%), with a third having debts in the bottom 25% as the poor tend to have difficulties securing loans.

---

[4]   They have a debt-to-asset ratio of 75% (OECD, 2015).

Youth, inequality and social mobility

In terms of income and wealth inequality, there were clearly winners and losers throughout the great recession. For example, a recent UK study showed that throughout the recession the top 20% of income earners were far more secure; in fact their median wealth (through savings) increased by 64% between 2005 and 2012/13. They were also less likely to be in debt compared to the middle- and low-income groups. The losers were the bottom 20%; their wealth was 57% lower in 2012 compared to 2005 (Broughton et al, 2015). In Canada we see similar trends – the median net worth of the top 10% increased by 41.9% between 2005 and 2015 while for the poorest 10% it fell by 150% (Broadbent Institute, 2014). Similar patterns can be found in Spain, New Zealand and Japan, showing increases in income and wealth for the top 10% throughout the great recession, while those in the bottom 10% to 20% saw their incomes and wealth either decline or not grow as fast as those of the top 10% (OECD, 2013d; Shorrocks et al, 2014).

This growth in inequality has had major impacts on young people. As we saw in Chapter Five, youth wage rates have been in decline throughout the recession. The youth wage has always been lower than that of adults and, over the last twenty years, the ratio has continued to decline (ILO, 2013). For example, Australia and Canada saw an erosion of the youth wage between the 1970s and 1990s, despite the shrinking supply of young workers, which ought to have improved their pay prospects (Blanchflower and Freeman, 1999). In 2006 the wage rate for 15–24-year-olds compared to the adult rate was 62%. Differences existed between countries, with the rate in Norway the highest at 73% and in the USA as low as 55%. Throughout the recession the youth wage has continued to drop: 'across the OECD countries, average household disposable income fell in real terms by around 1% per year among youth' (18–25-year-olds; OECD, 2014c, p.5). Significant losses took place in Spain (-5%) and the UK (-2%). In this there was a clear intergenerational impact in that '…over the four years since the onset of the crisis, young people (aged 18 to 25) suffered the most severe income losses, while elderly people (over 65) were largely shielded from the worse effects of the crisis.' (OECD, 2014c, p.5). The disposable income of the elderly increased in real terms or remained level in almost every country. In countries such as New Zealand and Slovakia, elderly people had gains of over 4% (compared to a 1% loss for young people aged 18 to 25). Even in countries where the wage rates either stayed flat or increased, the elderly's disposable income increased more than that of the young. For example, in both Australia and Norway the youth wage stayed flat, yet the elderly saw an increase of between 2.5% and 3% (OECD, 2014c). Such developments have seen the risk of income poverty for the young. While there has been a gradual trend across the OECD countries, from 2007 the risk of income poverty has shifted from the elderly to the young:

> Previous OECD reports highlighted that over the past 25 years youth replaced the elderly as the group experiencing the greater risk of income poverty. The recent crisis accentuated this trend. (OECD, 2014c, p.5)

The difference between countries can also be substantial. In 2011, the difference in poverty rates between 18–25-year-olds and the elderly in Norway was 28% for the former compared to 4.3% for the latter; in Spain it was 17.9% compared to 7%; in Canada 13.1% compared to 6.8% ; and in the UK 11.5% compared to 10.5%. Only two of our countries saw the trend reversed (Australia and Japan). The risk of income poverty among the 18–25-year-old group is also four times higher among the jobless. In addition, a young person working but in a single household has a risk of poverty around 50% higher than the rest of the population (OECD, 2014c). Austerity measures continue to reinforce generational inequality. A report by the Intergenerational Foundation in the UK showed that there has been a 10% decline since 2010 in young people's prospects. Older people have been less affected and the young seem to be paying a higher price as a result of the application of austerity measures. Recent announcements concerning the creation of a new and expanded minimum wage of £9 an hour that is not available to under-25s is an example of how such policies are unfair to the young (Intergenerational Foundation, 2014).

Inequality is growing between generations and the increasing levels of inequality have a negative impact on the young, particularly in terms of wellbeing and social mobility. While there may be some ambiguity about the relationship between inequality and the crisis, but we do know is that high levels of inequality are not good for societies and their members. Wilkinson and Pickett's (2009) now famous work *The Spirit Level* showed how the levels of inequality in a society correlate with a wide range of social problems. In other words, the more unequal a society is the more social problems it has. For example, in studying child wellbeing, Pickett and Wilkinson noted that:

higher levels of one or other of our inequality measures were significantly associated with worse outcomes for infant mortality, low birthweight, polio immunisation, average maths scores, the proportion of teenagers in further education, fewer children saying their peers are kind, teenage birth rates, experience of bullying, and childhood overweight. (2007, p.1083)

But it is not just wellbeing that is at stake. Evidence from the OECD indicates that income inequality 'has a negative and statistically significant impact on subsequent economic growth. In particular, what matters most is the gap between low income households and the rest of the population' (Cingano, 2014, p.6). For example, it is estimated that in New Zealand, economic growth should have been 44% between 1990 and 2010, yet due to the widening of the gap between social groups it was only 28%, representing a loss of 15.5%. This was the greatest loss across the developed OECD economies (Cingano, 2014).

Evidence also shows that rising inequality over this period led to young people whose parents had the lowest levels of education being affected most severely. Those young people whose parents had higher educational levels were largely unaffected by the crisis. The evidence shows that higher inequality 'lowers the probability of tertiary education for individuals from low background. Inequality is also associated to a significant increase in the probability that they attain, at most, lower secondary education' (Cingano, 2014, p.48). Those from the poorest groups are also more likely to be the long-term unemployed. 'Anti-poverty' programmes seem to have little effect. What is needed is cash and tax transfers and high quality education programmes targeted at the most vulnerable groups of young people (Cingano, 2014).

This raises issues about what happens to social mobility in those countries that have high levels of inequality. Michael Corak (2013) introduced the idea of the 'Gatsby Curve'. This shows that 'more inequality of incomes in the present is likely to make family background play a stronger role in determining the adult outcomes of young people, with their own hard work playing a commensurately weaker role' (Corak, 2013, p.1). Corak's analysis showed that those countries with high levels of inequality, such as the UK and the US, also had low levels of social mobility. While questions remain on the causal connection, it is clear from his analysis that social mobility is restricted when inequality is high (Corak, 2013). However, 'the reasons for the differences in the intergenerational elasticity across countries have to do with the different balances struck between the influence of families, the labor market, and public policy in determining the life chances of children' (Corak, 2013, p.7). As we have repeatedly seen, those with the most economic, social and cultural capital are more able not only to maintain their position and privilege but also, in many cases, to advance it. Some of the worst impacts of inequality (and the recent crisis) can be mediated by the broader social context, especially in terms of how privilege and power shape the life trajectories of the young.

As we have seen throughout this analysis, there remain at least three constants that reinforce the limited nature of social mobility for certain groups. Issues of inequality remain persistent, even in times of change. Three core themes have emerged in this analysis.

'Class' inequality

While it is difficult to construct a working definition of class that allows comparison across the case study countries, what is clear is that across all of our areas young people from the lowest socioeconomic status (SES) or bottom 20% of society have found their opportunities more limited since the great recession. Increased participation in post-16 education has been structured and experienced differently dependent on a person's SES. Across the UK, Australia, Canada and New Zealand, those from the low SES groups are consistently under-represented in higher education. When they do take part they are also more likely to go to the less successful universities and have high levels of attrition. The expansion of higher education has clearly benefited the middle classes. In our other four areas it was less clear, although there was evidence of class differences. In Japan and Poland the impact of the massification of higher education has seen high numbers of participants from all SES groups, while in Norway those from the middle class are four times more likely to be in higher education than those from lower SES groups. Spain presents a similar situation. In the post-16 field we also see segregation in the pathways taken by those from low SES groups. They are far more likely to be in vocational education and training (VET) programmes than at university. This was relevant in almost all of our case study areas. The low SES groups dominated vocational training, acquiring a range of skills and qualifications that have had mixed success in terms of accessing good jobs. The social reproduction of class identities that has always followed this division is alive and well in late modernity.

When it comes to unemployment and work, it is those groups at the bottom of the socioeconomic pile that have been hit the hardest. This was a constant across all of our case study areas. Unemployment hits the poorest groups most severely in all of our countries. Those of low SES, with low levels of qualifications, are more likely to be either unemployed or moving in and out of work, unemployment and training. While good social protection policies, such as those in Norway, can alleviate the worst impacts, most countries have cut back and limited this option for the poor. There are also important issues surrounding rural poverty in places like Spain and Poland, in that new jobs are being created in the cities and unemployment in some of the most deprived areas is exceptionally high. Precarious work in the shape of non-standard, temporary or part-time work almost always impacts most on low SES groups. While evidence suggests that graduate employment has been affected over the last seven years, and that the young middle class are struggling in the labour market, it also shows that, while their entry into good graduate jobs may be delayed, they do eventually get access to the best opportunities and jobs. However, in Spain and Poland even graduates are finding it increasingly difficult to find secure and well-paid work

Inequality and indigenous populations

A second theme shows the intersection between class and indigenous background. There remains a strong overlap between the experience of indigenous populations and those who are in the low SES bracket or who are working class. The previous chapters have shown that in countries such as New Zealand, Australia, Canada and Norway, indigenous youth populations tend to be at the bottom of the economic pile, being more likely to be poor and unemployed and in families without resources to help them get on in life. The recession has not reduced this; as the impact of the global crisis unfolded it was indigenous populations that suffered most, being hit hard by unemployment and slow to gain from the growth of jobs. Indigenous young people are less likely to go to university and, when they do, they have some of the highest non-completion rates. They are also, like others in low SES groups, more likely to end up in the vocational sector, undertaking low-level skill development, rather than having access to the best forms of apprenticeships. Being a young Maori in New Zealand, a young Aboriginal and Torres Strait in Australia, a First Nation young person in Canada, or a young Sami in Norway brings with it poverty and disadvantage. Inequality continues to operate in the lives of these young people.

Gender inequality

A final recurring theme is that major changes have been taking place around gender, which have changed young women's position in society. There has been a 'gender revolution' in higher education; across a wide range of countries more young women are entering university than young men. Parity was reached in the UK, Australia, Canada and New Zealand by the 1990s and since then more young women have been entering university than ever before. This was also the case in Poland, Spain and Norway, where gender has been a major driver in the expansion of the university sector. The only one of our case study areas that bucked this trend was Japan, where gender equality has been slow to take hold. This gender revolution is a global phenomenon and a trend that has become normalised worldwide. In a study of gender and higher education participation rates in 2005, it was found that, of 30 OECD countries, 25 now have higher education systems containing more young women than men. Countries such as Ireland (65%), Norway (60%), Sweden (60%) and New Zealand (59%) have the highest rates of female participation in higher education (Lancrin, 2008). However, in terms of types of degree, little has changed over time. In her article, *Some things never change*, Barone (2011) shows through a quantitative analysis of data from eight countries over three decades that gender segregation in terms of subjects studied at university has remained entrenched. Young women tend to do education, the arts, humanities and health, while young men do science, engineering and medicine.

In VET, this segregation continues. While we are starting to see more young women doing VET courses and apprenticeships, occupational segregation remains, in that young women remain dominant in hairdressing, social care and health, with young men doing engineering, ICT and manufacturing. While unemployment did not impact as significantly on young women, in the recovery and the creation of new jobs young women's employment tends to be part time, insecure and low paid. As we saw in Chapter Six, there are now three times more young women doing low-paid work than there were 20 years ago (Brinkley et al, 2013), and the percentage of young women aged between 16 and 24 working in low-paid occupations in countries such as the UK, Australia and Canada has increased from 7% to 21% (Corlett and Whitteker, 2014), while in Japan women make up over 70% of the non-regular labour force (Aoyagi and Garelli, 2013). These trends confirm that while the gender revolution may have increased participation, it has hardly touched the occupational segregation that has a long history in maintaining gender inequality.

Mobility: independent living and leaving home

While there is a range of diverse features defining independent living (Jones, 2009a) it is important to recognise that leaving home is a critical marker, not only for independent living but also for moving into adulthood (Jones, 2009a). What it means to leave home and become independent (as opposed to being dependent in the family home) has become increasingly complex and constantly in need of definition (Jones, 2009a). For example, the timing of movement out of the family home has consistently fluctuated over time and has national variations ranging between the late teens and the late thirties (Iacovou, 2011). For example, in the Nordic countries, the US, the UK, Norway, Japan and Australia it is not uncommon for the majority of young people to have left home before they reach the age of 30. Issues such as leaving to go to college or university, moving away for work and early marriage see the average age in these places being lower than other parts of the world (Brinton, 2011; Iacovou, 2011). For example, in Norway, evidence suggests that parents put in substantial support to help their children leave home early, unlike some of the Southern European states, where young people have strong family ties and weak social ties, meaning they stay at home longer (Iacovou, 2011). There is a strong cultural dominance in how families operate in such countries, with strong family ties being a critical feature of how young people's lives are structured (Holdsworth and Morgan, 2005). But, as we saw in Chapter Eight, there is also a lack of welfare support for leaving home, and youth wages remain low, alongside a lack of affordable housing stock that the young can access (Holdsworth and Morgan, 2005). Young people in Spain also spend longer in training and education, and take longer to get a permanent secure job (Holdsworth and Morgan, 2005). As a result of these factors, young people in countries such as Greece, Portugal, Italy and Spain are often still living at home in their thirties (Aassve et al, 2005). Similar patterns exist in Eastern European countries (Roberts, 2009), where poor wages, and the lack of availability of housing until they inherit from their parents, means that they live in the family home longer (Roberts, 2009). For example, in Poland over 50% of young people aged 18 to 34 are still living in the family home. The main reason for this is lack of income, with 50% of those living at home working on temporary contracts and only one in ten claiming their reason for living at home as being their own choice (Szafraniec, 2011).

Not only are there substantial national variations; variations also exist between genders and classes. It is usual that young women leave the family home earlier than young men in most advanced economies (Iacovou, 2011). For example, across Europe, young women usually leave home two to three years earlier than young men. This tends to occur as a result of young women entering into a relationship earlier than young men and either cohabiting or getting married (Iacovou, 2011). Similar patterns exist in Japan, where historically more than 90% of all young women would be married between the ages of 20 and 29 (compared to Spain where 75% of young women would be married by the age of 30). Young men tend to get married later and, as a result, young women leave the family home earlier than young men (Brinton, 2011). In terms of class there are long-standing patterns that show significant differences exist between social classes in terms of leaving home (Wallace and Jones, 1992). Evidence shows that those parents with strong social networks and economic and cultural capital are able to help their children leave home:

> there are three broad groups: young people on extended transitions who are able to receive parental support; young people on extended transitions who are not able to receive parental support; and those on fast track transitions who lack support (sometimes from both the family and the state) … (Jones, 2009a, p.142)

As Jones (2009a) goes on to show, the first group is dominated by the middle class, the second contains upwardly mobile young people from working-class backgrounds and the final group is from traditional groups who attempt to continue taking traditional routes yet find themselves in a risky situation regarding incomes and getting state support. They tend to become homeless as both the state and the family are unable (or unwilling) to support them. It is also the case that the 'missing middle' or 'squeezed middle' can find it increasingly difficult to leave home (Roberts, 2011). These are young people who are usually not attending higher education, have low skills and wages and few job prospects. Taking on high rents and regular payments becomes an increasing risk (Roberts, 2011).

So what has been happening to young people's movement into independent living since the 2008 crisis? As we have seen throughout this analysis, the context for young people moving towards independent living has been changing in most national settings. In our case study areas, youth wages have generally been on the decline, especially throughout the recession. At the same time, social benefits and welfare support were greatly reduced. The only country where this has not happened is Norway, where social protection for the young has remained stable over time. The decline of youth incomes is not just an issue for our case study areas; these are trends that can be found across a wide range of countries worldwide (ILO, 2013; OECD, 2014c). But clearly the structural changes we have identified are also of significance. For example, the growth of temporary work, while directly impacting on youth wages, also creates substantial obstacles to young people's ability to plan for the future. Similarly, as more students enter education and training where fees have risen and student debt has increased, leaving home and moving into independent living has changed.

The 'boomerang generation'?

One of the major impacts of the crisis has been the delayed movement of young people out of the family home. While the age of leaving home has been increasing since 2000, a number of countries are now finding that young people are staying at home longer (Australian Social Trends, 2013; Fry and Passel, 2014; Eurostat, 2015) Recent research in the UK (Figure 9.2) shows that while the population of young people aged 20 to 34 has stayed largely the same, since the recession

Figure 9.2 Young adults aged 20–34 living with parents in the UK, 1996–2013

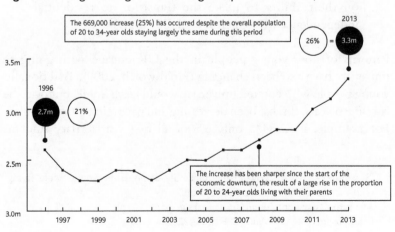

Source: ONS, 2014.

of 2008,[5] the numbers of those living at home have increased by over 25% (ONS, 2014). This is having a greater impact on the unemployed in that 13% of those still living at home are unemployed, compared to 6% of those who have left the family home (ONS, 2014). Clearly, those with low incomes and precarious work are less able to leave the family home (Berrington and Stone, 2013).

These are common trends. In the US, more young adults aged between 25 and 34 are living with multiple generations. By 2012, roughly one in four young adults (23.6%) lived in multi-generational households, up from 18.7% in 2007 and 11% in 1980. Again, it is the unemployed and those on insecure incomes with limited futures who tend to stay at home longer (Fry et al, 2014). In Australia a similar trend has been developing. In 2012–13, 31% of people aged 18 to 34 had never left their parental home to live elsewhere. This was an increase from 27% in 2006–7).[6] Living in the family home for longer has therefore continued to increase throughout the recession in some of the hardest hit countries. Alongside unemployment and insecurity, other major contributing factors have been the continued reduction of welfare and social benefit support for the young, the lack of cheap available housing, and limited opportunities, especially for poor young people to get into the housing market (Berrington and Stone, 2013). As a recent study into the interrelationship between precariousness in the labour market and residential independence shows:

> Almost all the indicators of precariousness were found to be associated with a higher likelihood of living in the parental home, suggesting that these young adults face constraints on their ability to make the transition to residential independence. (Berrington et al, 2014, p.1)

Patterns of how young people in the UK engage with going to university have also been changing (Holdsworth, 2009). Traditionally, young people who entered university would leave home, but over the last fifteen years, this has been decreasing and becoming more complex. For example, in 1984/5 only 8% of all first-year tertiary students

---

[5]   See: http://www.ons.gov.uk/ons/rel/family-demography/young-adults-living-with-parents/2013/sty-young-adults.html

[6]   See: http://www.abs.gov.au/ausstats/abs@.nsf/Latestproducts/4442.0Main%20Features22012-13?opendocument&tabname=Summary&prodno=4442.0&issue=2012-13&num=&view=

stayed at home, but by 2007 this figure had increased to 20% (HEFC, 2009). It was primarily young women and young people from lower SES groups that stayed at home while doing a degree (HEFC, 2009). How the increased participation of low-to-middle-income students, alongside the increased tuition fees for higher education, is affecting the ways young people organise their living arrangements remains unclear, although it would suggest that more young people will stay at home (Berrington and Stone, 2013). Of course such an issue is also not always relevant in other countries such as New Zealand, Australia and Canada, where young people tend to go to their local universities rather than travel long distances.

The process of leaving home has become increasingly complex. Rugg et al (2004) identified five different housing pathways that existed among a wide range of young people in the UK, and Jones (2001) proposes we think about young people's relationship with leaving home as a housing career. However, more recently, the focus has been on the 'boomerang generation'. This concept has been popularised in the media, along with the idea that all young people are now using the family home as a place to find safety and to relaunch themselves (Barrington and Stone, 2013a; Sage et al, 2013). What is suggested is that the strategy of 'boomeranging', where young people move in and out of the family home over a prolonged period of time, operates as a safety net towards securing permanent independent living (Sage et al, 2013). It can then be seen as a part of the increase of the 'yo-yo generation', where the young are constantly on the move (Walther, 2006). For example, in Australia the numbers who have left the family home and then returned at some stage have been increasing (Warner et al, 2012). Similarly, Mitchell (2006) and Iacovou and Parisi (2009) showed a more frequent rate of return for young adults in Southern European countries, Canada, the USA and the UK, than for those in countries such as Germany. As has been noted, 'an increasing degree of financial independence via regular employment increases the likelihood that they will pay their own living costs and live away from the parental home permanently' (Berngruber, 2015, p.13). Those living in rural areas also face substantial difficulties in moving out of the family home (Jones, 2001). However, the lack of detailed evidence makes it difficult to assess how prevalent 'boomeranging' is among the young, especially across national borders. What is clear is that there seems to have been an increase of groups using this method as a way of managing the impact of the recession (Stone et al, 2011) and that those with degree qualifications are 'boomeranging' more than others (Sage et al, 20012). Stone et al (2011) showed that holding a higher education qualification was in fact the strongest determinant of a young person returning to the family home. In a UK-based study, graduates leaving university would undertake between five and eight moves before they found permanent accommodation. In the first instance, over 32.7% would return to the family home after graduating and they would stay for a year or more, with 12.2% staying for over five years. From this base they were likely to move to other parts of the country in the search for work (Sage et al, 2013). A large proportion would return to their graduating city and others would eventually end up in London. Throughout this process the young graduates showed evidence of a 'double boomerang' effect (Sage et al, 747), where they would move back to the family home, finding it a place of safety and somewhere that helped them financially. For example, of those who returned, 56% lived rent free, 54.9% did not contribute to household bills and 57.7% received meals at no cost. Short-term stays of less than three months (17.4%) or 3–6 months (15.6%) were also common. In fact over 50% returned to the family home in a five-year period, which suggests that over 320,000 graduates were likely to return home on a regular basis (Sage et al, 2013). What was not explored in this study was the different nature of these experiences depending on SES, gender or ethnicity. Overall, the evidence suggests that those with a higher qualification and from higher SES groups are more likely to leave home permanently sooner than those from lower SES groups (Stone et al, 2011).

One final point to recognise is how the media have started to represent and construct this debate. For example, a number of national newspapers have focused on the increased problems the 'returnees' are creating for their parents (Sage et al, 2013). *The Independent* newspaper raised questions over KIPPERS ('Kids in Parents' Pockets Eroding Retirement Savings', 17 June 2007). Others have focused on the Nesters, that is, those who become comfortable in the family home and refuse to leave, creating increased intergenerational conflict and a financial burden on parents, limiting their ability to enjoy their lifestyle of choice (Centre for Modern Family, 2014). In Japan, this debate created a moral panic over 'freeters' in the early 2000s. They were associated with a national scare in the media over young people's diminishing commitment to work. Statistics seemed to suggest that over 2 million had adopted a stay-at-home lifestyle that included working part time (Toivonen, 2013). Panic over youth staying at home increased when it was argued that there was a class of young people defined as 'parasite singles', usually young women who delayed marriage and enjoyed a 'life of luxury and leisure at the expense of their hard-working parents' (Toivonen, 2013, p.13). As we saw in

Chapter Eight, these panics in Japan were not supported by evidence and were usually related to middle-class anxieties over the growth of youth unemployment.

Mobility: migration and movement across borders

In this final section we explore the impact of the crisis and the great recession that followed on youth migration. As Bauman suggested: 'mobility has become the most powerful and most coveted stratifying factor' in the world today (1998, p.9). Those who are mobile and freely move around the globe can gain substantial privilege and advantage while the losers are relegated to poverty and insecurity (Bauman, 1998). As we will see, these patterns are clearly evident today among the young, with some able to move while others have limited economic, cultural or social capital. Some who do move also find themselves in situations that can be as bad if not worse than the ones they left. Migration does not always pay the dividends that many would hope for (United Nations, 2013).

The reasons for migration are complex and many, but a number of important trends can be seen that are clearly linked to recent events. Migration is becoming one way in which the young have responded to the crisis. There are many forms of migrants and many ways they can be categorised. In this discussion we will focus on international migrants and those young people who move across national borders. International migrants are those defined as 'any person who changes his or her country of usual residence ... for a period of at least 12 months', although international figures also tend to include short-term migrants who stay for a period longer than 3 months but shorter than 12 months[7] (United Nations, 2013, p.20). This can include undocumented or irregular migrants,[8] refugees and asylum seekers. Importantly for our discussion, these definitions also include international students.

International migration has been increasing over the last thirty years; the number of migrants has grown from 154 million in 1990 to 175 million in 2000, 221 million in 2010 and 232 million in 2013, the latest year for which data are available. Young people are more likely to migrate than older people (Cortina et al, 2014). The age

---

[7] Not including visits that are for recreation, holiday visits to friends and relatives, business, medical treatment or religious pilgrimage.

[8] These are usually illegal and 'in violation of the regulations on entry and residence, either when entering or after having entered the country' (United Nations, 2013, p.20).

distribution of migrants peaks in the middle to late twenties, with most being between 23 and 27 (Cortina et al, 2014). Young people aged between 15 and 24 have accounted, on average, for one in four of all international migrants. Over 28.2 million young people aged 15 to 24 migrated in 2013 (Cortina et al, 2014). In 2013, developed countries had approximately 59% of all international migrants and almost half of these were aged between 15 and 24 (49%). The largest numbers were living in Asia (10.3 million – 36% of all migrants), Europe (7.3 million – 26%) and North America (5.4 million – 19%). However, youth migration was not simply a movement of youth from developing to developed nations. Strong evidence also shows movement across developing nations and between developing and least developed nations (United Nations, 2013). Migration is also regional: in Japan most migrants are from the South Asian region (China and Korea); in the UK and Norway they are mainly from Europe; and Australia and New Zealand share migrants, in that many New Zealanders and Australians work across the national borders of the two countries (OECD, 2013c). There are also significant gender differences; young men are more likely to migrate than young women (Cortina et al, 2014). Across the globe 46.5% of 15–24-year-olds who migrate are women. This has remained reasonably consistent over time and, while there has been a decrease of women migrating to developing and less developed nations, the proportion of women migrating to developed countries has remained reasonably stable over time (Cortina et al, 2014).

So why do young people migrate? Decisions to migrate are not simply related to 'pull and push' factors. 'Migration is a process involving various family members and other acquaintances which together create a broader form of community which stretches beyond borders' (Geisen, 2010, p.12). In fact migration itself needs to be recognised within a life-course analysis that shows how it connects to the life planning and biography-building that may see it leading to a permanent move over a longer period of time (Geisen, 2010). Decisions to migrate are not taken lightly; they are usually strongly related to the young making major life transitions, especially around getting an education, a job and getting married or building a family. A core factor is often comparisons between the opportunities they perceive in their own countries and those of the countries they move to:

> Often, the main driving force behind youth migration
> (particularly international migration) is the magnitude
> of perceived inequalities in labour market opportunities,
> income, human rights and living standards between the

countries of origin and destination. (Cortina et al, 2014, p.22)

Throughout the economic crisis and the early years of the recession that hit most of the developed countries, migration either dropped or stagnated. The use and uptake of temporary labour was stagnant across OECD countries and a number of nations increased restrictions on labour movement to help protect local workers, but by 2010 countries started to relax temporary labour restrictions or introduce new legislation as a way of creating an international temporary 'reserve army' that was flexible and available for local employers as economies tried to rebuild. Poland, for example, received labour migrants from the Ukraine and introduced new legislation in 2012 that saw the criteria relaxed, allowing increased numbers.

Similar changes took place in Australia and New Zealand, where new legislation was introduced that allows more seasonal and temporary workers into both countries. This has seen a sharp increase of temporary migrants in Australia and a 7% increase in seasonal workers in New Zealand (OECD, 2013c). Apart from Spain, all of our case study countries have seen an increase in temporary and/or seasonal workers from 2011. Even Norway has begun to see a strong influx of labour migrants, with a 13% increase in 2011. Its strong economy has attracted a large number of Polish young people and other Europeans. Spain is the exception; since the economic crisis there has been a huge drop in the number of migrants entering the country, with levels 55% lower in 2011 than in 2007. There has also been a recent trend of existing migrants leaving Spain, alongside a small but growing number of Spanish nationals also leaving the country to look for work overseas (OECD, 2013c).

The crisis has, however, increased the risk of unemployment for migrants who arrive with low levels of skills and, at the same time, there has been a growing trend to reduce social rights and access to benefits for temporary migrants. On average, the unemployment rate among migrant populations worldwide increased by 5% between 2008 and 2010, compared to 3% for native citizens. Unsurprisingly, young people have been hit the hardest, especially if they have low education and poor language skills (United Nations, 2013). This is not simply a result of the recession as it is historically a fact of the migrant experience (Cortina et al, 2014). For example, young Polish workers in the UK have historically tended to be overqualified, underpaid and working in some of the most insecure and temporary jobs (Migration Advisory Committee, 2014). This trend continued throughout the recession.

In the UK, approximately 60% of migrants (2.1 million in 2013) are in low-skilled jobs. Of these, 1.2 million come from non-European Union (EU) countries. Since 2010 there has also been a large increase in migrant workers in the UK coming from Spain, Portugal and Italy; again they tend to be employed in low-paid occupations (Migration Advisory Committee, 2014). Migrants who have stayed in Spain have also suffered badly as a result of the crisis and recession. Spain has a very high rate of unemployment. The impact has been even harsher among the migrant population. For example, the average rate of unemployment among migrant workers in Spain is 36.5% compared to 24% for Spanish nationals. This was even higher among the young. While Spain has not made any legislative changes with regard to migration, the harsher implementation of the existing registration system has seen permanent renewal visas, family reunification and temporary work visas harder to get. As a way of supporting migrants, Spain has helped them to maintain their legal status, although some reforms have restricted their right to certain health benefits (OECD, 2013c).

However, it is important to recognise that migrants are not just poor people trying to find a new life. One of the growth areas in migration has been the movement of an affluent middle class who have wealth to spend and invest. Evidence shows that large numbers of migrants are highly skilled and bring with them substantial economic resources to set up businesses or invest (United Nations, 2013). In countries such as New Zealand, Australia and Canada, highly skilled migrants are also sought after to overcome skill shortages. For example, in New Zealand, with the rebuilding of Christchurch after the earthquake, a major recruitment drive has been necessary (alongside legislative changes) that has brought thousands of skilled builders to the country (OECD, 2013c). Australia also makes special provision for those migrants within skill shortage areas, and recent legislation created special sponsorship for 1,700 migrants in the iron ore industry in Western Australia. Australia has the second highest number of migrants per unit of population of all OECD countries (New Zealand has the fourth highest, and Canada the fifth highest) and is strongly reliant on migrants to fill skill gaps. It has a strong pool of migrants who have degrees and other higher qualifications and are working in sectors that require specialised skills. Many of its migrants are earning good incomes and making major contributions to the economy (Miranti et al, 2010). However, there remains a large pool of young workers who tend to be low-skilled, temporary, underemployed and on low pay (Miranti et al, 2010).

As noted, there has been an increase in middle-class migrants who are able to self-finance and buy into businesses and property. Countries such as the UK, Japan, Canada and Australia have extended their skill categories. For example, Japan created a preferential channel for highly skilled foreigners. This gives special treatment to those with high skills, such as academics, researchers, doctors and corporate executives, but tests of language and work experience requirements have also been increased (OECD, 2013c). The growth of middle-class migration is strongly fueled by Asia and China in particular. It is claimed that over 10 million Chinese people migrated in 2013, and over 60% of them had over US$1.5 million in assets (Rietig, 2014).

> the primary destinations for Chinese elites are the United States, Canada, Australia, New Zealand, and European countries. Investor and skilled worker visas are among the preferred routes for this emerging emigrant class. (Rietig, 2014, p.1)

Over 80,000 Chinese people migrated to Australia on either skilled worker visas or employer- sponsored visas between 2009 and 2012. Many were from the new emerging middle class, with large economic resources[9] (Alongside this, since 2008, a number of nation states have introduced or increased entrepreneurial categories. In the UK, Australia, New Zealand and Canada, major changes have taken place in the availability of visas for entrepreneurs who want to start up businesses. In Australia, the 'Business Innovative Stream' was set up in 2012. This requires migrants to have AU$800,000 and substantial experience in starting up businesses. Australia also introduced a special category that aims to provide entry if a person is bringing in a business and has also created an economic migrant category that gives easy access to entry if potential migrants have AU$5 million to invest. This has seen over 700 new permanent residents arrive in Australia, of whom 90% are from the Chinese middle class.[10] In the UK, entrepreneurs with at least £200,000 of their own money plus investment from a UK source will be granted a visa. Canada and New Zealand have similar

---

9   http://www.economist.com/news/china/21601305-more-middle-classes-are-leaving-search-cleaner-slower-life-yearning-breathe

10   http://www.economist.com/news/china/21601305-more-middle-classes-are-leaving-search-cleaner-slower-life-yearning-breathe

criteria[11] that allow people with economic capital to enter. There are also success criteria, which usually include job creation and increased profits, but those with the resources are able to get 'special treatment' (Sumption, 2012). In other words, if a person has substantial economic resources, they can 'buy' entry. Of course, most of these migrants will be older and already have established their wealth. For countries such as Australia, New Zealand, Canada and the UK, attracting the more wealthy migrants has been a core strategy in increasing private sector development.

International student migration

Globally, the largest group of migrants is international students. As part of their search for new incomes and markets, universities around the world have developed a strategy of recruiting more overseas students (Olssen and Peters, 2005). As we saw in Chapter Four, as neoliberal policies and pressures reduce the public funding of higher education sectors, universities need to seek out new sources of income (Streitwieser, 2014). In 2012, UK university sector funding sourced from non-European registrations was £3.5 billion. Since 2008, there has been year-on-year growth, and income non-European registrations has risen from 8% to 12% of all university income (Universities UK, 2014). Governments not only support this strategy (as it reduces state costs of public education) but also use it as a way of trying to attract highly skilled graduates to their shores (Choudaha and De Wit, 2014). For example, over 25% of all international students tend to remain in the countries where they are educated, in many cases creating a highly skilled workforce (Sykes, 2012). Universities in the US, UK and Australia have also set about developing campuses and courses in other countries. For example, over 600,000 such students were registered on UK-supported degree programmes in 2012. Similarly the development of online courses has been seen as a future growth area for capturing international student income (Universities UK, 2014).

However, the drives and the 'pull' factors related to why young people study abroad are complex and not always clearly understood. There can be substantial differences in both choice and resources between young people coming from developing or developed economies. There are also class differences that affect where they may end up. Some, with less resources, will end up in universities with low fees and poorer records

---

[11]   Although New Zealand does not have a set limit – the system works on a case-by-case basis.

of success, while others will be able to enter better universities as a result of financial help from their families. This is not a level playing field, yet little is known about how this situation affects the lives of the young (Choudaha and De Wit, 2014). For example, writing about student mobility within the UK, Holdsworth argues that we need to recognise that 'differential experiences of stasis/mobility [of students] not only reflect access to resources, but mobility strategies can reinforce inequalities in education experiences and outcomes' (2009, p.1852). This suggests that we need to try to understand more about the power differentials between international student groups and also their relationships with the receiving countries. As yet, little research has explored young people's reasons for moving to another country or the circumstances that may have influenced their decisions to be mobile. Most research explores their experience of the systems and country they arrive in. Yet, as we shall see below, this is a massive growth area in youth mobility.

While migration for paid work slowed on average across the globe, the numbers migrating to get higher education qualifications increased by up to 6% during the recession (OECD, 2014a). Clearly young people, especially from some of the developing countries, saw the global market place created by the internationalisation of the higher education sector as a way of improving their life chances and future work prospects, although this had already been a growing trend for a number of years. For example, in 2000 over 2 million students were enrolled outside their country of citizenship; by 2005 the number had reached 3 million and by 2008 it was 3.5 million. After the crisis, the number jumped to over 4.3 million in 2011 (OECD, 2014a). The countries that received the most students were the US (16.5%), the UK (13%) and Germany (6.3%). European countries accounted for over 40% of all students studying abroad, although 75% of these were from countries within the eurozone. North America (US and Canada) was the second most popular place to study, with 21% of international students. However, 57% of Canadians studying abroad study in the US and 15% of Americans study in Canada (OECD, 2014a). In Australia, New Zealand and the UK, international students now represent over 10% of the graduate student body and over 30% of enrolments in advanced programmes of study (OECD, 2014a). This is partly a result of government and university strategies. For example, in Australia international students accounted for 37% of all temporary migrants entering the country in 2011, which was a 1% increase (over 2,500 more students than the previous year). Australia also implemented new visa regulations that aimed to streamline and improve the application process while giving migrants the right to work (OECD, 2014a). Not all international students go into degree or higher degree programmes. In New Zealand only 60% of international students go into degree-type programmes, with 32%[12] entering vocational programmes. Similar trends can be seen in Spain (51% in degree and 30.7% in vocational) and Japan (68% in degree and 22% in vocational).

Asian students are the biggest movers into OECD and G20 countries, with 53% of all international students being from this region of the world. The proportion of Asian students in the international student population is highest in Japan (93%), Australia (81%) and New Zealand (68%). In total, 21% of all Asian students are from China and 25% of them study in the US. The second largest group of international students comes from India (6.5%). European students tend to be highly concentrated in European countries although they account for 23.1% of all international students (OECD, 2014a).

In terms of costs to students, living in a foreign country is a huge investment for most, although the fees for being an international student vary by country. In the UK and Poland, international students pay higher fees than domestic students, although eurozone citizens are treated the same as UK and Polish citizens and only pay domestic fees. In Australia, New Zealand and Canada all international students pay higher fees than domestic students, while in Norway (and Finland and Iceland) there are no tuition fees for international students. Spain and Japan charge international students the same fees as domestic students (OECD, 2014a). International students also have their opportunities to work restricted, meaning that funding has to come from parents, savings or national loans. Scholarships have always been a key way of helping students manage the high costs of overseas education, but these have become more restricted since the 2008 crisis (OECD, 2014a).

Conclusion

This chapter has explored the impact of the crisis and the great recession that followed on young people's mobility. While mobility can be understood in a variety of ways, no matter how it is approached it has become more central to the process of growing up. As we saw with the growth of inequality, social mobility for the young within nation states has become increasingly difficult. Not only is there growing intergenerational inequality of access to resources between the old and the young but also certain forms of inequalities for those aged 15 to 25

---

[12] This figure does not include students who are entering higher degree programmes.

remain entrenched, even in times of rapid social change. In accepting a Bourdieusian model of class in our analysis we have seen, in a number of the discussions in previous chapters, not only clear economic differences within and across the younger generation but also how cultural and social capital operates to help either maintain privilege or increase disadvantage. These patterns of winners and losers among the young continue when we examine patterns of leaving home. Clearly, leaving home and becoming independent has become more difficult for the young since the 2007 crisis. Again, there are clear differences between those who have the resources to be mobile and those who do not. Having financial and cultural resources allows young people to be able to engage in 'yo-yo' activities, moving back and forth from the family home, knowing they have a safety net, usually provided by parents, which makes it easier for them both to maintain periods of independent living and move to areas where some of the best jobs are located. Finally, the largest movement of the young is those crossing international borders as migrants, with over 28 million young people moving in 2013. There are two drivers for this. The first is the search for work and the second the seeking out of a good education. In terms of work, the young tend to arrive as temporary workers, as they do not have the wealth to fund migration as entrepreneurs; this makes them more vulnerable. While there was an initial drop in migrant labour post-2007, we are now seeing it increase again, although new patterns are emerging in which young people from the Southern European states are moving to other countries in search for work. However, the fastest area of growth has been in student mobility and, while we do not know enough about the drivers and how they contribute to (or address) inequality, it is clear that young people, especially from the Asian region, are seeing studying overseas as a way of acquiring the cultural capital to find jobs in a highly competitive environment. What impact this has on their host nations (or the countries they leave) requires more investigation.

TEN

After the crisis: social change and what it means to be young

This book emerged out of an interest in filling a 'gap' in youth sociology. As outlined in Chapter One, while there has recently been significant attention to the concept of youth agency, there has been less systematic focus on the concepts of 'structures' and the 'structuring processes' that create the environment that young people have to manage today. By drawing on eight case study countries in the advanced economies, we have explored the current political ecological context for young people aged 16 to 24. For these young people, the post-school field of practice is structured by the interplay of specific local, national and international activities that have embedded within them cultural norms and understandings of 'the rules of the game' regarding how life should be organised (Bourdieu, 1993a). Within this environment a number of subfields operate separately but must be seen in relation to each other, constructing the pathways that are available to young people (France et al, 2012). For this age group, work, training, education and the social welfare system are core institutional aspects of life, and bring with them their own structural arrangements. A range of processes and practices then operate at the macro, meso, exo and micro levels to influence the everyday social life of the young. As I have suggested throughout the discussion, to understand the social and political processes that underpin developments in these areas, we need to recognise the role of youth policy and capital, and the relationship between the two. The activities of the state, corporations and private sector business all shape young people's post-school experience (Ball, 2008).

This book has shown that the field of education, training, work and welfare for those young people who leave compulsory schooling has undergone significant changes over the past thirty years, which have been further accelerated as a result of the global crisis in 2007 and the expansion of a range of austerity measures that followed. What is evident is that not all of the changes discussed in this book can be attributed to the crisis or austerity alone, although what can be claimed is that both of these have accelerated processes that have been in place for a number of years. By drawing on material from eight different national contexts, we have identified how embedded and extensive some of these changes have been. Writers and researchers in the field of youth sociology have been drawing our attention to this for some years (du Bois-Reymond, 1998; Dwyer and Wyn, 2001: Furlong and Cartmel, 2007; Walther, 2006; Wyn and Woodman, 2006; MacDonald, 2011; Antonucci et al, 2014), highlighting how some of the processes we have explored here have infiltrated the lives of young people in different parts of the world. A number of trends have been identified throughout the book. While there are clearly variations across and even within countries in how these are experienced, all of the eight countries examined in this book have been introducing changes in post-compulsory schooling that were significantly restructuring what it means to be young. These changes are as follows.

1. *The growth and expansion of education and training.* As have seen, not only in our case study areas but globally, education and training have become a fundamental aspect of the experience of young people aged 16 to 24. It is clear that in this highly competitive labour market young people believe that qualifications make a difference. This is reinforced by the political discourses and narratives around social policy that suggest those without qualifications are being irresponsible and increasing their risk of being unemployed and poor. Not only have young people increased their participation but there has also been a fundamental shift in 'who pays', in that we are now seeing the responsibility for paying for education and training is now fundamentally with the individual. The reconfiguring of education and training to be the dominant field for the young started as early as the 1980s and it has continued to grow in all of our eight case study countries. As we saw, the crisis has not slowed this process; in fact, since 2010, young people's involvement in education and training has grown even faster than before. As we saw in Chapter Nine, there was also a massive increase in young people travelling to our core case study countries as migrants throughout the great recession, accessing local educational institutions as a way of trying to increase their opportunities for high quality work in the future. As national states have increased opportunities to participate, who benefits still remains strongly shaped by class, gender and race.

2. *Unemployment and underemployment.* High unemployment among the young is not a new phenomenon. For example, youth unemployment in most of our countries (and most of the globe) has been an ongoing problem, especially since the late 1990s; while there was a period of improvement in the mid-2000s, the 2007 crisis and recession that followed pushed the rates back up to levels that were

evident in 2000. In times of crisis, young people are always hit the hardest and this has clearly been the case in our case study countries. Almost universally, youth unemployment increased at a faster rate than adult unemployment from 2008 onwards. We have seen that the level and impact of unemployment (and its continuation) is mediated by the local context. However, this is not simply a problem of unemployment, but one of underemployment that is being embedded as a social problem. As young people have increased their skills and qualifications, the jobs they were led to believe would emerge in the knowledge economy have not appeared. As a result, we see a large number of graduates unemployed or underemployed for the level of qualification they have. One of the major strategies in most of our case study countries is the use of apprenticeships. These now tend to be almost completely funded by national governments; consequently, what we see is the private sector getting huge subsidies as a way of tackling the youth unemployment problem. Again, the impacts of unemployment and underemployment are not evenly distributed. The most vulnerable suffer most, especially in those countries that have been removing social protection and increasing the responsibilising agenda of neoliberalism.

3. *The growth of non-standard and precarious work.* Since the late 1990s, there has been a massive expansion of 'precarious' and insecure work. While large numbers of young people have always worked in occupations that are temporary and insecure, with wages that are lower than those of older groups, this has been growing to the extent that young people are more likely than any other group to be employed on these types of contracts. Even in countries with strong forms of social protection (Norway) and a history of structured and secure transitions into work (Japan) we have seen temporary and part-time work becoming normalised. This has been partly driven by the 'need' of business and enterprise to have a flexible workforce, which has then been supported by legislative changes to increase flexible working. We have seen country after country re-regulating the youth labour market, increasing legislation that gives employers greater control over their workforce. While the movement of migrant temporary labour decreased through the first part of the great recession, it has subsequently been growing, again supported by legislative changes on immigration. New jobs for the young in most countries hit hard by the crisis have also been mainly either temporary or part-time. Graduate work and well-paid work has been slow to grow in most countries. In fact, as the recession took hold, the expansion of zero contracts and internships became

a normal way of young people getting experience and a foothold in the labour market. Unfortunately, many of these unpaid or low-paid experiences bring no guarantees of subsequent full-time employment. It those with extensive cultural and social capital who are most able to navigate their way through the complex challenges this context produces. If you come from a privileged background, your chances of maintaining your class position in this process are enhanced by such resources.

4. *Complex lives, fragmented transitions, 'yo-yo' lifestyles and increased mobility.* Notions of a standardised transition or single pathways into work have been challenged throughout this analysis. For many young people, the simple method of leaving school and getting a job does not seem to exist in any of the case study countries. Life is complex and young people find themselves consistently having to manage their lives and make decisions about the next stage. This brings them into 'yo-yo' lifestyles in a wide range of areas. Many move into education and training, then periods of unemployment, back to education, and then into a job. As we saw, many are being churned around the system, finding no way of breaking into the stable futures they desire. Even those with more resources and qualifications are finding it increasingly difficult; they may have up to five jobs before they find a career of choice, and this can take anything between five and ten years to achieve. Many of those in education are also having to combine work with study. The simple distinction between one subfield and another is becoming more blurred. The 'yo-yo' lifestyle can also be seen in the ways the young are trying to manage their movement to some form of independent living. Moving in and out of the family home over time as a way of managing the insecurity of the labour market has become a strategy common to many young people. As a result, many are not leaving home until their late twenties and early thirties. Youth migration has also been on the rise. Even though it stalled after the crisis, young people are increasingly seeing the need to search beyond national borders to find security. Again, who can participate in this context and who has the resources to take risks is influenced by the social and cultural capital they either possess or have access to.

Youth and citizenship after the crisis

The impact of these changes is significant. As we saw in Chapters Two and Seven, young people's experience of being and becoming citizens has been strongly influenced since the 1990s in countries such as the UK, Australia, New Zealand, Canada and Poland by the neoliberalisation of public policy. Again, since the crisis this process has been accelerated. Even in our other three countries, these principles and ideas have influenced political views of how economies and civil societies should be organised. Clearly countries such as Norway, Japan and Spain have a form of citizenship for the young that has been conceived and enacted in particular ways as a result of their histories, culture and political ideologies, yet even in those countries, policy is actively helping to create neoliberal citizens. The concept of austerity popularised in the crisis and great recession is another word for neoliberal economic and social policies. Resistance is slowly eroding; approaches to getting the young back to work (through the introduction of active labour markets policies [ALMPs]) and various welfare programmes, especially since the 2007 crisis, are underpinned by and emphasise neoliberal principles. While not all of our case study areas have bought in to the ideology and principles of neoliberalism, it is clear that there is a growing hegemony and rationality that suggests there is now only one way of tackling the problems created by the crisis. As we have seen with the recent cases of Greece and Spain, even those countries that resist or reject the idea of neoliberalism through austerity are finding themselves forced by loan requirements or international pressure to conform to such practices. As the crisis unfolded, neoliberalism became not only the dominant economic and social doctrine driving policy; it also became normalised and embedded in national psyches as the way to solve the problem. There seems to be no alternative. As we saw in Chapter Two, the causes of this crisis were the actions of bankers and unregulated financial sectors, yet when it comes to blame, state spending or the actions of individual benefit claimants are consistently portrayed in political discourses – and accepted by large sections of the public – as the problems to be tackled.

Welfare regimes are among the significant institutional arrangements that are shaping young people's life paths (Heinz, 2009) and, as we have seen, major changes have taken place in all our case study countries, conferring different rights and responsibilities, and creating different models of semi-dependence or semi-independence (Walther, 2006). As we saw in Spain, the strong familism embedded both ideologically and culturally has produced a distinctive welfare model in the Southern European states (Micheli and Rosina, 2009). While the use of welfare regimes is useful in thinking about how states operate, such concepts have limitations in the present climate. In trying to make sense of the clustering of welfare regimes, they focus more on outcomes than on process (Antonucci et al, 2014). A better way of conceptualising the organisation of welfare in different states is recognising the 'welfare mix'. This helps to clarify 'how the different combination of welfare sources in each country leads to different levels of de-commodification and de-familisation in young people's lives' (Antonucci et al, 2014, p.57). In this context we need to recognise how welfare is being delivered across the state, the market and the family, although I suggest we also need to recognise how young people are now having to provide their own welfare, especially in terms of 'taking responsibility'.

The commodification of youth citizenship

As we have seen in the discussions throughout this book, one of the major drivers in economic and welfare provision has been the increased use of neoliberal policies and practices in constructing the architecture of the state. New ways of organising welfare provision across education, training, employment services and welfare support have arisen and expanded throughout the crisis. For example, we see quasi markets and increased competition in education and other social welfare organisations, a massive unregulated subsidising of the private sector to provide apprenticeships and training, a re-regulation of the youth labour market towards flexibility and the privatisation of a wide range of welfare services, including the introduction of payment by results, which has seen youth policy in all of our eight countries being reconfigured in some way in relation to market principles. Welfare services are now more likely than ever before to be delivered and operated around market principles, with the private sector more likely to be providers of services. Even in Norway, a strongly social democratic nation with a well-established welfare state, we see services contracted out to the private sector. While the state may commission and even pay for welfare services, their delivery by the private sector is common. As a result, young people find themselves continually in some form of *market relationship*, being either a commodity or a purchaser, where failure to succeed is then seen as their own fault.

There has been increased use of ALMPs targeted at the vulnerable. ALMPs have been among the fastest growing and strongest policy areas targeting the young. During the recession, countries increased the resourcing of such programmes to try to tackle the unemployment problem. Anxiety over the problem, of NEETS (those not in employment, education and training) alongside the desire to find solutions to the problem of youth unemployment, have seen the growth of ALMPs across those countries with a more liberal tradition (the UK, Australia, New Zealand and Canada). They have tended to construct policies around a narrative of problem youth, creating programmes that not only individualise the problem of unemployment but also have sanctions and punishments embedded in them as a way of forcing young people into jobs that may not be ones they would choose or suitable for them. Those more social democratic states such as Norway and even Spain buy into such programmes less and tend to see them more as a way of supporting the young back into work, yet they still see them as the way to do business. It is clear that across the advanced economies, paid work is now a core obligation of citizenship and the only option, regardless of its quality. Without it, the present and future is increasingly precarious for young people as state benefits and support are now being continually eroded and withdrawn. As neoliberal governments in a number of our case study countries take stronger hold, this is becoming more obvious. After the crisis, this strategy accelerated as a part of the austerity programmes, especially in countries such as the UK, with less resources being made available and more sanctions being imposed for non-compliance. For example, recent announcements in the 2015 budget statement in the UK saw proposals to remove all housing benefits for young people under the age of 21 and to restrict access to a higher minimum wage to those over the age of 25.

Privatisation of responsibility and inequality

Finally, what we have seen throughout the discussions in this book is growing evidence of 'a shift in emphasis from social responsibilities to private responsibilities … [that] reflects neoliberal governmental style of thinking about and acting on problems' (Ilcan, 2009, p.203). This privatisation of responsibility exists not only in structural arrangements (shifting responsibility onto individuals or others) but also in the level of ideas and discourses about how social life should be organised (Ilcan, 2009). It can transform the way that relationships between groups are configured and can limit other options. For example, it can reconfigure gender relationships, family practices (especially around the provision of support), and the social obligations of individuals. It forms what is a climate of normality around responsibility (Antonucci et al, 2014) or a 'responsibility ethos' (Ilcan, 2009, p.209), creating a form of citizenship that shapes the choices and options young people may have. Traditionally, the social welfare model that had great influence between the 1970s and 1990s in many advanced economies was largely concerned with 'shifting harm and risk from the level of the individual citizen, groups, and firms to society' (Ilcan, 2009, p.210). Since then, the state has been increasingly reconfigured towards market principles, where citizens must become 'more self-disciplined, multi-skilled, entrepreneurial and resilient' (Stasiulis and Bakan, 2003, p.22), while the state also uses institutional changes to provide new definitions of responsible citizens (Ilcan, 2009). This ethos of responsibility is not simply a reworking of the state but '…new ways of thinking and acting, which stress a neoliberal governing rationality' (Ilcan, 2009, p.212), where '…individuals make choices, pursue references and seek to maximise the quality of their lives' (Ilcan, 2009, p.213).

Of course, placing responsibility on the young and their families through youth policy is not new (Kelly, 2000; Antonucci et al, 2014), but what we have been seeing, especially since the 2007 crisis and throughout the great recession, is an expansion of policies and practices across our eight case study areas that shift the responsibility to the individual and towards the families of the young, especially in relation to the 16-plus age group. For example, in Australia and Canada the state has been trying to make parents responsible if their children do not participate in the new compulsory educational arrangements for 16–18-year-olds. Similarly, it is being proposed that in the future income support for under-22-year-olds in Australia will be paid to the family, not the young person, and that its availability will be determined by the parent's income, not the young person's needs. Some of these shifts towards parental responsibility for the young have also been emerging through the removal of social benefits to the young. For example, the new UK conservative government's plan to remove access to housing benefits for young people under the age of 21 means that they have no support available other than that of parents when leaving the family home, and if they stay at home then the expectation is that parents will continue to support them.

The growing responsibilities within the family for the young, particularly for their welfare needs and for the support they may need to manage and negotiate their way through the complex social milieu that now surrounds them after leaving school are greatly shaped by the resources available within families, and the relationships young people have with their parents. Those with parents who have high levels of economic, cultural and social capital are more able to negotiate their way through the system. It is relevant that a strong focus in higher education policy across a number of our eight countries has been on widening participation and this has targeted young people from families with no history of entering university. These parents do not have the social networks or cultural capital to help their children in the system. Throughout the expansion of higher education it has been the middle classes that have benefited and been able to use it to maintain their position of privilege (Elias and Purcell, 2012), and even when opportunities for extra financial support have been developed, those from middle-class backgrounds have been able to benefit more than those from low socioeconomic status (SES) groups (Harrison and Hatt, 2012).

Similar patterns have emerged over how parents can and do help young people into work. As we saw, middle-class parents have been exceptionally good at helping their children to access internships and also in providing resources for them to 'boomerang' in and out of the family home, providing cheap living and also a safety net and a place to re-energise (Sage et al, 2013). These examples are strong indicators of how parents from different classes can draw upon their own cultural and social capital to help (or not) their children throughout the post-school period. However, there remains much we do not know about other ways this may happen. For example, there is anecdotal evidence of parents paying university fees, buying their young people houses to live in and rent out while at university, and helping them with deposits to ensure they get into the housing market. These are not only helping, in many cases, to maintain privilege and reinforce inequality between groups, but are a form of wealth transference, ensuring that family resources are passed onto the next generation at an earlier stage.

Conclusion

What we have seen throughout the analysis in this book is that growing up today is complex and, for many young people, exceptionally challenging. Managing expectations that they should be responsible citizens and demands that they should be better qualified while also having to 'pay their way' puts young people under sustained and constant pressure. At the same time, life is clearly precarious; insecurity in employment, high debt and low incomes are now becoming the 'norm'. Managing this on a day-to-day basis is not easy and the risk of failure is high, with the consequences being increased surveillance and sanctions. While welfare policies can provide some form of social protection, especially in those countries that see its value, it is individualised or family forms of social, cultural and economic capital that are now providing the best (and sometimes only) forms of social protection for the young. As we have seen, these are not evenly distributed across social groups; it is clear that winners and losers are being created by the relationship a young person has with these types of resources. It also seems that the future quality of life for some young people is being protected and maintained by parents who can invest in their son or daughter early in their life course. This becomes a form of wealth transference across generations in family households. Yet what we know about this process, especially since the 2007 crisis, is limited. How it operates in the transmission of position and privilege, or disadvantage and exclusion, is still unclear. However, as we have discovered in this analysis, the evidence suggests it is becoming critical in maintaining and perpetuating social inequality *between* and *across* young people aged 16 to 24 years, and it is essential that we gain a better understanding of the likely consequences of current policies relating to this age group.

Finally, how the changes we have identified here are impacting on developing economies across the globe was not a part of this analysis, yet we know that the 2007 global crisis and the great recession that followed had, and is still having, a massive and sustained impact on the poorer nations and especially their young people (ILO, 2013; OECD, 2014a). Levels of inequality between the advanced and developing economies are increasing, and poverty and unemployment among the young remain at endemic levels (OECD, 2015). We are also seeing increasing movements of economic migrants, refugees and asylum seekers in search of security and safety (OECD, 2013c). In such an environment we can be reasonably confident in claiming that growing up through the economic crisis and great recession that followed has had even greater consequences for young people in these developing nations, although what these look like in different countries would need further investigation.

References

Aassve, A., Mazzuco, S., and Mencarini, L. (2005) Childbearing and wellbeing: a comparative analysis of welfare regimes in Europe, *Journal of European Social Policy*, 15, 3 , 283–99

Abbott, M.J. (2004) *Commercial risks and opportunities in the New Zealand tertiary education sector,* Auckland: AIS St Helens, Centre for Research in International Education

ABS (Australian Bureau of Statistics) (2014) 'Exploring the gap in labour market outcomes for Aboriginal and Torres Strait Islander Peoples', available at: www.abs.gov.au/ausstats/abs@.nsf/Lookup/4102.0main+features72014

Ainley, P. (1997) 'Towards a learning or a certified society? Students in Britain', *Youth and Policy*, 4–13

Ainley, P. and Allen, M. (2010) *Lost generation? New strategies for youth and education,* London: Continuum London, International Publishing

Aldridge, H., Kenway, P., MacInnes, T. and Parekh, A. (2012) *Monitoring poverty and social exclusion,* York: Joseph Rowntree Foundation

Allais, S. (2012) '"Economics imperialism", education policy and educational theory', *Journal of Education Policy*, 27, 2, 253–74

Allen, J. (2006) 'Welfare regimes, welfare systems and housing in southern Europe', *International Journal of Housing Policy*, 6, 3, 251–77

Allen, S. (1968) 'Some theoretical problems in the study of youth', *Sociological Review*, 16, 3, 319–31

Anderson, G. and Quinlan, M. (2008) 'The changing role of the state: regulating work in Australia and New Zealand 1788–2007', *Australian Society for the Study of Labour History*, 95, 111–32

Andres, L. (2010) 'New pathways to what? The dynamics of education, work, and family', *Éducation et Sociétés*, 26, 2, 45–69

Andres, L. and Wyn, J. (2010) *The making of a generation: The children of the 1970s in adulthood,* Toronto: University of Toronto Press

Antonucci, L., Hamilton, M. and Roberts, S. (2015) *Young people in Europe: Dealing with risk, inequality and precarity in time of crisis,* London: Palgrave Macmillan

Aoyagi, C., Ganelli, G. and Murayama, K. (2015) *How inclusive is Abenomics?* IMF Working Paper, New York: IMF

Arthur, L. (2006) 'Higher Education and the Knowledge Society: issues, challenges and responses in Norway and Germany', *Research in Comparative and International Education*, 1, 3, 241–51

Ashton, D.N., Maguire, M. and Spilsbury, M. (1990) *Restructuring the labour market: The implications for youth,* London: Macmillan

Atkinson, W. (2010) 'The myth of the reflexive worker: class and work histories in neo-liberal times', *Work, Employment and Society,* 24, 3, 413–29

AUCC (2011) *Trends in higher education,* Canada: Association of Universities and Colleges of Canada

Australian Labor Party (2010) *Creating opportunity, requiring responsibility: Modernising Australia's welfare system,* Canberra: Australian Labor Party

Australian Social Trends (2012) 'Vocational education and training', available at: http://tinyurl.com/jru8lpb

Australian Social Trends (2013) 'Young adults: then and now', available at: www.abs.gov.au/AUSSTATS/abs@.nsf/Lookup/4102.0Main+F eatures40April+2013#livingar

Ball, S.J. (1997) 'Policy sociology and critical social research: a personal review of recent education policy and policy research', *British Educational Research Journal,* 23, 3, 257–74

Ball, S.J. (2008) *The education debate: Policy and politics in the twenty-first century,* Bristol: Policy Press

Ball, S.J. and Exley, S. (2010) 'Making policy with "good ideas": policy networks and the "intellectuals" of New Labour', *Journal of Education Policy,* 25, 2, 151–69

Ban, C. (2011) *Neoliberalism in translation: Economic ideas and reforms in Spain and Romania,* PhD thesis, College Park, University of Maryland

Banting, K. (1987) *Federalism and the welfare state in Canada,* Montreal: McGill-Queen's University Press

Banyuls, J. and Recio, A. (2012) 'Spain: the nightmare of Mediterranean neoliberalism', in *A triumph of failed ideas: The European models of capitalism in crisis,* Brussels, ETUS

Barlett, G. (2014) *Young and restless: A look at the state of youth employment in Canada,* Vancouver: TD Economics

Barone, C. (2011) 'Some things never change: gender segregation in higher education across eight nations and three decades', *Sociology of Education,* 84, 2, 157–76

Bates, I., Clarke, J., Cohen, P., Finn, D., Moore, R. and Willis, P. (1984) *Schooling for the dole? The new vocationalism,* London: Macmillan

Bates, I. and Riseborough, G. (1993) *Youth and inequality,* Milton Keynes: Open University Press

Batterham, J. and Levesley, T. (2011) *New directions: Young people's and parents' views of vocational education and careers guidance,* London: Centre for Skills Development

Bauman, Z. (1998) *Globalization: The human consequences,* New York: Columbia University Press

Beck, U. (1992) *Risk society: Towards a new modernity,* London: Sage

Beeson, M. (2007) 'Competing capitalisms and neoliberalism: the dynamics of, and limits to, economic reform in Asia-Pacific', in K. England and K. Ward (eds) *Neoliberalism: States, networks, people*, Oxford: Blackwell

Belka, M. and Krajewski, S. (1995) 'Polish transformation after 5 years – some general remarks', in M. Belka and H.G. Petersen (eds) *Economic transformation in Poland: Reforms of institutional settings and macroeconomic performance*, New York: Campus Verlag

Bennett, A. (1999) 'Subcultures or neo-tribes? Rethinking the relationship between youth, style and musical taste', *Sociology*, 33, 3, 599–617

Bennett, A. (2011) 'The post-subcultural turn: some reflections 10 years on', *Journal of Youth Studies*, 14, 5, 493–506

Berger, J., Motte, A. and Parkin, A. (2009) *The price of knowledge. Access and student finance in Canada*, Montreal: Canada Millennium Scholarship

Berger, M.T. (1999) 'Feature review – Up from neoliberalism: free-market mythologies and the coming crisis of global capitalism', *Third World Quarterly*, 20, 2, 453–63

Berglund, T. (2010) *Labour market mobility in Nordic welfare states*, Copenhagen: TemaNord, Nordic Council of Ministers

Bernardi, F. and Requena, M. (2010) 'Inequality in educational transitions: the case of post-compulsory education in Spain', *Revista de Educación*, 93–118

Berngruber, A. (2015) '"Generation boomerang" in Germany? Returning to the parental home in young adulthood', *Journal of Youth Studies*, 18, 10, 1274–90

Berrington, A. and Stone, J. (2013) 'Young adults' transitions to residential independence in Britain: the role of social and housing policy', in L. Antonucci, M. Hamilton and S. Roberts (eds) *Young people and social policy in Europe: Dealing with risk, inequality and precarity in times of crisis*, Basingstoke: Palgrave Macmillan

Berrington, A., Tammes, P. and Roberts, S. (2014) *Economic precariousness and living in the parental home in the UK*, Southampton: ESRC Centre for Population Change

Bessant, J. (2008) 'Hard wired for risk: neurological science, "the adolescent brain" and developmental theory', *Journal of Youth Studies*, 11, 3, 347–60

Bevins, V. and Cappitt, O. (2009) 'FT timeline: the history of finance', available at: www.ft.com/intl/cms/s/0/334eea46-ce0d-11de-95e7-00144feabdc0.html#axzz3grtH3PaN

Bexley, E., Daroesman, S., Arkoudis, S. and James, R. (2013) *University student finances in 2012: A study of the financial circumstances of domestic and international students in Australia's universities*, Melbourne: The University of Melbourne, Centre for the Study for Higher Education

Billones, C. (2013) 'Japanese students in debt with $5 billion loans', *Japan Daily Press*, 18 March.

Bix, H. (2013) 'Japan under nationalist, neoliberal rule: moving towards an abyss?', *Asia-Pacific Journal*, 11, 15, available at: www.japanfocus.org/-Herbert_P_-Bix/3927/article.html

Blair, T. (2005) '"Restless for change" in education. Prime Minister's speech on education in his constituency of Sedgefield', available at: www.number10.gov.uk/output/Page8547.asp

Blanpain, R. (2010) *Labour law and industrial relations in industrialized market economies*, Dordrecht: Kluwer

Boesler, M. (2013) 'Everything you need to know about 'Abenomics': the Japanese economic experiment that's captivating the world', Business Insider, available at: www.businessinsider.com.au/what-is-abenomics-2013-3

Bolton, S. and Laaser, K. (2013) 'Work, employment and society through the lens of moral economy', *Work, Employment and Society*, 27, 3, 508–25

Bonoli, G. (1997) 'Classifying welfare states: a two-dimensional approach', *Journal of Social Policy*, 26, 3, 351–72

Bonoli, G. (2010) 'The political economy of active labour-market policy', *Politics and Society*, 38, 4, 435–57

Booth, A.L. and Kee, H.J. (2009) *The university gender gap in Australia: A long-run perspective*, Canberra: Australian National University, Centre for Economic Policy Research

Boston, J., Dalziel, P. and John, S.S. (1999) *Redesigning the welfare state in New Zealand: Problems, policies, prospects*, Auckland: Oxford University Press

Bottrell, D. and France, A. (2015) 'Boudieusian cultural transitions: young people negotiating fields', in D. Woodman and A. Bennett (eds), *Youth cultures, belonging and transitions*, London: Palgrave Macmillan

Bourdieu, P. (1975) 'L'ontologie politique de Martin Heidegger', *Actes de la recherche en sciences sociales*, 5, 6, 109–56

Bourdieu, P. (1988) *Homo academicus*, Cambridge: Polity Press

Bourdieu, P. (1990) *The logic of practice*, Stanford, CA: Stanford University Press

Bourdieu, P. (1993) *The field of cultural production*, Cambridge: Polity Press

Bourdieu, P. (1998) 'The abdication of the state', in P. Bourdieu (ed) *The weight of the world: Social suffering in contemporary society,* Cambridge: Polity Press

Bourdieu, P. (2005) *The social structures of the economy,* Cambridge: Polity Press

Bourdieu, P. and Passeron, J. (1977) *Reproduction in society, education and culture,* London: Sage

Bourdieu, P. and Wacquant, L. (1992) *An invitation to reflexive sociology,* Cambridge: Polity Press

Bradley, D., Noonan, P., Nugent, H. and Scales, B. (2008) *Review of Australian higher education: Final report (Bradley review),* Canberra: Department of Education, Employment and Workplace Relations

Brandal, N., Bratberg, Ø. and Thorsen, D.E. (2013) *Nordic model of social democracy,* London: Palgrave Macmillan

Brenner, N. and Theodore, N. (2002) 'Cities and the geographies of "actually existing neoliberalism"', *Antipode,* 34, 3, 349–79

Brinkley, I. (2015) *Employment regulation and the labour market,* Lancaster: Work Foundation

Brinkley, I., Jones, K. and Lee, N. (2013) *The gender jobs split,* London: Touchstone Publications

Brinton, M.C. (2011) *Lost in transition: Youth, work, and instability in postindustrial Japan,* Cambridge: Cambridge University Press

British Columbia Ministry of Human Resources (2002) Employment and Assistance Act, British Columbia: BCMHR

Broadbent Institute (2014) *Have's and Have not's,* Ottawa, Ontario: Broadbent Institute

Bronfenbrenner, U. (1979) *The ecology of human development,* Cambridge, MA: Harvard University Press

Broughton, N., Kanabar, R. and Martin, N. (2015) *Wealth in the Downturn: Winners and Losers,* London: Social Market Foundation

Brown, P., Lauder, H. and Ashton, D. (2011) *The global auction,* Oxford: Oxford University Press

Brown, R. (2005) 'Education, education, education – but will government policies produce an excellent higher education system?', *Higher Education Review,* 38, 1, 3–31

Brzeziński, M. and Kostro, K. (2010) 'Income and consumption inequality in Poland, 1998–2008', *Bank i Kredyt,* 41, 4, 45–72

Brzeziński, M., Jancewicz, B. and Letki, N. (2011) *Growing inequality and the impact in Poland,* Amsterdam: GIN Country Report

Byrne, D. (2005) *Social Exclusion,* 2nd edn, Maidenhead: Open University Press

Cabinet Office (2012) *Fair access to professional careers: A progress report by the Independent Reviewer on Social Mobility and Child Poverty.* London: Information Policy Team

Cahill, D. (2010) '"Actually existing neoliberalism" and the global economic crisis', *Labour and Industry: a Journal of the Social and Economic Relations of Work,* 20, 3, 298–316

Callender, C., Wilkinson, D. and Hopkin, R. (2009) *The impact of institutional financial support in England: Higher education students' awareness, knowledge and take-up of bursaries and scholarships,* Bristol: Office of Fair Access

Campbell, I. and Brosnan, P. (2005) 'Relative advantages: casual employment and casualisation in Australia and New Zealand', *New Zealand Journal of Employment Relations,* 30, 3, 1–14

Canada Budget Statement (2013) Available at: www.budget.gc.ca/2014/docs/bb/brief-bref-eng.html

Carrington, K. and Pratt, A. (2003) *How far have we come: Gender disparities in the Australian higher education system,* Canberra: Information and Research Services, Department of the Parliamentary Library

Carroll, W. and Little, W. (2001) 'Neoliberal transformation and antiglobalization politics in Canada: transition, consolidation, resistance', *International Journal of Political Economy,* 31, 3, 33–66

Carter, M. (1966) *Into Work,* London: Penguin Books

Case, S. and Haines, K. (2009) *Understanding youth offending risk factor research: Policy and practice,* Cullompton: Willan

Castles, F. and Ferrera, M. (1996) 'Home ownership and the welfare state: is Southern Europe different?', *South European Society and Politics,* 1, 2, 163–84

Centre for the Modern Family (2014) *Meet the full nesters,* Edinburgh: CFMF

Chan, S. (2011) *Belonging, becoming, and being: First year apprentices' experience in the workplace,* Wellington: National Centre for Tertiary Teaching Excellence, Ako Aotearoa

Chapman, B. and Higgins, T. (2014) *HELP interest rate options: Equity and costs,* available at: http://images.theage.com.au/file/2014/07/31/5639573/Help_interest_rate_options_report.pdf

Chatterton, P. and Hollands, R. (2003) *Urban nightscapes: Youth cultures, pleasure spaces and corporate power,* London: Routledge

Child Hill, R., Bae-Gyoon, P. and Saito, A. (2012) 'Introduction: locating neoliberalism in East Asia', in P. Bae-Gyoon, R. Child Hill and A. Saito (eds) *Locating neoliberalism in East Asia,* Chichester: Wiley-Blackwell

Chisholm, L., Kovacheva, S. and Merico, M. (2011) *European youth studies,* Innsbruck: M.A. EYS

Choudaha, R. and De Wit, H. (2014) 'Challenges and opportunities for global students mobility in the future: comparative and critical analysis', in B. Streitwiseser (ed) *Internationalism of higher education and global mobility,* Oxford: Symposium Books

Choudhury, S. (2010) 'Culturing the adolescent brain: what can neuroscience learn from anthropology?', *Social Cognitive and Affective Neuroscience,* 5, 2–3, 159–67

Cingano, F. (2014) *Trends in income inequality and its impact on economic growth,* Paris: OECD

Clarke, J. and Newman, J. (2012) 'The alchemy of austerity', *Critical Social Policy,* 32, 3, 299–319

Coffey, J. and Farrugia, D. (2014) 'Unpacking the black box: the problem of agency in the sociology of youth', *Journal of Youth Studies,* 17, 3–4, 461–74

Cohen, S. (1973) *Folk Devils and Moral Panic,* London: Routledge

Cohen, P. and Ainley, P. (2000) 'In the country of the blind? Youth studies and cultural studies in Britain', *Journal of Youth Studies,* 3, 1, 79–95

Commonwealth of Australia (2015) *A new system for better employment outcomes and social outcomes,* Canberra: Commonwealth of Australia

Corak, M. (2013) *Income Inequality, Equality of Opportunity, and Intergenerational Mobility,* (No. IZA DP No. 7520), Bonn: Institute for the Study of Labor

Corak, M. (2013) *Income inequality, equality of opportunity, and intergenerational mobility,* Bonn: Institute for the Study of Labor

Corlett, A. and Whittaker, M. (2014) *Low pay Britain,* London: Resolution Foundation

Cortina, J., Taran, P. and Raphael, A. (2014) *Migration and youth: Challenges and opportunities,* Paris: UNICEF

Corver, M. (2010) *Have bursaries influenced choice between universities?* Bristol: Office of Fair Access

Côté, J.E. (2014) 'Towards a new political economy of youth', *Journal of Youth Studies,* 17, 4, 527–43

Craig, D. and Porter, D. (2006) *Development beyond neoliberalism? Governance, poverty reduction and political economy,* Cambridge: Cambridge University Press

Craig, D. and Cotterell, G. (2007) 'Periodising neoliberalism?' *Policy and Politics,* 35, 3, 497–514

Crawford, C. and Jin, W. (2014) *Payback time? Student debt and loans repayments: What will the 2012 reforms mean for graduates,* London: Sutton Trust

Crisp, R. and Fletcher, R. (2008) *A comparative review of workfare programmes in the United States, Canada and Australia,* London: Department of Work and Pensions

Crompton, R. (1997) *Women and work in modern Britain,* Thousand Oaks, CA: Sage

Crotty, J. (2009) 'Structural causes of the global financial crisis: a critical assessment of the "new financial architecture"', *Cambridge Journal of Economics,* 33, 4, 563–80

Crowley, L. and Cominetti, N. (2014) *The geography of youth unemployment: A route map for change,* London: The Work Foundation

Cuervo, H., Crofts, J. and Wyn, J. (2013) *Generational insights into new labour market landscapes for youth,* Melbourne: Youth Research Centre, University of Melbourne

Curtis, D. and McMillan, J. (2008) *School non-completers: Profiles and initial destinations, Longitudinal Studies of Australian Youth (LSAY),* Victoria: Australian Council for Educational Research

Davies, B. (1999) *From volunteerism to welfare state,* Leicester: National Youth Agency

Davis, J. (1990) *Youth and the condition of Britain: Images of adolescent conflict,* London: Athlone Press

Dearing, R. (1997) *The Dearing Report,* London: HMSO

Debrett Foundation (2015) *Intern Britain,* London: Debrett Foundation

Deeming, C. (2014) 'Social democracy and social policy in neoliberal times', *Journal of Sociology,* 50, 4, 577–600

Delors, J. (1996) *Learning, the Treasure Within: Report to UNESCO of the International Commission on Education for the Twenty-First Century:[summary],* Paris: UNESCO

Department for Education (2011) *Raising expectations: Staying in education and training post 16,* Norwich: HMSO

Department for Education and Skills (2004) *Higher education bill,* London: HMSO

Department for Education and Skills (2007) *Raising expectations: Staying in education and training post-16,* Norwich: DFES

Department of Business, Innovation and Skills (2014) *Further education and skills: Learner participation, outcomes and level of highest qualification held,* London: Skills Funding Agency

Department of Employment (2013) *Jobs and Training Compact Evaluation,* Canberra: Australian Government

Department of Work and Pensions (2010) *Universal credit: Welfare that works,* London: Department of Work and Pensions

Department of Work and Pensions (2014) *Work Programme Evaluation: Operation of the Commissioning Model, Finance and Programme Delivery,* (No. 893), London: Department of Work and Pensions

Djernaes, L. (2013) 'A Nordic perspective on youth unemployment', *Lifelong Learning in Europe (LLinE),* 1, 1–6

du Bois-Reymond, M. (1998) I Don't Want to Commit Myself Yet': Young People's Life Concepts, *Journal of Youth Studies,* 1(1), 63–79

du Bois-Reymond, M. (2009) 'Models of navigation and life management', in A. Furlong (ed) *Youth and young adulthood,* London: Routledge

Duménil, G. and Lévy, D. (2005) *The neoliberal (counter-)revolution,* London: Pluto Press

Duménil, G. and Lévy, D. (2011) *The crisis of neoliberalism,* Cambridge, MA: Harvard University Press

Dwyer, P. and Wyn, J. (2001) *Youth education and risk: Facing the future,* London: Routledge Falmer

Eisenstadt, S.N. (1956) *From generation to generation: Age groups and social structure,* Piscataway, NJ: Transaction Publishers

Elder, S. (2015) *What does NEETs mean and why is the concept so easily misinterpreted?* Geneva: International Labour Organization

Elias, P. and Purcell, K. (2012) 'Higher education and social background', in *Understanding society: Findings,* Institute for Social and Economic Research, Colchester, University of Essex

Ellem, B. (2006) 'Beyond industrial relations: Work Choices and the reshaping of labour, class and the Commonwealth', *Australian Society for the Study of Labour History,* 90, 211–20

Ellis, K. and France, A. (2012) 'Being judged, being assessed: young people's perspective of assessment in youth justice and education', *Children and Society,* 26, 2, 112–23

Enders, J. and Jongbloed, B. (2007) *Public–private dynamics in higher education: Expectations, developments and outcomes,* Bielefeld: Transcript Verlag

Engel, L. (2007) '"Rolling back, rolling out": exceptionalism and neoliberalism of the Spanish state', *Critical Studies in Education,* 48, 2, 213–27

Equality Challenge Unit (2013) *Equality in higher education: Statistical report,* London: Equality Challenge Unit

Esping-Andersen, G. (1990) *The three worlds of welfare capitalism,* Princeton, NJ: Princeton University Press

Eurociett (2014) *Europe 2020 From Strategy to Action: Ensuring Inclusive Growth,* Brussels: Eurociett

Eurofound (2012) *NEETs – young people not in employment, education or training: Characteristics, costs and policy responses in Europe,* Dublin: Eurofound

Eurofound (2013) *Young people and temporary employment in Europe,* Luxembourg: European Union

Eurofound (2015) *Youth entrepreneurship in Europe: Values, attitudes, policies,* Luxembourg: European Union

European Commission (2013) *Entrepreneurship 2020 Action Plan: Reigniting the entrepreneurial spirit in Europe,* COM (2012) 795 final. Brussels: European Commission

Evans, J., Rich, E., Allwood, R. and Davies, B. (2008) 'Body pedagogies, P/policy, health and gender', *British Educational Research Journal,* 34, 3, 387–402

Eurostat (2015) *Being young in Europe today,* Luxembourg, Eurostat

Fairclough, N. (1992) *Discourse and social change,* Cambridge: Polity Press

Farnsworth, K. (2012) 'From economic crisis to a new age of austerity: the UK', in K. Farnsworth and Z. Irving (eds) *Social policy in challenging times,* Bristol: Policy Press

Farnsworth, K. and Irving, Z. (2012) 'Varieties of crisis, varieties of austerity: social policy in challenging times', *Journal of Poverty and Social Justice,* 20, 2, 133–47

Fawcett Society (2009) *Are women bearing the brunt of the recession?* London: Fawcett Society

Ferguson, I. (2004) 'Neoliberalism, the third way and social work: the UK experience', *Social Work and Society,* 2, 1, 1–9

Ferguson, S.J. and Wang, S. (2014) *Graduating in Canada: Profile, labour market outcomes and student debt of the class of 2009–2010,* Ottawa: Statistics Canada

Fergusson, R. (2013) 'Against disengagement: non-participation as an object of governance', *Research in Post-Compulsory Education,* 18, 1–2, 12–28

Fergusson, R. and Yeates, N. (2013) 'Business, as usual: the policy priorities of the World Bank's discourses on youth unemployment, and the global financial crisis', *Journal of International and Comparative Social Policy,* 29, 1, 64–78

Ferrer-i-Carbonell, A., Ramos, X. and Oviedo, M. (2013) 'Spain: what can we learn from past decreasing inequalities?', in E. Saalverda and D. Checchi (eds) *Changing inequalities and societal impacts in thirty rich countries,* Oxford: Oxford University Press

Fevre, R. (2007) 'Employment insecurity and social theory: the power of nightmares', *Work, Employment and Society*, 21, 3, 517–35

Filmer-Sankey, C.M. and McCrone, T. (2012) *Developing indicators for early identification of young people at risk of temporary disconnection from learning*, London: NFER

Finn, D. (1987) *Training without jobs: New deals and broken promises*, London: Macmillan Education

Finn, D. (2009) *Differential pricing in contracted out employment programmes: Review of international evidence*, London: Department of Work and Pensions

Fisher, D., Rubenson, K., Jones, G. and Shanahan, T. (2009) 'The political economy of post-secondary education: a comparison of British Columbia, Ontario and Québec', *Higher Education*, 57, 5, 549–66

Fong, B. and Phelps, A. (2007) *Apprenticeship pay: 2007 survey of earnings by sector*, London: Department for Innovation, Universities and Skills

Foster, K. (2012) *Youth employment and un(der) employment in Canada*, Ontario: Canadian Centre for Policy Alternatives

Fowkes, L. (2011) *Thinking Australia's employment services*, Sydney: Whitlam Institute, University of Western Australia

France, A. (1996) 'Youth and citizenship in the 1990s', *Youth and Policy*, 53, 28–43

France, A. (2007) *Understanding youth in late modernity*, Buckingham: Open University Press

France, A. (2008a) 'Being to becoming: the importance of tackling youth poverty in transitions to adulthood', *Social Policy and Society*, 7, 4, 495–505

France, A. (2008b) 'Risk factor analysis and the youth question', *Journal of Youth Studies*, 11, 1, 1–15

France, A. (2009) 'Anti-social behaviour', in A. Furlong (ed) *Youth and young adulthood*, London: Routledge

France, A. (2012) '"It's all in the brain": science and the "new" construction of the youth problem in New Zealand', *New Zealand Sociology*, 27, 2, 76

France, A. and Roberts, S. (2015) 'The problem of social generations: a critique of the new emerging orthodoxy in youth studies', *Journal of Youth Studies*, 18, 2, 215–30

France, A., Freiberg, K. and Homel, R. (2010) 'Beyond risk factors: Towards a holistic prevention paradigm for children and young people', *British Journal of Social Work*, 40, 4, 1192–210

France, A., Bottrell, D. and Armstrong, D. (2012) *A political ecology of youth and crime*, London: Palgrave Macmillan

Freud, D. (2007) *Reducing dependency, increasing opportunity: Options for the future of welfare to work,* Leeds: Department of Work and Pensions

Friedman, M. and Friedman, R. (1980) *Free to choose,* New York: Harcourt Brace Jovanovich

Fry, R. (2012) *A record one-in-five households now owe student loan debt,* Washington, DC: Pew Research Center

Fry, R. and Passel, J.S. (2014) *In post-recession era, young adults drive continuing rise in multi-generational living,* Washington, DC: Pew Research Center

Fuller, A. and Unwin, L. (2013) *Gender segregation, apprenticeship and the raising of the participation age in England: Are young women at a disadvantage?* London: Centre for Learning and Life Chances in Knowledge Economies and Societies

Furlong, A. (2006) 'Not a very NEET solution: representing problematic labour market transitions among early school-leavers', *Work, Employment and Society,* 20, 3, 553–69

Furlong, A. (2013) *Youth studies: An introduction,* New York: Routledge

Furlong, A. and Cartmel, F. (2007) *Young People and Social Change,* Buckingham: Open University Press

Furlong, A. and Cartmel, F. (2009) *Higher education and social justice,* Buckingham: Open University Press

Furlong, A. and Kelly, P. (2005) 'The Brazilianisation of youth transitions in Australia and the UK?', *Australian Journal of Social Issues,* 40, 2, 207–25

Furlong, A., Woodman, D. and Wyn, J. (2011) 'Changing times, changing perspectives: reconciling "transition" and "cultural" perspectives on youth and young adulthood', *Journal of Sociology,* 47, 4, 355–70

Galabuzi, G. (2005) *Canada's economic apartheid: The social exclusion of racialised groups in the new century,* Toronto: Canadian Scholars Press

Galbraith, J.K. (2012) *Inequality and instability: A study of the world economy just before the great crisis,* Oxford: Oxford University Press

Gale, T. and Parker, S. (2013) *Widening participation in Australian higher education,* Leicester: CFE Research

Gale, T. and Tranter, D. (2011) 'Social justice in Australian higher education policy: an historical and conceptual account of student participation', *Critical Studies in Education,* 52, 1, 29–46

García. J. (2011) *Youth unemployment in Spain: Causes and solutions,* Madrid: BBVA Research

Gardiner, L. (2014) *Totaling the hidden talent,* London: Local Government Association

Gazso, A. and McDaniel, S. (2010) 'The "Great West" experiment: neo-liberal convergence and transforming citizenship in Canada', *Canadian Review of Social Policy,* 63, 15–35

Gebel, M. (2008) 'Labour markets in Central and Eastern Europe', in I. Kogan, M. Gebel and C. Noelke (eds) *A handbook of education, labour and welfare regimes in Central and Eastern Europe,* Bristol: Policy Press

Geisen, T. (2010) 'New perspectives on youth and migration: belonging, cultural repositioning and social mobility', in D. Cairns (ed) *Youth on the move: European youth and geographical mobility,* Wiesbaden: VS-Verlag/Springer

Genda, Y. (2005) *A nagging sense of job insecurity: The new reality facing Japanese youth,* Tokyo: LTCB International Library Trust

Genda, Y. and Maganuma, M. (2004) *NEET: Furī tā demo naku, Shitsugy ōsha demo naku (NEET: Neither freeter nor unemployed),* Tokyo: Gentōsha

Gerrard, J. and Farrell, L. (2013) '"Peopling" curriculum policy production: researching educational governance through institutional ethnography and Bourdieuian field analysis', *Journal of Education Policy,* 28, 1, 1–20

Giddens, A. (1991) *Modernity and self-identity,* Cambridge: Polity Press

Gifford, C., Mycock, A. and Murakami, J. (2014) 'Becoming citizens in late modernity: a global–national comparison of young people in Japan and the UK', *Citizenship Studies,* 18, 1, 81–98

Goldson, B. (1997) 'Children, crime, policy and practice: neither welfare nor justice', *Children and Society,* 11, 2, 77–88

Goldson, B. (2002) *New Punitiveness: the politics of child incarceration,* London: Sage

Goldthorpe, J.H. (1998) 'Rational action: theory for sociology', *British Journal of Sociology,* 49, 167–92

Golsch, K. (2003) 'Employment flexibility in Spain and its impact on transitions to adulthood', *Work, Employment and Society,* 17, 4, 691–718

Gooderham, P., Steen E., Olsen, K. and Steen, C. (2014) *The labor market regimes of Denmark and Norway – One Nordic model?* Copenhagen: Kobenhavns Universitet

Goodman, R. (2012) 'Shifting landscapes: the social context of youth problems in an aging nation', in R. Goodman, Y. Imoto and T. Toivonen (eds) *A sociology of Japanese youth,* Abingdon: Routledge

Goodman, R., Hatakenaka, S. and Terri, K. (2009) 'The changing status of vocational higher education in contemporary Japan and the Republic of Korea: a discussion paper', Bonn: UNESCO-UNEVOC International Centre for Technical and Vocational Education and Training

Goodwin, J. and O'Connor, H. (2005) 'Exploring complex transitions: looking back at the "golden age" of youth transitions', *Sociology*, 39, 2, 201–20

Gorard, S. (2008) Who is missing from higher education? *Cambridge Journal of Education*, 38, 3, 421–37.

Gottfried, H. (2014) 'Precarious work in Japan: old forms, new risks?', *Journal of Contemporary Asia*, 44, 3, 464–78

Gough, I. (2011) 'From financial crisis to fiscal crisis', in K. Farnsworth and Z. Irving (eds), *Social Policy in Challenging Times*, Bristol: Policy Press

Government of Canada (2002) *Knowledge matters: Skills and learning for Canadians*, available at: www.eric.ed.gov/PDFS/ED473598.pdf

Grey, S. and Scott, J. (2012) 'When the government steers the market: Implications for the New Zealand tertiary education system', Working paper for National Tertiary Education Union Future of Higher Education Conference, University of Sydney, 22-23 February

Griffin, C. (1985) *Typical girls? Young women from school to the job market*, London: Routledge and Kegan Paul

Grisoni, L. and Wilkinson, J. (2005) 'Undergraduate business and management students as consumers of identity', Paper 3.20 presented at Society for Research in Higher Education Annual Conference 2005, Edinburgh, 13–15 December

Guillén, A. and Lugue, D. (2014) 'Evolving social policy languages in Spain: what did democracy and EU membership change?', in D. Veland and K. Petersen (eds) *Analysing social policy concepts and language*, Bristol: Policy Press

Hahn-Bleibtreu, M. and Molgat, M. (2012) *Youth policy in a changing world*, Berlin: Barbara Budrich Publishers

Hall, G.S. (1904) *Adolescence, 2 vols*, New York: Appleton

Hall, S. (1985) 'Authoritarian populism: a reply to Jessop et al', *New Left Review*, 151, 1, 115–23

Hall, S. (2003) 'New Labour has picked up where Thatcherism left off', *The Guardian*, 6 August

Hall, S. and Jefferson, T. (1976) *Resistance through rituals*, London: Hutchinson

Hall, S., Clarke, J., Critcher, C., Jefferson, T. and Roberts, B. (1978) *Policing the crisis: Mugging, law and order and the state,* London: Macmillan

Halvorsen, R. and Hvinden, B. (2014) 'Nordic reforms to improve the labour market participation of vulnerable youth: An effective new approach?' *International Social Security Review,* 67, 29–46

Hamilton, M. (2014) 'The "new social contract" and the individualisation of risk in policy', *Journal of Risk Research,* 17, 4, 453–67

Hardy, J. (2009) *Poland's new capitalism,* London: Pluto Press

Harrison, N. (2011) 'Have the changes introduced by the 2004 Higher Education Act made higher education admissions in England wider and fairer?', *Journal of Education Policy,* 26, 3, 449–68

Harrison, N. and Hatt, S. (2012) 'Expensive and failing? The role of student bursaries in widening participation and fair access in England', *Studies in Higher Education,* 37, 6, 695–712

Harvey, D. (2005) *A brief history of neoliberalism,* Oxford: Oxford University Press

Harvey, D. (2010) *The enigma of capitalism and the crises of capitalism,* New York: Oxford University Press

Hawke, G. (1988) *Hawke Committee on Tertiary Education,* Wellington: Department of Education

Haworth, N. (2011) 'A political economy of "the hobbit" dispute', *New Zealand Journal of Employment Relations,* 36, 3, 100–9

Hayek, F.A. (1944) *The Road to Serfdom,* Chicago: University of Chicago Press

Healey, N. and Gunby, P. (2012) 'The impact of recent government tertiary education policies on access to higher education in New Zealand', *Journal of Educational Leadership, Policy and Practice,* 27, 1, 29

HEFC (2009) *Patterns in higher education: Living at home,* Bristol: Higher Education Funding Council

HEFC (2014) *Higher education in England: Analysis of latest shifts and trends,* Bristol: Higher Education Funding Council

Heinen, J. and Portet, S. (2002) 'Political and social citizenship: an examination of the case of Poland', in M. Molyneux and S. Razavi (eds) *Gender justice, development, and rights,* Oxford: Oxford University Press

Heinz, W.R. (2009) 'Youth transitions in an age of uncertainty', in A. Furlong (ed) *The handbook of youth and young adulthood: New perspectives and agendas,* London: Routledge

Herndon, T., Ash, M. and Pollin, R. (2014) 'Does high public debt consistently stifle economic growth? A critique of Reinhart and Rogoff', *Cambridge Journal of Economics,* 38, 2, 257–79

Heyes, J. and Lewis, P. (2014) 'Employment protection under fire: labour market deregulation and employment in the European Union', *Economic and Industrial Democracy*, 35, 4, 587–607

Higgins, J. (2002) 'Young people and transitions policies in New Zealand', *Social Policy Journal of New Zealand*, 18, 44–61

Hinton-Smith, T. (2012) *Widening participation in higher education: Casting the net wide?* London: Palgrave Macmillan

Holdsworth, C. (2004) 'Family support during the transition out of the parental home in Britain, Spain and Norway', *Sociology*, 38, 5, 909–26

Holdsworth, C. (2009) '"Going away to uni": mobility, modernity, and independence of English higher education students', *Environment and Planning A*, 41, 8, 1849–64

Holdsworth, C. and Morgan, D. (2005) *Transitions in context*, Milton Keynes: Open University Press

Hollands, R.G. (1990) *The long transition: Class, culture and youth training*, London: Macmillan Education

Hollands, R. (2002) 'Divisions in the dark: youth cultures, transitions and segmented consumption spaces in the night-time economy', *Journal of Youth Studies*, 5, 2, 153–71

Hollands, R. (2015) 'Waiting for the weekend? Nightlife studies and the convergence of youth transitions and youth cultural analysis', in D. Woodman and A. Bennett (eds) *Youth cultures, transitions, and generations: Bridging the gap in youth research*, London: Palgrave Macmillan

Honda, Y. (2005) '"Freeters"; Young Atypical Workers in Japan', *Japan Labor Review*, 2, 1, 5–25

Hoogvelt, A. (2001) *Globalization and the postcolonial world: The new political economy of development*, 2nd edn, London: Palgrave

Horiguchi, S. (2012) 'Hikikomori: how private isolation caught the public eye', in R. Goodman, Y. Imoto and T. Toivonen (eds) *A sociology of Japanese youth*, Abingdon: Routledge

Hovdhaugen, E. (2013) *Widening participation in Norwegian higher education*, Leicester: CFE

Hudson, M., Phillips, J., Ray, K., Vegeris, S. and Davidson, R. (2010) *The influence of outcome-based contracting on provider-led pathways to work*, Norwich: Department of Work and Pensions

Human Resource and Skills Development (2009) *Summative Evaluation if Youth Employment Strategy*, Ottawa: Human Resource and Skills Development

Hummeluhr, N. (1997) *Youth Guarantees in Nordic Countries*, Paris: OECD

Humpage, L. (2011) 'Neo-liberal reform and attitudes towards social citizenship: a review of New Zealand public opinion data 1987–2005', *Social Policy Journal of New Zealand*, 37, 83–96

Humpage, L. and Craig, D. (2008) 'From welfare to welfare-to-work', in N. O'Brien, M. Lunt and B. Stephens (eds) *New Welfare, New Zealand*, Melbourne: Cengage Press

Iacovou, M. (2011) *Leaving home: Independence, togetherness and income in Europe*, New York: United Nations

Iacovou, M. and Parisi, L. (2009) 'Leaving home', in J. Ermisch and M. Brynin (eds) *Changing relationships*, London: Routledge

Ikuo, A. (2014) 'Globalization and higher education reforms in Japan: Obstacles and greater international competitiveness', available at: http://www.nippon.co,/en/in-depth/a02801

Ilcan, S. (2009) 'Privatizing responsibility: public sector reform under neoliberal government', *Canadian Review of Sociology*, 46, 3, 207–34

ILO (2013) *Global trends for youth: A generation at risk*, Geneva: International Labour Organization

IMF (2011) *World economic outlook: Recovery, risk, and rebalancing*, Washington, DC: International Monetary Fund

Intergenerational Foundation (2014) *Young people and employment*, London: Intergenerational Foundation

Inui, A. (2003) 'Restructuring youth: recent problems of Japanese youth and its contextual origin', *Journal of Youth Studies*, 6, 2, 219–33

IPPR (2010) *Trends in part-time and temporary work for the young*, London: IPPR

Istance, D., Rees, G. and Williamson, H. (1994) *Young People Not in Education, Training or Employment in South Glamorgan*, Cardiff: South Glamorgan Training and Enterprise Council

James, R., Bexley, E., Anderson, A., Devlin, M., Garnett, R., Marginson, S. and Maxwell, L. (2008) *Participation and equity: A review of the participation in higher education of people from low socioeconomic backgrounds and Indigenous people*, Melbourne: University of Melbourne, Centre for the Study of Higher Education

Jesson, B. (1992) *Lobbying and protest: Patterns of political change at the informal level*, Auckland: Longman Paul

Jessop, B. (2002) 'Liberalism, neoliberalism, and urban governance: a state-theoretical perspective', *Antipode*, 34, 3, 452–72

Jobs Australia (2011) Jobs Australia: Submission on ways to improve employment services with Job Services Australia (JSA), available at: www.deer.gov.au/Employment/Consultation/2012/Subs/Page/2012submissions.aspx

Jones, G. (2001) 'Fitting homes? Young people's housing and household strategies in rural Scotland', *Journal of Youth Studies*, 4, 1, 41–62

Jones, G. (2002) *The youth divide: Diverging paths to adulthood*, York: Joseph Rowntree Foundation

Jones, G. (2009a) *Youth*, Cambridge: Polity

Jones, G. (2009b) 'Sectors, institutional types and the challenges of shifting categories: a Canadian commentary', *Higher Education Quarterly*, 63, 4, 371–83

Jones, G. (2012) *Higher education in Canada: Different systems, different perspectives*, New York: Routledge

Kalleberg, A.L. (2008) 'The mismatched worker', *Industrial and Labor Relations Review*, 61, 3, 84

Kalleberg, A.L. (2012) 'Job quality and precarious work clarifications, controversies, and challenges', *Work and Occupations*, 39, 4, 427–48

Kariya, T. (2012) 'Is everyone capable of becoming a "good citizen" in Japanese society? Inequality and the realization of the "good citizen" education', *Multicultural Education Review*, 4, 1, 119–46

Keep, E. and Mayhew, K. (2010) 'Moving beyond skills as a social and economic panacea', *Work, Employment and Society*, 24, 3, 565–77

Kelly, P. (2000) 'The dangerousness of youth-at-risk: the possibilities of surveillance and intervention in uncertain times', *Journal of Adolescence*, 23, 4, 463–76

Kelly, P. (2006) 'The entrepreneurial self and "youth at risk": exploring the horizons of identity in the twenty-first century', *Journal of Youth Studies*, 9, 1, 17–32

Kelly, P. (2012) 'The brain in the jar: a critique of discourses of adolescent brain development', *Journal of Youth Studies*, 15, 7, 944–59

Kelsey, J. (1993) *Rolling back the state: Privatisation of power in Aotearoa/New Zealand*, Wellington: Bridget Williams Books

Kildal, N. (2001) *Workfare tendencies in Scandinavian welfare policies*, Geneva: International Labour Organization

King, L., Kitson, M., Konzelmann, S. and Wilkinson, F. (2012) 'Making the same mistake again – or is this time different?' *Cambridge Journal of Economics*, 36, 1, 1–15

Kirby, D. (2011) 'Strategies for widening access in a quasi-market higher education environment: recent developments in Canada', *Higher Education*, 62, 3, 267–78

Kirkup, G. (2011) 'Preparing women for dead-end jobs? Vocational education and training (VET) for information and communication technology (ICT) jobs', *International Journal of Gender, Science and Technology*, 3, 2, 460–82

Kluve, J. (2014) *Active labour market policies with a focus on youth,* Turin: European Training Foundation

Konzelmann, S.J. (2014) 'The political economics of austerity', *Cambridge Journal of Economics,* 38, 4, 701–41

Kwiek, M. (2013) 'From system expansion to system contraction: access to higher education in Poland', in P. Zgaga, U. Teichler and J. Brennan (eds) *The globalisation challenge for European higher education,* Frankfurt am Main: Peter Lang

Labonté, R. (2012) 'The austerity agenda: how did we get here and where do we go next?', *Critical Public Health,* 22, 3, 257–65

Laeven, L. and Valencia, F. (2012) 'The use of blanket guarantees in banking crises', *Journal of International Money and Finance,* 31, 5, 1220–48

Lancrin, V. (2008) *The reversal of gender inequalities in higher education: The ongoing trends in OECD, higher education trends to 2030,* Paris: OECD

Lane, P., Foster, R., Gardiner, G., Lanceley, L. and Purvis, A. (2013) *Work programme evaluation procurement, supply chains and implementation of the commissioning model,* London: Department for Work and Pensions

Lang, D. (2013) 'Incentives in financing higher education', in C. Amrhein and B. Baron (eds) *Building success in a global university,* Berlin: Lemmens

Lange, C.M. and Sletten, S.J. (2002) *Alternative education: A brief history and synthesis,* Alexandria, VA: Project Forum at National Association of State Directors of Special Education, available at: http://www.nasdse.org/forum.htm

Larner, W. (1996) 'The "new boys": restructuring in New Zealand, 1984–94', *Social Politics: International Studies in Gender, State and Society,* 3, 1, 32–56

Larner, W. (2003) 'Neoliberalism?', *Environment and Planning D,* 21, 5, 509–12

Larner, W. and Le Heron, R. (2005) 'Neo-liberalizing spaces and subjectivities: Reinventing New Zealand universities', *Organization,* 12, 6, 843–62

Leccardi, C. (2005) 'Facing Uncertainty: Temporality and biographies in the new century', *Young,* 13, 2, 123–46

Levitas, R. (2012) 'The just's umbrella: austerity and the Big Society in coalition policy and beyond', *Critical Social Policy,* 32, 2, 320–42

Lewis, S., Brannen, J. and Nilsen, A. (2009) 'Research Design and Methods: doing comparative cross-national research', in J. Brannen, A. Nilsen and S. Lewis (eds), *Work, families and organisations in transition: European perspectives,* Bristol: Policy Press

Lister, R. (2009) 'A Nordic Nirvana? Gender, citizenship, and social justice in the Nordic welfare states', *Social Politics*, 16, 2, 242–78

Lister, R. (2010) *Understanding theories and concepts in social policy*, Cambridge: Policy Press

Lister, R. and Bennett, F. (2010) 'The new "champion of progressive ideals"? Cameron's Conservative Party: poverty, family policy and welfare reform', *Renewal*, 18, 1/2, 84–109

Little, M. and Marks, L. (2006) 'A closer look at the neo-liberal petri dish', *Canadian Review of Social Policy*, 57, 16–45

López, I. and Rodríguez, E. (2011) 'The Spanish model', *New Left Review*, 69, May–June, 5–29

Lunt, I. (2010) 'Beyond tuition fees', in G. Walford (ed) *Blair's educational legacy?* London: Routledge

McBride, S. (2004) *Challenging the market: The struggle to regulate work and income*, Montreal: McGill-Queen's University Press

McBride, S. (2005) *Paradigm shift: Globalization and the Canadian state*, Black Point: Fernwood Publishing

McBride, S. and McNutt, K. (2007) 'Devolution and neoliberalism in the Canadian welfare state ideology, national and international conditioning frameworks, and policy change in British Columbia', *Global Social Policy*, 7, 2, 177–201

MacDonald, M. (1999) 'Restructuring, gender and social security reform in Canada', *Journal of Canadian Studies*, 34, 2, 57–88

MacDonald, R. (ed) (1997) *Youth, the 'underclass' and social exclusion*, London: Routledge

MacDonald, R. (2009) 'Precarious work', in A. Furlong (ed) *A handbook of youth and young adulthood: New perspectives and agendas*, London: Routledge

MacDonald, R. (2011) 'Youth transitions, unemployment and underemployment: *plus ça change, plus c'est la même chose?*', *Journal of Sociology*, 47, 4, 427–44

MacDonald, R. (2013) 'Underemployment and *precarité*: the new condition of youth?', Lifelong Learning in Europe (LLinE), available at: www.elmmagazine.eu/articles/underemployment-and-precarit-the-new-condition-of-youth

MacDonald, R. and Marsh, J. (2005) *Disconnected youth? Growing up in Britain's poor neighbourhoods*, London: Palgrave Macmillan

McDowell, L. (2003) *Redundant masculinities? Employment change and white working class youth*, Oxford: Wiley-Blackwell

McDowell, L. (2004) 'Work, workfare, work/life balance and an ethic of care', *Progress in Human Geography*, 28, 2, 145–63

McKay, S., Jefferys, S., Paraksevopoulou, A. and Keles, J. (2012) *Study on precarious work and social rights,* London: Metropolitan University, Working Lives Research Institute

MacLeavy, J. (2007) 'Engendering New Labour's workfarist regime: exploring the intersection of welfare state restructuring and labour market policies in the UK', *Gender, Place and Culture,* 14, 6, 721–43

MacLeavy, J. (2011) 'A "new politics" of austerity, workfare and gender? The UK coalition government's welfare reform proposals', *Cambridge Journal of Regions, Economy and Society,* 4, 3, 355–67

MacPhail, F. and Bowles, P. (2008) 'Temporary work and neoliberal government policy: evidence from British Columbia, Canada', *International Review of Applied Economics,* 22, 5, 545–63

McRobbie, A. (1978) 'Working Class Girls and Femininity', *Women's Studies Group (CCCS), Women Take Issue. Aspect of Women's Subordination,* London: Hutchinson

McRobbie, A. and Thornton, S.L. (1995) 'Rethinking "moral panic" for multi-mediated social worlds', *British Journal of Sociology,* 46, 4, 559–74

Madsen, P., Molina, O., Møller, J. and Lozan, M. (2013) 'Labour market transitions of young workers in Nordic and southern European countries: the role of flexicurity', *European Review of Labour and Research,* 19, 3, 325–43

Maguire, S. (2013) 'Will raising the participation age in England solve the NEET problem?', *Research in Post-Compulsory Education,* 18, 1–2, 61–76

Mahoney, P. (2003) *Higher education funding – Overseas models,* Wellington: Parliamentary Library

Maki, K. (2011) 'Neoliberal deviants and surveillance: welfare recipients under the watchful eye of Ontario Works', *Surveillance and Society,* 9, 1/2, 47–63

Malbon, B. (1999) *Clubbing: Dancing, ecstasy and vitality,* London: Routledge

Mannheim, K. (1952) 'The problem of generation', in K. Mannheim (ed) *Essays on the sociology of knowledge,* London: Routledge and Kegan Pau

Marginson, S. (2013) 'The impossibility of capitalist markets in higher education', *Journal of Education Policy,* 28, 3, 353–70

Marquardt, R. (1998) 'Labour market policies and programmes affecting youth in Canada'. Background paper prepared for the Thematic Review of the Transition from Initial Education to Working Life, Paris: OECD

Marston, G. (2000) 'Metaphor, morality and myth: a critical discourse analysis of public housing policy in Queensland', *Critical Social Policy*, 20, 3, 349–73

Martin, J. (2014) *Activation and active labour market policies in OECD countries: Stylized facts and evidence on their effectiveness*, Bonn: Institute for the Study of Labor

Martinez Lucio, M. and Stuart, M. (2003) 'Training and development in Spain: the politics of modernisation', *International Journal of Training and Development*, 7, 1, 67–77

Meager, N., Newton, B., Sainsbury, R., Corden, A. and Irvine, A. (2014) *Work programme evaluation: The participant experience report*, Norwich: Department for Work and Pensions

Micheli, G. and Rosina, A. (2009) 'The vulnerability of young adults on leaving the parental home', in C. Ranci (ed) *Social vulnerability in Europe: The new configuration of social risks*, Basingstoke: Palgrave Macmillan

Migration Advisory Committee (2014) *Migrants in low-skilled work: The growth of EU and non-EU labour in low-skilled jobs and its impact on the UK*, London: Home Office

Milburn, A. (2012) *University Challenge: How Higher Education Can Advance Social Mobility*, London: HMSO.

Miles, R. and Bickert, M. (2007) *Women and VET: Strategies for gender inclusive VET reform*, Sydney: Security4Women

Miles, S. (2000) *Youth lifestyles in a changing world*, Milton Keynes: McGraw-Hill International

Minas, C., Jacobson, D., Antoniou, E. and McMullan, C. (2014) 'Welfare regime, welfare pillar and southern Europe', *Journal of European Social Policy*, 24, 2, 135–49

Minguez, A. (2013) 'The employability of young people in Spain: the mismatch between education and employment', *US–China Education Review*, 3, 5, 334–44

Ministry of Education (2002) *New Zealand's Tertiary Education Sector 2001– Profile and Trends*, Wellington: Ministry Education

Ministry of Education (2013) *New Zealand tertiary education sector: Profile and trends*, Wellington: Ministry of Education

Ministry of Education (2014) *Education counts*, Ministry of Education, New Zealand, available at: www.educationcounts.govt.nz/statistics/tertiary_education/participation

Ministry of Labour (2010) *Regulatory impact statement – Minimum wage review 2010*, available at: www.dol.govt.nz/publications/general/ris-min-wage-review-2010/

Miranti, R., Nepal, B. and McNamara, J. (2010) *Calling Australia home: The characteristics and contributions of Australian migrants,* Sydney: AMP

Mitchell, B. (2006) 'The boomerang age from childhood to adulthood: emergent trends and issues for aging families', *Canadian Studies in Population,* 33, 2, 155–78

Mizen, P. (1995) *The state, young people and youth training: In and against the training state,* London: Mansell

Mizen, P. (2004) *The changing state of youth,* Basingstoke: Palgrave Macmillan

Moreno, A. (2012) 'The transition to adulthood in Spain in a comparative perspective: the incidence of structural factors', *Young,* 20, 1, 19–48

Moreno, L. (2013) 'Spain's catch up with the EU core: the implausible quest of a "flying pig"?', *South European Society and Politics,* 18, 2, 217–36

Moreno, L. and Marí-Klose, P. (2013) 'Youth, family change and welfare arrangements', *European Societies,* 15, 4, 493–513

Morgan, J. (2009) 'The limits of central bank policy: economic crisis and the challenge of effective solutions', *Cambridge Journal of Economics,* 33, 4, 581–608

Mortimer, J.T. (2009) 'Changing experiences of work', in A. Furlong (ed) *Handbook of youth and young adulthood: New perspectives and agendas,* London: Routledge

Mosca, I. and Wright, R.E. (2011) *Is graduate under-employment persistent? Evidence from the United Kingdom,* Bonn: Forschungsinstitut zur Zukunft der Arbeit

Moulton, B.R. (2014) 'The 2007-2009 Financial Crisis and Recession: Reflections in the National Accounts', *Eurostat Conference the Accounts of Society National Accounts at the Service of Economic and Monetary Policy Making Luxembourg, Alvisse Parc Hotel,* Luxembourg: Eurostat

Muncie, J. (1984) *The trouble with kids today: Youth and crime in post-war Britain,* 1st edn, London: Hutchinson

Muncie, J. (2009) *Youth and crime,* London: Sage

Murray, C. (1984) *Losing ground: American policy 1950–1980,* New York: Basic Books

Mydske, P., Claes, D. and Lie. A. (eds) (2007) *In Nyliberalisme – ideer og politisk virkelighet,* Oslo: Universitetsforlaget

Næss, T. (2011) *Graduate employment in the knowledge society,* Bologna: AlmaLaurea

Naidoo, R. and Jamieson, I. (2005) 'Empowering participants or corroding learning? Towards a research agenda on the impact of student consumerism in higher education', *Journal of Education Policy,* 20, 3, 267–81

Naidoo, R., Shankar, A. and Veer, E. (2011) 'The consumerist turn in higher education: policy aspirations and outcomes', *Journal of Marketing Management,* 27, 11–12, 1142–62

Nairn, K., Higgins, J. and Sligo, J. (2012) *Children of Rogernomics: A neoliberal generation leaves school,* Otago: Otago University Press

National Assembly for Wales (2000) *Extending entitlement: Supporting young people in Wales,* Cardiff: Corporate Policy Unit

Navarro, V. (2013) 'The social crisis of the eurozone: the case of Spain', *International Journal of Health Services,* 43, 2, 189–92

NCVER (2014) *Apprentices and Trainees,* Adelaide: NCVER

Newby, H., Weko, H., Breneman, D., Johanneson, T. and Maassen, P. (2009) *OECD review of tertiary education in Japan,* Paris: OECD

Nielsen, J. and Andreasen, L. (2015) 'Higher education in Scandinavia', in P. Blessinger and J. Anchan (eds) *Democratizing higher education: International comparative perspectives,* London: Routledge

O'Connor, K., Stimpson, R. and Daly, M. (2001) *Australia's changing economic geography,* Melbourne: Oxford University Press

OECD (1996) *The knowledge based society,* Paris: OECD

OECD (2003) *Norway – Marketisation of government services – State-owned enterprises,* Paris: OECD

OECD (2005) *Education at a glance,* Paris: OECD

OECD (2008) *Tertiary education for the knowledge society: OECD thematic review of tertiary education,* vol. 2, Paris: OECD

OECD (2009) *The role of welfare and activation policies in Poland,* Paris: OECD

OECD (2010) *Activation policies in Japan,* Paris: OECD

OECD (2012) *The labour market reform in Spain: A preliminary assessment,* Paris: OECD

OECD (2013a) *Employment outlook,* available at: *www.dx.doi. org/10.1787empl_outlook-2013-en,* Paris: OECD

OECD (2013b) *Activating job seekers: How does Australia do it?* Paris: OECD

OECD (2013c) *Crisis squeezes income and puts pressure on inequality and poverty,* Paris: OECD

OECD (2013d) *International migration outlook,* Paris: OECD

OECD (2014a) *Education at a glance,* Paris: OECD

OECD (2014b) *Inequality and growth,* Paris: OECD

OECD (2014c) *Raising inequality: Youth and poor fall further behind,* Paris: OECD

OECD (2015) *In it together: Why less inequality benefits all,* Paris: OECD

Office of Fair Access (2014) *Do Bursaries have an effect on retention rates?* Bristol: Office of Fair Access

Office of Ministry of Social Development (2012) *Welfare reform: Availability and preparation for work for solo parents, widows, women alone and partners,* Wellington: OMSD

O'Hara, M. (2014) *Austerity bites A journey to the sharp end of cuts in the UK,* Bristol: Policy Press

Ohtake, F., Kohara, M., Okuyama, N. and Yamada, K. (2013) *Growing inequalities and their impacts in Japan: Country report for Japan,* Amsterdam: Gini Reports

Oliveira, L., Carvalho, H. and Veloso, L. (2011) 'Youth and precarious employment in Europe', in R. Price, P. McDonald, J. Bailey and B. Pini (eds) *Young People and Work,* Farnham: Ashgate

Olofsson, J. and Wadensjö, E. (2012) *Youth, education and labour market in the Nordic countries: Similar but not the same,* Berlin: Friedrich Ebert Stiftung

Olssen, M. and Peters, M.A. (2005) 'Neoliberalism, higher education and the knowledge economy: from the free market to knowledge capitalism', *Journal of Education Policy,* 20, 3, 313–45

ONS (Office of National Statistics) (2014) *Unemployment by age 15–24 year olds,* available at: www.ons.gov.uk

Ontario Legislative Assembly (1995) *Official reports of debates* (Hansard), 1st session, 36th legislature, 28 September

O'Reilly, K. (2012) *International migration and social theory,* London: Palgrave Macmillan

Ortiz, I. and Cummins, M. (2012) *A recovery for all: Rethinking socio-economic policies for children and poor households,* New York: Unicef

Parsons, T. (1942) 'Age and sex in the social structure of the United States', *American Sociological Review,* 7, 5, 604–16

Peacock, D., Sellar, S. and Lingard, B. (2014) 'The activation, appropriation and practices of student-equity policy in Australian higher education', *Journal of Education Policy,* 29, 3, 377–96

Peck, J. (2001) *Workfare states,* New York: Guilford Press

Peck, J. (2010) *Constructions of neoliberalism,* Oxford: Oxford University Press

Peck, J. and Theodore, N. (2012) 'Reanimating neoliberalism: process geographies of neoliberalisation', *Social Anthropology,* 20, 2, 177–85

Peck, J. and Tickell, A. (2002) 'Neoliberalizing space', *Antipode,* 34, 3, 380–404

Peiró, J, Sora, B. and Caballer, A. (2012) 'Job insecurity in the younger Spanish workforce: Causes and consequences', *Journal of Vocational Behaviour,* 80, 444–53

Pempel, T.J. (1999) 'The development regime in a changing world economy', in *The developmental state,* Ithaca, NY: Cornell University Press

Perugini, C., Hölscher, J. and Collie, S. (2016) 'Inequality, credit and financial crises', *Cambridge Journal of Economics* 40,1, 227–57.

Pickett, K. and Wilkinson, R. (2007) 'Child wellbeing and income inequality in rich societies: ecological cross sectional study', *British Medical Journal,* 333, 1080–5

Picketty, T. (2013) *Capital in the twenty-first century,* Cambridge, MA: Harvard University Press

Pitts, J. (2001) *The new politics of youth crime,* London: Palgrave

Polakowski, M. (2012) *Youth unemployment in Poland,* Berlin: Friedrich Ebert Stiftung

Polanyi, K. (1944) *The great transformation: The political and economic origins of our time,* Boston, MA: Beacon Press

Pollock, G. (2002) 'Contingent identities: updating the transitional discourse', *Young,* 10, 1, 59–72

Poznanski, K.Z. (1996) *Poland's protracted transition: Institutional change and economic growth 1970–1994,* Cambridge: Cambridge University Press

Pring, R. (2010) '14–19', in G. Walford (ed) *Blair's legacy?* London: Routledge

Puhani, P.A. (1999) *Evaluating active labour market policies,* Berlin: Springer-Verlag

Putman, T. and Gill, J. (2011) 'The Bradley challenge: a sea change for Australian universities', *Issues in Educational Research,* 21, 2, 176–91

Quinlan, M. (2012) 'The "pre-invention" of precarious employment: the changing world of work in context', *Economic and Labour Relations Review,* 23, 4, 3–34

Rae, G. (2012) *Austerity policies in Europe: The case of Poland,* Berlin: Friedrich Ebert Stiftung

Rashid, M., Rutkowski, J. and Fretwell, D. (2005) 'Labor markets', in N. Barr (ed) *Labor markets and social policy in Central and Eastern Europe,* Washington, DC: World Bank

Rasmussen, E., Fletcher, M. and Hannam, B. (2014) 'The major parties: National's and Labour's employment relations policies', *New Zealand Journal of Employment Relations,* 39, 1, 21–32

Rees, J., Taylor, R. and Damm, C. (2013) *Does sector matter? Understanding the experiences of providers in the Work Programme,* Birmingham: Third Sector Research Centre

Reinhart, C. and Rogoff, K. (2009) *This time is different: Eight centuries of financial folly,* Princeton, NJ: Princeton University Press

Rhoades, G. and Torres, C. (2006) *Globalization and higher education in the Americas,* Stanford, CA: Stanford University Press

Richards, J. (2008) *Closing the Aboriginal/non-Aboriginal education gaps,* Toronto: C.D. Howe Institute

Rietig, V. (2014) *Migration with Chinese characteristics: Hukou reform and elite emigration,* Washington, DC: Migration Policy Institute

Roberts, K. (1995) *Youth and employment in modern Britain,* Oxford: Oxford University Press

Roberts, K. (2003) 'Change and continuity in youth transitions in Eastern Europe: lessons for western sociology', *The Sociological Review,* 51, 4, 484–505

Roberts, K. (2009) 'Opportunity structures then and now', *Journal of Education and Work,* 22, 5, 355–68

Roberts, S. (2011) 'Beyond "NEET" and "tidy" pathways: considering the "missing middle" of youth transition studies', *Journal of Youth Studies,* 14, 1, 21–39

Rodger, J.J. (2008) *Criminalising social policy: Anti-social behaviour and welfare in a de-civilized society,* Cullompton: Willan Publishing

Rodríguez Cabrero, G. (2011) 'The consolidation of the Spanish welfare state (1975–2010)', in A. Guillén and M. León (eds) *The Spanish welfare state in European context,* Farnham: Ashgate

Rønsen, M. and Skarŏhamar, T. (2009) 'Do welfare-to-work initiatives work? Evidence from an activation programme targeted at social assistance recipients in Norway', *Journal of European Social Policy,* 19, 1, 61–77

Roper, B. (2005) *Prosperity for all? Economics, social and political change in New Zealand since 1935,* Melbourne: Cengaga Learning

Rose, L. and Heidar, K. (2007) 'Oppfatningen om den gode samfunnsborger: har nyliberalisme avsatt noen spor?' in P. Mydske, D. Claes and A. Lie (eds) *Nyliberalisme – ideer og politisk virkelighet,* Oslo: Universitetsforlaget

Rose, N. (1996) 'Governing "advanced" liberal democracies', in A. Barry, T. Osborne and N. Tose (eds) *Foucault and political reason: Liberalism, neo-liberalism and rationalities of government,* London: UCL Press

Rothman, S., Shah, C., Underwood, C., McMillan, J., Brown, J. and McKenzie, P. (2014) *National report on social equity in VET,* Melbourne: NVEAC

Rowley, J. (2002) 'Using case studies in research', *Management Research News,* 25, 1, 16–27

Rugg, J., Ford, J. and Burrows, R. (2004) 'Housing advantage? The role of student renting in the constitution of housing biographies in the United Kingdom', *Journal of Youth Studies,* 7, 1, 19–34

Ryan, C. (2014) *Impact of the Australian higher education funding reforms,* Melbourne: Melbourne Institute of Applied Economic and Social Research

Ryan, R. (2011) *How the VET Responds; A Historical Perspective,* Adelaide: Commonwealth of Australia

Sachs, J.D. (2005) *The end of poverty,* New York: Penguin

Sage, J., Evandrou, M. and Falkingham, J. (2013) 'Onwards or homewards? Complex graduate migration pathways, well-being and the "parental safety net"', *Population, Space and Place,* 19, 6, 738–55

Sánchez, F. (2012) *Youth unemployment in Spain,* Berlin: Friedrich Ebert Stiftung

Savelsberg, H.J. (2010) 'Setting responsible pathways: the politics of responsibilisation', *Journal of Education Policy,* 25, 5, 657–75

Sayer, A. (2005) 'Class, moral worth and recognition', *Sociology,* 39, 5, 947–63

Scott, D. (2003) *Participation in tertiary education,* Wellington: Ministry of Education

Scraton, P. (1997) *'Childhood' in 'crisis'?* London: Taylor & Francis

Seccareccia, M. (2012) 'The role of public investment as principal macroeconomic tool to promote long-term growth: Keynes's legacy', *International Journal of Political Economy,* 40, 4, 62–82

Sejersted, F. (2014) *The age of social democracy: Norway and Sweden in the twentieth century,* Princeton, NJ: Princeton University Press

Sgritta, G. (2001) 'Family and welfare systems in the transition to adulthood: an emblematic case study', in L. Chisholm, A. de Lillo, C. Leccardi and R. Richter (eds) *Family forms and the young Generation in Europe,* Report by the European Observatory on the Social Situation, Demography and the Family, Vienna: Österreichisches Institut für Familienforschung.

Shaker, E. and MacDonald, D. (2013) *Degrees of uncertainty: Navigating the changing terrain of university finance,* Ontario: Canadian Centre for Policy Alternatives

Sharpe, A. and Gibson, J. (2005) *The apprenticeship system in Canada: Trends and issues,* Ottawa: Centre for the Study of Living Standards

Sharrock, G. (2014) *Fee deregulation and HELP debts after the 2014 budget: Some scenarios,* Melbourne: Martin Institute

Sheller, M. and Urry, J. (2006) 'The new mobilities paradigm', *Environment and Planning A,* 38, 207–26

Shibata, K. (2008) 'Neoliberalism, risk and spatial governance in the developmental state: Japanese planning in the global economy', *Critical Planning*, 15, 1, 92–118

Shildrick, T., MacDonald, R., Webster, C. and Garthwaite, K. (2012) *Poverty and insecurity: Life in low-pay, no-pay Britain*, Bristol: Policy Press

Shorrocks, A., Davies, J. and Lluberas, R. (2014) *The global wealth report*, Zurich: Credit Suisse

Shulruf, Boaz, Tumen, Sarah and Hattie, John. (2010) 'Student Pathways in a New Zealand Polytechnic: Key factors for completion', *International Journal of Vocational and Technical Education, 2*, 4 August, 67–74

Simmons, R. (2008) 'Raising the age of compulsory education in England: a NEET solution?', *British Journal of Educational Studies*, 56, 4, 420–39

Simmons, R., Thomson, R. and Russell, L. (2014) *Education, work and social change: Young people and marginalization in post-industrial Britain*, London: Palgrave Macmillan

Sissons, P. (2011) *The hourglass and the escalator: Labour market change and mobility*, London: The Work Foundation

Siwinska, B. (2011) 'Poland private higher education under threat', *University World News*, 193

Skóvra, M. (2013) *Austerity policies and gender impacts in Poland*, Berlin: Friedrich Ebert Stiftung

Smith, D.E. (1999) *Writing the social: Critique, theory, and investigations*, Toronto: University of Toronto Press

Smith, D.E. (2001) 'Texts and the ontology of organizations and institutions', *Studies in Cultures, Organizations and Societies*, 7, 2, 159–98

Smith, D.E. (2005) *Institutional ethnography: A sociology for people*, Toronto: AltaMira Press

Smith, M.K. (2007) 'The Connexions service in England', available at: www.infed.org/personaladvisers/connexions.htm

Social Mobility and Poverty Commission (2013) *Higher education: The fair access challenge*, London: Social Mobility and Poverty Commission

Southgate, E. and Bennett, A. (2014) 'Excavating Widening Participation Policy in Australian Higher Education', *Creative Approaches to Research*, 7,1, 21–45

Souto-Otero, M. and Bjørn Ure, O. (2012) 'The coherence of vocational education and training in Norway and Spain: national traditions and the reshaping of VET governance in hybrid VET systems', *Journal of Comparative and International Education*, 21, 1, 91–111

Spoonley, P., Du Puis, A. and De Bruin, A. (2004) *Work and working in the 21st century New Zealand,* Palmerston North: Dunmore Press

Springhall, J. (1986) *Coming of age: Adolescence in Britain, 1860–1960,* Dublin: Gill and Macmillan

St John, S. and Rankin, K. (1997) *Quantifying the welfare mess,* Auckland: Child Poverty Action Group

St John, S. and Rankin, K. (2009) *Escaping the welfare mess?* Auckland: Child Poverty Action Group

Standing, G. (2011) *The precariat: The new dangerous class,* London: Bloomsbury

Standing, G. (2012) 'The precariat: from denizens to citizens?' *Polity,* 44, 4, 588–608

Stanford, J. (2014) 'Canada's transformation under neoliberalism', *Canadian Dimension,* 29 March

Stanwick, J., Lu, T., Karmel, T. and Wibrow, B. (2013) *How young people are faring 2013: The national report on the learning and earning of young Australians,* Melbourne: Foundation for Young Australians

Starke, P. (2013) 'Antipodean social policy responses to economic crises', *Social Policy and Administration,* 47, 6, 647–67

Stasiulis, D. and Bakan, A. (2003) *Negotiating citizenship: Migrant women in Canada and the global system,* New York: Palgrave Macmillan

Statistics Canada (2014a) Canadian post-secondary enrolments and graduates 2012/13, 25 November, Daily Report, Ottawa, Statistics Canada

Statistics Canada (2014b) 'Unemployment by age 15–24 year olds', available at: www.statcan.gc.ca

Statistics New Zealand (2008) *Hot Off The Press, Survey of Working Life: March 2008 quarter,* Wellington: Statistics New Zealand

Statistics New Zealand (2011) *Introducing the youth not in employment, education, or training indicator,* Wellington: Statistics New Zealand

Statistics New Zealand (2012) *Flexibility and security in employment: Findings from the 2012 Survey of Working Life,* Wellington, New Zealand Government

Statistics New Zealand (2014) *Youth employment 16 - 24,* available at: www.stats.govt.nz

Stewart, A. and van der Waarden, N. (2011) *Regulating youth work: Lessons from Australia and the United Kingdom,* Farnham: Ashgate

Stone, J., Berrington, A. and Falkingham, J. (2011) 'The changing determinants of UK young adults' living arrangements', *Demographic Research,* 25, 20, 629–66

Strathdee, R. (2013) 'Reclaiming the disengaged: reform of New Zealand's vocational education and training and social welfare systems', *Research in Post-Compulsory Education,* 18, 1–2, 29–45

Strathdee, R. and Engler, R. (2012) 'Who is missing from higher education in New Zealand?', *British Educational Research Journal,* 38, 3, 497–514

Streitwieser, B. (ed) (2014) *Internationalism of higher education and global mobility,* Oxford: Symposium Books

Sumption, M. (2012) *Visas for entrepreneurs: How countries are seeking out immigrant job creators,* Washington, DC: Migration Policy Institute

Sunley, P., Martin, R. and Nativel, C. (2006) *Putting workfare in place,* Oxford: Blackwell

Swartz, D. (1997) *Power and culture: The sociology of Pierre Bourdieu,* Chicago: University of Chicago Press

Sykes, B. (2012) *Mobile talent? The staying intentions of international students in five EU countries,* Berlin: Sachverstandigenrat deutscher Stiftunger fur Integration und Migration

Szafraniec, K. (2011) *Youth 2011,* Warsaw: The Chancellery of the Prime Minister

Sztandar-Sztanderska, K. (2009) 'Activation of the unemployed in Poland: from policy design to policy implementation', *International Journal of Sociology and Social Policy,* 29, 11/12, 624–36

Tapia, J.A. (2013) 'From the oil crisis to the great recession: five crises of the world economy', *Marxismo Critico,* available at: http://marxismocritico.com/2013/05/08/from-the-oil-crisis-to-the-great-recession-five-crises-of-the-world-economy/

Taylor, L., Proaño, C.R., de Carvalho, L. and Barbosa, N. (2012) 'Fiscal deficits, economic growth and government debt in the USA', *Cambridge Journal of Economics,* 36, 1, 189–204

Tebbit, A. (2007) *Does the UK still have a flexible labour market?* London: Institute of Directors

Theodaropoulou, S. and Watt, A. (2011) *Withdrawel Symptons: An assessment of the austerity,* Working Paper 2011.02, Brussels, European Trade Union Institute

Thompson, E.P. (1971) *The making of the English working class,* New York: Vintage Books

Thompson, J. and Bekhradnia, B. (2010) *Male and female participation and progression in higher education: Further analysis,* Oxford: Higher Education Policy Institute

Thomson, P. (2008) 'Field', in M. Grenfell (ed) *Pierre Bourdieu: Key concepts,* Durham: Acumen

Thomson. R., Holland, J., McGrellis, S., Henderson, S. and Sharpe, S. (2004) 'Inventing adulthoods: a biographical approach to understanding youth citizenship', *Sociological Review*, 52, 2, 218–39

Thornton, S. (1995) *Club cultures: Music, media and subcultural capital*, Cambridge: Polity Press

Thun, C. (2012) 'Norwegianness as lived citizenship: religious women doing identity work at the intersections of nationality, gender and religion', *Nordic Journal of Religion and Society*, 25, 1, 1–25

Tiberghien, Y. (2012) 'The global economic crisis and the politics of regime change in Japan', in J. Pontusson (ed) *Coping with crisis*, London: Russell Foundation

Toivonen, T. (2013) *Japan's emerging youth policy*, London: Routledge

Tomlinson, S. (2013) *Ignorant yobs? Low attainers in a global knowledge economy*, London: Routledge

Torfing, J. (1999) 'Workfare with Welfare: Recent Reforms of the Danish Welfare State', *Journal of European Social Policy*, 4, 485–510

Trappmann, V. (2011) 'Precarious employment in Poland – a legacy of transition or an effect of European integration?', *Employment and Economy in Central and Eastern Europe*, 3, 1, 1–22

Tregenna, F. (2009) 'The fat years: the structure and profitability of the US banking sector in the pre-crisis period', *Cambridge Journal of Economics*, 33, 4, 609–32

Trevena, P. (2011) 'A question of class? Polish graduates working in low-skilled jobs in London', *Studia Migracyjne: Przeglad Polonijny*, 1, 71–96

Trow, M. (1974) 'Problems in the transition from elite to mass higher education', in *Policies for Higher Education*, from the General Report on the Conference on Future Structures of Post-Secondary Education, Paris: OECD, 55–101

Tsukamoto, T. (2012) 'Neoliberalization of the developmental state: Tokyo's bottom-up politics and state rescaling in Japan', *International Journal of Urban and Regional Research*, 36, 1, 71–89

TUC (Trade Union Congress) (2014) *Casualisation and low pay*, London: Trade Union Congress

Tweedie, D. (2013) 'Precarious work and Australian labour norms', *The Economic and Labour Relations Review*, 24, 3, 297–315

Tyler, I. (2013) *Revolting subjects: Social abjection and resistance in neoliberal Britain*, London: Zed Books

Tyyskä, V. (2014) *Youth and society: The long and winding road*, Toronto: Canadian Scholars' Press

Ungerleider, C. (2008) *Evaluation of the Ontario Ministry of Education's Student Success / Learning to 18 Strategy*, Ontario: Canadian Council of Learning

United Nations (2013) *Youth and migration*, New York: United Nations

Universities UK (2014) *International students in higher education: The UK and its competition*, London: Universities UK

Urry, J. (2007) *Mobilities*, Cambridge: Polity Press

Vallas, S. and Prener, C. (2012) 'Dualism, job polarization, and the social construction of precarious work', *Work and Occupations*, 39, 4, 331–53

Van Bavel, B. and Frankema, E. (2013) *Low income inequality, high wealth inequality: The puzzle of the Rhineland welfare states*, Utrecht: Centre for Global Economic History

Wacquant, L. (2009) *Punishing the poor: The neoliberal government of social insecurity*, Durham, NC: Duke University Press

Wacquant, L. (2010) 'Crafting the neoliberal state: workfare, prisonfare, and social insecurity', *Sociological Forum*, 25, 2, 197–220

Wacquant, L. (2011) 'The wedding of workfare and prisonfare revisited', *Social Justice*, 18, 1–2, 1–16

Wacquant, L. (2012) 'Three steps to a historical anthropology of actually existing neoliberalism', *Social Anthropology*, 20, 1, 66–79

Walford, G. (2010) *Blair's educational legacy?* London: Routledge

Wallace, C. and Jones, J. (1992) *Youth, family and citizenship*, Milton Keynes: Open University Press

Wallace, C. and Kovatcheva, S. (1998) *Youth in society: The construction and deconstruction of youth in East and West Europe*, Basingstoke: Macmillan

Walther, A. (2006) 'Choice, flexibility and security in young people's experiences across different European contexts', *Young*, 14, 2, 119–39

Warner, E., Henderson-Wilson, C. and Andrews, F. (2012) 'Everyones life is different', *Journal of Youth Studies*, 31, 4, 28–33

Watts, B., Fitzpatrick, S., Bramley, G. and Watkins, D. (2014) *Welfare sanctions and conditionality in the UK*, York: Joseph Rowntree Foundation

Western, M., Baxter, J., Pakulski, J., Tranter, B., Western, J., Van Egmond, M. et al. (2007) 'Neoliberalism, inequality and politics: the changing face of Australia', *Australian Journal of Social Issues*, 42, 3, 401

Wheelahan, L. (2008) 'Neither fish nor fowl: the contradiction at the heart of Australian tertiary education', *Journal of Access Policy and Practice*, 5, 2, 133–52

White, R. and Wyn, J. (2008) *Youth and society*, 2nd edn, Melbourne: Oxford University Press

Wierenga, A., Landstedt, E. and Wyn, J. (2013) *Revisiting disadvantage in higher education*, Melbourne: Youth Research Centre, University of Melbourne

Wilkinson, R. and Pickett, K. (2009) *The spirit level: Why greater equality makes societies stronger,* London: Bloomsbury Press

Williamson, H. (2002) *Supporting young people in Europe: Principles, policy and practice,* Strasburg: Council of Europe

Williamson, H. (2008) *Supporting young people in Europe,* vol. 2, Strasbourg: Council of Europe

Williamson, H. (2012) 'Youth policy reviews of the Council of Europe and their impact on national youth policies', in M. Hahn-Bleibtreu and M. Molgat (eds) *Youth policy in a changing world,* Berlin: Barbara Budrich Publishers

Williamson, J. (1990) 'What Washington means by policy reform', in J. Williamson (ed) *Latin American adjustment: How much has happened?* Washington, DC: Institute for International Economics

Wilson, K., Stemp, K. and McGinty, S. (2011) 'Re-engaging young people with education and training', *Youth Studies Australia,* 30, 2, 32–9

Wolf, M. (2014) *The shifts and the shocks,* New York: Penguin

Woodman, D. (2012) 'Life out of synch: how new patterns of further education and the rise of precarious employment are reshaping young people's relationships', *Sociology,* 46, 6, 1074–90

Woodman, D. and Bennett, A. (eds) (2015) *Youth cultures, belonging and transitions,* London: Palgrave Macmillan

Woodman, D. and Wyn, J. (2014) *Youth and generation: Rethinking change and inequality in the lives of young people,* London: Sage

World Bank (2006) *World development report 2007: Development and the next generation,* Washington, DC: World Bank

Wright, S. (2011) 'Can welfare reform work?', *Poverty,* 139, 5–8

Wyn, J. (2012) 'The long-term effects of youth policies in Australia', in M. Hahn-Bleibtreu and M. Molgat (eds) *Youth policy on a changing world,* Berlin: Budrich Publishers

Wyn, J. (2013) 'Young Adulthood in Australia and New Zealand: Pathways to belonging', in Evans, K. and Helve, H. (eds) *Youth and work transitions in changing social landscapes,* London: Tufnell Press

Wyn, J. and Woodman, D. (2006) 'Generation, youth and social change in Australia', *Journal of Youth Studies,* 9, 5, 495–514

Wynd, D. (2013) *Benefit sanctions: Creating an invisible underclass of children,* Auckland: Child Poverty Action Group

Yin, R. (2014) *Case study research: Design and methods,* 5th edn, Washington, DC: Sage

Young, N. (2008) 'Radical neoliberalism in British Columbia: remaking rural geographies', *Canadian Journal of Sociology,* 33, 1, 1–36

Index

References to tables and figures are in *italics*